[M]REEN LIPMAN, actress and author, has triumphed in [telev]ision (*Agony*, the British Telecom ads), films (Roman Polanski's [*The*] *Pianist*, on stage (particularly her one-woman show as Joyce [Gre]nfell) and in print (her memoirs and magazine columns). She [was] married to Bafta Award-winning Jack Rosenthal, who died in [200]4. In 1999, Maureen Lipman was awarded a CBE and she has won [nu]merous awards for her theatrical and television work.

Also by Maureen Lipman:

How Was It For You?
Something To Fall Back On
You Got an 'Ology?
Thank You For Having Me
When's It Coming Out?
You Can Read Me Like a Book
Lip Reading
The Gibbon's In Decline, But The Horse Is Stable
Past-it Notes

With Jack Rosenthal:

By Jack Rosenthal: An Autobiography in Six Acts

I Must Collect Myself

. . . Choice Cuts From A Long Shelf Life

Maureen LIPMAN

SIMON &
SCHUSTER

London · New York · Sydney · Toronto

A CBS COMPANY

First published in Great Britain by Simon & Schuster UK Ltd, 2010
This paperback edition first published in Great Britain by
Simon & Schuster UK Ltd, 2011
A CBS COMPANY

Simon & Schuster UK Ltd
1st Floor
222 Gray's Inn Road
London
WC1X 8HB

www.simonandschuster.co.uk

Simon & Schuster Australia
Sydney

A CIP catalogue record for this book
is available from the British Library

ISBN: 978-1-84739-368-5

Typeset by M Rules
Printed in the UK by CPI Cox & Wyman, Reading, Berkshire RG1 8EX

I dedicate this book to my friends who now live without their soul mates, namely, Karen Segal, Cleo Laine, Shirley Plater, Pat Pilkington, Linda Agran, Liz Clapp, Anne Coren, Valerie Hall, Pat Nimmo, Beryl Vosborough, Dannie Abse, Greville Janner, Lady Cotton, Colin Shindler, Mavis Nicholson, Diana Towb, Stephanie Crawford and Caroline Kington. No matter how you spin it, it's not fair!

Contents

Prologue	1
Acknowledgements	6
Holding My Brain In	7
I Call It Schaden*fraud*	11
Kimberley-Kate	15
IT Girl	18
West Side Glory	22
The Best Hundred Best List	25
Lydia	31
Mayor Culpa	35
I Go to Pieces	40
Animal Writes	45
Street Furniture	49
Doctor Who's Who	53
Glamour, Us?	55
No Smoke Without Being Fired	59
The Archers of Umbridge	64
Hull Is Other People	67
Pauline Buchanon	71
Be Careful What You Say In PC World	77
Rage Roader	81
Hockney Practice	85
Art at Sea	91

Rivet, Rivet   96
Napoleon's Extraction   99
Ready When You Are, Lord Reith   101
Ninety-Nine, Not Out   108
Luke Warm Tickets   112
Dinah   115
Mugger All   120
De-Scent of a Woman   124
Model Habits   127
Brought Up By a Guardian   131
Cut From the Same Cloth   134
JR's Last Act   136
Fan Tango   139
Barkless Up the Wrong Tree   142
Bette, Baseball Mom   147
Sporting Chance   151
The King's Ears   153
Dead Pirate Sketch   155
A Practically Perfect Day   159
Driving Miss Maisie   163
Freedom Past   167
One Day At A Time   171
Twelve Things I've Never Done   173
Twelve Things I've Done   174
Shock and Law   176
Midge Darke   181
Drying Up   185
The Rangoon Show (1)   189
The Lady's Not For Burma   191
The Rangoon Show (2)   196
Posey   199
On Aiming to Get Michelle Obama's Arms before
    She Notices and Wants Them Back   204
Spiegel in Spiegeltent   207
Elsa's Dad   211
Osbourne No Show   216
Competitions   219

Contents

Brittney's Got Talent	223
Wimborne Every Minute	226
You Can Take the Girl Out of Hull	230
Micheline	239
Memorials Are Made of This	243
And That's Jazz	246
Ladies of Letters	252
Shut Up	261
Disco Must Go On	263
Awards	266
Daftas	269
Happenstance in France	274
There's No Such Thing As Happenstance	280
Caviar Caveat	283
Endgame	285
Darius	289
Met My Metamorphosis	292
Spiked	295
A Day in Reality	301
Niamh the Naive	307
Maintaining Your Election	312
Artie: Play To The Gallery	317
If You Want to Put Something Back, Make it the Seat of the Lavatory	321
A Little Night-Night Music	326
Rosh Hashana Dinner	331
Diary of a Woman Not in Total Control of Her Freedom Pass	336
Sandi or 'No Probs'	343
Crosspatch Sit by the Latch	347
Picture Credits	352

Prologue

This book will be called *One Good Turn* or *Holding My Own*, or *Why Did I Ever Agree To Do This?*, or even, *Don't Get A Round Much Any More*. Another favourite, at five o'clock in the morning over hot milk and nutmeg and, much later, a Temazipan, was *Earning My Lines* and involved a high-definition photo of my furrowed brow and meandering cheek bones. For some reason, this failed to excite my publishers in the same way it did me. Certainly, by the time you read this prologue, you will know the name of the book you've paid over the odds for . . . As of now, though, the writer doesn't. It depends very much on what comes up as the best photo at the shoot on 25 May. *Recycled Clips* is another 3 a.m. regular, as is one of Zelma, my late mother's standards: 'Shall I tell you something about me? No matter what I've been doing, whether it's late or early, no matter how tired I am or what I have to do next day, come rain or shine, every night that dawns, I wash out my underwear.' So, *Every Night That Dawns* by Maureen Lipman.

The trouble is that with my other books, none of which I actually remember writing, the titles just appeared like the transformation scene in a panto. It looks like magic but you had to be there at the technical rehearsal to know how much blood and throat slashing and injured fly-men went into getting it to appear like magic. Now, looking back on those books, I'm misty eyed and nostalgic because they are the nearest I'll ever get, with my disintegrating memory, to a diary of my life.

Whereas Zelma's diaries, which sit on my shelf in the study where I work, go like this:

Monday, washed windows. Tea with Freda.

Tuesday, turned mattress. Bernard's shampoo and set.

Wednesday, kitchen cupboards. Harold Flasher for filling.

Thursday, coin-op with nets. Kalooki. Buy loaf. Tall tin salmon.

Friday, scalded chicken, Silvo'd candlesticks/cutlery. Spoke to Mo. Amy chickenpox.

Saturday, shul, changed girdle for 42 inch, Marks. Jean's evening.

Sunday, ride out for ice cream. Joyce and Louis. Saw Lily. Tea, Beverley Arms.

In short, not a thought, feat of imagination or feeling is captured from January to December. Just an aide memoire of another year. I don't know if she was happy or sad, contented or forlorn. Her diary, like most diaries, was for her consumption alone and there is nothing in its numerous pages, save accuracy, which would communicate to you her enormous personality or her idiosyncratic nature. It's been up to me to do that. There are few moments more precious to me than the laughter her comments still ellicit from audiences, young and old, all over the country. The only person reaping more pleasure from the sound would have been Zelma herself.

Still, I hope this 'diary' conveys the kaleidoscope of the last few years. Accuracy . . . I can't vouch for, because, I realize more and more, everything I read or experience is subjective. When I read Lynda Bellingham's riveting autobiography, *Lost and Found*, I was transfixed by how different her experience of working on the play *The Sisters Rosensweig* was from mine. She recalled a fellow actress being a bit late for the half-hour call, me getting upset and she keeping the peace. I recall rising panic at the five-minute call, virtually on a nightly basis, as we dressed her quivering understudy. We are neither of us liars.

When, on a recent Mark Lawson interview, I told the story of Frank Finlay being rubbed down on the set of *The Pianist* with an immense German sausage by director Roman Polanski, it was virtually *all* I remembered of the shoot. I had dined out on it. Frank, conversely, could scarcely remember the incident at all.

When two of my girl friends and I first met my friend, chap, *consort*, Guido, we all saw a man with silver hair, no beard and a grey suit, who kissed my hand. He was, actually, nobly bald, bearded, wearing navy and insists he doesn't make a habit of kissing ladies' hands. We are none of us fantasists. 'Half the truth is often the whole lie,' said Burke. It's perfectly clear to us that Shakespearian fairy dust was sprinkled in our eyes.

Somewhat nervously, I'm injecting a little fantasy of my own into the anecdotal format and I'm quietly confident you'll take on board this new spin on the old formula. Included here are my 'Partly Pieces' – twenty solo monologues or character sketches in homage to Joyce Grenfell and her second cousin by marriage, the revered solo artiste, Ruth Draper. Joyce's sketches stayed in my head for a long time after I completed five years on and off in the West End hit *Re: Joyce*. This July, along with the actress/teacher Jane Bower, I've just tried out a show, *Mrs Grenfell and Miss Ruth*, illuminating the huge influence the established star Ruth Draper had on the shy, amateur Joyce Grenfell. It was a steamy hot night and I lost my nerve a bit and began to panic. I finally turned to the audience, Joyce-like, shook myself from top to toe and yelled 'Nerves!' They gave me a round of applause. Then we got on with the show. Afterwards I was wrung out like a wet-wipe, but the standing ovation we got reflected, I think, an audience thrilled to have participated in something rather than having it spoon-fed to them.

It seems to me that in a monologue, the writer/performer has the advantage of working *with* an audience, much more than an actress who just *includes* them obliquely. Our audiences had to work hard to *see and hear* the invisible people we were conjuring up. As Alan Bennett proved with his *Talking Heads*, to really *get it* the audience has to meet the speaker halfway. We do it all the time with novels, but on television, as my great grandma would have said, they hit us over the head with a teapot. 'Passengers on their way to airports,' says the announcer, then follows a shot of suitcase, feet, baggage handlers – 'faced queues' – shot of lines of cars on motorway – 'and a spokesman' – shot of man emerging from office with clipboard . . . You get the picture? Imagination by-pass.

Monologues work as if you were a child again. 'You be Miss Peterson and I'll be the naughty schoolgirl!' or 'We can't go to the palace unless we swim the mighty river!' or 'Let's make this sideboard into a boat!' is the scenario, genially crossed with Radio 4's *Afternoon Theatre*, listened to whilst doing the ironing. As if. The last time I ironed was just after sweet rationing.

So, interspaced between the stories, the whinges, the nostalgia, the jokes and the helpless refrain 'It could only happen to me', my editor has sprinkled my bevy of characters. They range from 'No Smoke Without Being Fired', where a sour and jaded woman executive, smoking outside the trophy building, finds herself in the company of a born-again Christian from the sorting department, to 'Brittney's Got Talent', where a hot-panted young wannabe faces an *X-Factor* celebrity panel, to 'Driving Miss Maisie', where a woman practises returning the child she won custody of to her ex-husband. We have, en route, 'Sandi or "No Probs"', the Aussie mammographer with the bedside manner of a hydrangea, and 'Midge Darke', the tough, relentless army sergeant, who has a soft way with her privates.

They are in there for you to try out on your friends, as audition pieces, or for a musical festival, if such things still exist, or as a bit of a concert on a dark and stormy night, when 200 channels prove as entertaining as the Test Card and you've exhausted your Australian drinking games. I hope they come to life when they're inflated by the human voice. I've tried a few out on captive audiences and they do what it says on the tin – embarrass the shit out of you – no, what I'd like to think is they create short cocktails with a twist of lemon and a dash of Angostura, which leave you refreshed but with a thirst for more . . . but I won't say that on the grounds that it would be fantastically pretentious. Not altogether to my surprise, they are all rather angry women.

Look, it's a hybrid, an amalgam, a crossbreed, a homogenized melting pot, a concoction, a patchwork, a scrambled edge, a jumble tale, a combination, a medley of mania, a mixer match, a mongrel feast. A mo-latto . . . what you will. It's . . . hell, it's my new book.

Anyway, before I make the final decision, I really Must Collect Myself.

As I began this book, I was starting a new play named *Glorious*, which was going to rehearse in Birmingham, tour for six weeks and come into the Duchess Theatre for a six-month run. It told the story of the American philanthropist and entertainer, Florence Foster Jenkins, a woman so adorably deluded about the greatness of her vocal powers that she hired Carnegie Hall at vast expense and sent her fans crying into the street – with laughter. During Florence's 'Queen of the Night' aria, Tallulah Bankhead, allegedly, wet herself and had to be carried out of her box. Jenkins' long-playing record, issued after her death, was entitled 'Murder on the High Cs'. I would, of course, be performing eight shows a week . . . three arias a show.

I was also writing a weekly opinion column for the *Guardian* newspaper. I did this for a year whilst trying to decorate a flat, obedience-train a puppy, keep up with my friends and apply myself to a new relationship. I was happy but, looking back at the scribbled notes, something had to give . . .

Acknowledgements

As well as Collecting myself, I must thank Others. My PA amanu-ensis and dog handler, Natalie, for explaining things to me not once, not twice, but daily, and for collating things neatly – then finding them again, when I've filed them under a pile of laundry.

Invaluable help came from Karen Segal who read through and said, 'No, Mo, it's NOT a pile of old teabags.' To my editor Angela Herlihy, gently insistent as one must be, and Suzanne Baboneau for buying the idea. Designer Rafi Romaya and photographer Johnny Ring for doing exactly what it says on the job description with the minimum of fuss, Jane Pizzey for organizing photos and proofs, and encouraging words about the manuscript, and my agent Charlie Viney for keeping my simmering pan from boiling over and braising my sneakers. My thanks to Ray Harris who took the brief 'I want a dress that looks like my dog' – and elegantly ran with it. For the lights in my life Amy, Adam, Taina and Guido.

To the *Guardian* newspaper, who have let me recycle some of my work onto these pages, my thanks and further gratitude to the *Oldie*, *Radio Times* and *Good Housekeeping*.

Holding My Brain In

There are times when I think I'm losing my brain. As if bits of it are evaporating through the pores of my head into the air, to be picked up by other people from a central pool of knowledge, leaving my head with just coarse yellow Emmenthal where there used to be springy white Rosenthal.

How could I forget the word indomitable? Oh sure, I know it *now*, but where was it when I was describing a friend who *is*? But perhaps I should slow down a bit and stop being so bloody in . . . indem . . . inevit . . . *whatsit*! Or the surname of Michael, who was the administrator of the Old Vic when I was there from 1970 to 1973? I've got it *now*, it was Halifax, but when I needed it – in its exact place in the story I was telling – it vanished. The whole rhythm of the story was thrown, as, indeed, was I, which reminds me, as most things do, of a joke.

Millie, an elderly lady, was out driving one day with her friend Dorothy, when she drove straight through a red light. The friend was shocked but, sure it wouldn't happen again, refrained from saying anything. At the next lights, Millie accelerated and once again shot through them. Shaken, Dorothy prepared to say something when, to her horror, Millie slowed down at green, revved up during yellow and screamed into full throttle on red.

'Millie!' said her friend. 'For heaven's sake! You've just gone through three red lights. What are you thinking of?'

'Me?' said Millie in amazement. 'Do you mean to say that I'm driving?'

Why are you laughing? That's not funny, that's tragic. Good friends understand when I invite them to lunch, then go out to open a fete or take the dog out for a really long walk, but it doesn't work so well the other way round. The organizers can get justifiably shirty if you turn up, as they're clearing away the coconut shy, in wellies and a track suit with a poo bag in your hand. Actually, that's another irritant, forgetting the poo bag on a walk and having to scrabble around with leaves or a discarded Kentucky Fried chicken box. I've taken to carrying a disposable rubber glove around with me but it can be equally embarrassing when one drops out of your bag as you pay for a posh bra and pants in Bravissimo.

It's also *hard* being a dumb brunette, and I feel only sympathy for the woman in the car park of a Texan supermarket who was spotted by passers-by, sitting, for over an hour, in her car, eyes shut, both hands on the back of her head. Finally, someone went over and tapped on the car window, whereupon she opened her eyes and mouthed the words, 'Help me! I've been shot in the head.' Paramedics were called and the door of the car forced open, but she refused to move or take her hands off her head because she insisted her brains were oozing out of her skull. When they examined the car, they found that in the midday heat, a packet of Pillsbury dough on the back seat had exploded with a sharp retort, sending mounds of dough flying onto her head. She'd been sitting in her car for an hour pressing bread to her scalp. The last sentence of the article was, 'The woman was blonde.'

Which reminds me of another joke: a blonde on a flight to Toronto suddenly ups sticks from Economy, parks herself in First Class and orders champagne. The stewardess politely tells her that she cannot serve her and she has to move back into her seat in Economy. The blonde just purrs, 'Look, honey, I'm blonde, I'm beautiful and I'm staying in First till we get to Toronto, so fetch me a drink, OK?' Worried, the stewardess goes to consult with her senior steward, who straightaway goes over to reason with the blonde, who naturally is having none of it. She stretches her fabulous legs, bats her lashes and says, 'Look, honey, I'm blonde, I'm beautiful and I'm damned if

I'm moving from this seat till I get to Toronto.' The senior steward
scratches his head and returns to the front of the plane to consider.
Several other stewards and stewardesses have the same lack of success. Finally, someone tells the pilot about the dilemma and asks
what he would do in the situation. The pilot smiles and hands over
the controls to his co-pilot. 'Leave this to me,' he crows. 'I speak
blonde.' They stare at him. He continues, 'I'm married to a blonde.'
With a swagger, he walks over to the blonde and whispers something
in her ear. Immediately, she leaps up from her seat, thanks him and
returns to Economy. Amazed, the stewards gather round and ask him
what he could possibly have said to make her behave so obediently
when they had all failed to move her. 'Oh, it's simple really,' he says,
taking back the controls from his partner, 'I asked her where she was
heading. She told me she was going to Toronto, so I told her I was
very sorry she hadn't been told this at Heathrow, but the front part
of this plane doesn't go to Toronto.'

Last week, by dint of spending the previous night in the right
area, I did make it, on time and wearing a fetching *het,* to open a fete
at a Leonard Cheshire Home for the disabled in Brampton, near
Huntingdon. I'm so glad I did. It was a pleasure. It was a gorgeous
summer day and the balloons and bunting were shimmering on a
real old-fashioned English 'do'. There were homemade cakes, a
fancy-dress competition with all of two entrants, ringed plastic ducks
in a paddling pool, book, video and knick-knack sales and a dis-
arming police . . . er . . . dis-arming demonstration. And owls. Owls!
Four of them from a local owl sanctuary, sitting on the gloved arms
of their trainers. I've never been that close to a real owl before, let
alone been allowed to stroke its downy breast, and it was stirring to
the soul. They are incredibly beautiful creatures in Calvin Klein white
and beige, tan, amber and brown – which just happened to be exactly
the colours I was wearing to open the fete.

Wildly overexcited, I asked the organizers to please take photos of
me, covered in snowy barn owl, on my camera, which for once in a
millennium I had remembered to bring along. It goes without saying
that when I'd finished the reel and taken it proudly to the developer
the following day, he reminded me that with these camera things, it's
quite important to remember to put in a film first.

Still, I won't forget the wheelchair-bound residents and the carers of the Leonard Cheshire Home, because, without exception, they were, as the Irish say, up for the craic. A lovely young lad called Jonah had seen me in *Doctor Who* and gave me one of the two coconuts he'd won on the shy.

We drove home on my favourite road, the old A1, passing a village called Braughing. My companion remarked that he'd never, in thirty years of driving to Cambridge, known how Braughing was pronounced. 'Why don't we ask some inhabitants?' was my practical suggestion.

'It's Braughing like laughing,' said one of the two ladies with a basset hound we stopped.

'Yes, but is that as pronounced in the south or the north? I mean we laff and you lahf.'

'And have you seen our ford? No? Well you should. Turn left and follow the road and you can drive round the village square and back.'

Which we did. My first ever drive-through ford. A perfect day, a coconut on the back seat and, conveniently, a hammer in the boot.

I Call It Schaden*fraud*

A word of advice. If you're going to be defrauded don't let it happen after 5.30 p.m. or before 9.30 a.m. Or over a weekend. Or a Bank Holiday. The Fraud Helpline helps you during office hours only. This makes sense to Mr Big of the Fraud Helpline and his young and probably burgeoning family, but makes *ashenblotty*, as my late father would have called it, of your nerves, your bank accounts, credit cards and assorted finances. On reflection, it might be an idea to call the Fraud Helpline in advance, and ask them when it would be most convenient for them for you to be defrauded.

This week, whilst I was rehearsing in Birmingham, some sub-normal crook tried to open two bank accounts, start an Amex account and an online account, not only in my name but in the name of my late husband. Clearly he or she is not an obituary reader. They had my address, so a cheque-book robbery was suspected. My loved and trusted accountant was given shrift of the short variety when he tried to speak to the fraud line at the building society involved. They told him they could only accept calls from the fraudee, or whatever I'm termed. The society will remain anonymous, though if I say the whole thing made me cross, you might be getting warm.

I was called out of rehearsals, given a list of reference numbers as long as Giselle Bundchen's arm, and told to contact the building society, and there began the attempt to defraud my brain. Much has been written about BT's numbing 'If you want to tear out every hair on your leg press one, if you wish to invade Poland press two', so I won't add to that cry from every overcharged subscriber in the land. However, when you press the number indicated only to find a set of seven further choices and then finally hear, to a backing of porpoise music, that you are a valued customer but there is no one to take your call as all operators are busy so please call back later because you are still a valued customer, you find you have paid for 13 futile minutes of phone time.

'I'm being robbed, for Christ's sake!' you scream at a pre-recorded voice. 'Give me a human being! A walking, talking human bloody being, a serial wife beater even, a gormless twitcher from Ballyback o' Beyond.'

Which, lo and behold, is more or less what I got.

'H'lloy,' said a nasal but chirpy voice.

'I don't believe it!' I gasped. 'Are you real? Are you a person?'

'Hoykenoyholpeu?' said the real person.

'Pardon?' said I.

'Frahd Holploin. Hoykenoyhalpyeu?'

Believe me, I have a decent ear for accents, and I love the Irish second only to the other eleven tribes, but the number of times I said, 'I'm sorry, but could you say that again – slowly' became embarrassing. It was a call centre in Belfast and by the time I got through to someone I could understand I'd used up every shred of patience and, yes, I'm humiliated enough to admit, every trump card in my pack, including 'I'm Maureen Lipman.' ('Huy?') And, even more desperately, 'I shall be writing about this in my column!' It was only shame that stopped me invoking the name of Esther Rantzen.

One of the last exchanges I ever had with my late mother was a call I shall always treasure.

'You'll never guess what,' she stated emphatically from her Hull living room. 'I've just had the funniest conversation on the phone. Have you got a minute?'

I had.

'Well,' she continued, 'I was just phoning up for cheaper calls, you know, and this woman answered and she had ever such a funny accent, all up and down, and I said to her, "Haven't you got a lovely accent? Are you Welsh?" And she said, "No, I'm Indian." So I said, "Oh, where are you then?" And what do you think she said? She said "I'm in India." So I said, "You're not are you? Really? What's the weather like?"'

It's a shame they're not still making those BT ads.

Anyway, by this time I'd given my mother's maiden name and my birth date so many times that I began to think I was giving *her* birth date and *my* name when I finally got through to a Mr Big, a twelve-year-old Jane Horrocks soundalike from Lancashire. He gave me his name and his direct number and suggested I should perhaps contact the police in my own locale. Well, I said, I'm in Birmingham and they took away the local police station in my home borough, and what were *they* going to do if my friends in Belfast wouldn't take their calls and I've a play to get on stage. Later that day, after taking advice from my bank, I rang my new friend back and heard, not his warm and welcoming northern tones, but, instead, 'Welcome to Fraud Helpline. If you wish to report a theft, please press one. If you wish to bury a phone operator alive with a hyena, please press two . . .' etc. There is no end to this story. I just have to watch all my bank returns and see if I suddenly start buying yachts in the Bahamas or investing in a vineyard in Mongolia.

It's a thought-provoking thing, though. If it's that hard to report a couple of minor scams, it's no wonder Enron got away with it for so long – the missing tsunami money, Food for Aid, Yasser Arafat's millions, Robert Mugabi's fleets of Mercedes – greed and corruption (to Madoff and beyond) with no retribution in sight.

'Love thyself last; cherish those hearts that hate thee. Corruption wins not more than honesty.' Lines from *Henry VIII*, a man to whom corruption was not unknown, written by Shakespeare . . . or possibly Bacon . . . or Sir Philip Sydney . . . or most likely the Earl of Oxford?

Before my Greek holiday, I went to a large, important post office to renew my international driving licence. I parked my car, walked through twenty minutes of 'summer rain' – the type that acts as warm-up man for the announcement of profits of billions for Thames Water and the annual hose-pipe ban – and joined the other fifty-three people shuffling round the barriers and jumping to attention whenever the pre-recorded voice yodelled, 'Cashier number FOUR.'

Finally, I'm there. Nirvana. I show her my papers and flash my new driving licence card.

'I need the proper, paper licence,' says she behind glass.

I show her a printed copy of the proper paper licence.

'Sorry, I need the real thing.'

But . . . *they* sent me this card. *They* didn't say I was supposed to carry two around with me.

'I require the actual paper licence, thank you,' she repeats and turns away.

'Cashier number four,' coos the tannoy.

I gaze wearily at racks of obscure DVDs on sale and leaflets alerting me to the fact that I can do my travel insurance, my will, my floral arrangements and probably my monthly dog worming through the post office. What I can't do is weigh a letter without joining an enormous queue, buy a stamp in less than half an hour or renew my sodding licence without carrying the contents of the filing cupboard . . . and yes, I would be the first in the protest demo when they suggest closing down my local p.o.

Post office mortem: when I get home, frothing, a friend tells me the regular licence works fine in Greece.

Kimberley-Kate

Kimberley-Kate works at a call centre, manning the enquiries and complaints. She is sunny, amiable, not awfully bright but terribly willing to help. She has the gift of empathy and frequently finds herself listening to tales of woe at the bus stop. She loves small animals and is hopeful of meeting Mr Right and settling down in a small house with pretty curtains. She enjoys her work.

Kimberley-Kate

(As many upward inflections as possible turn her statements into questions.)

Hello, Customer Services, Kimberley-Kate speaking. How can I help you? Yes, I *am* a real person.

Oh, I *know* – you're not the first to complain about it. It's not my choice believe me . . . Dizzy Rascal. Oh, was you? Well, you *can* complain if you like but . . . Aww . . . That's rubbish. How long did they leave you hanging on? Oh. Bummer . . . That's like, before I came *on*.

We do apologize for any inconvenience. Now how can I . . .?

Cool . . . Cool . . . Cool . . . So you need to send them on your PX221 like, urgently? I can quite understand that. You're a photo*grapher* are you? Oh, cool. I love photographs. I've got zillions on my iPhone. OK. Shall we just calm down, and see what we can do? No probs.

Soooo. I could look up your reference *from* the shop but we might as well start afresh for you. Could I have your mobile number now? Sorry, yes, I know, but you haven't, like, given it to *me* . . . Right that's 07748 985908 . . . Yes, I – I'll repeat that back: 07784 958 908. Sorry. So, what was it again? Brilliant!

No, nothing's *actually* brilliant. It's just a vigorous peach – a vigorous peach – like . . . OK or wicked or whatever, know what I mean? I just meant I'd – like got it up on screen. You're 'aving me on . . . straight up? I never knew that . . . Speech is it? Figure? Of? No! Reelly?

I don't get it. All them years I thought . . . All my family, like, say vigorous peach. Somefing new every day in this job. Thanks, dude.

Now, can I first have some proof of your identity? What is your password? Oh I know . . . It's easily done. Well, let me give you some help – er, yes – the first part's right but the last two letters . . . ooh, sooo nearly.

Nope. That's not it. Oh *isn't* it irritating? I *know* – there's such a *lot* to remember these days. Sooo? Got it yet? Oooh . . . Nope, s'not it.

I'll tell you what *I* do – my date of birth and the year. Like, say I'm the twelfth of the twelfth eighty-six – then I always know. Would you like to do that? So, right, that'd be two ten forty-six. Forty-six? Oh, you sound younger – bear with me while I just change that over.

Bear with me one sec . . . Oops, sorry, I didn't mean to put you back on music. I do apologize. I never meant to . . . are they OK now, your ears? Cool . . . cool . . . cool.

Now. Have you got a pen? One eight four four. So. OK. I've texted it to you, sir, no probs . . .

Sooo . . . (*She sings softly to herself.*) Done. Awesome . . . Na, sir, nothing's *actually* awesome. It's just a *figure* of speech? (*Giggles*) D'you mind my asking, is that – I mean like in, like, figure? Like, in *Dancing on Ice*? Are you sure? Figure of speech – all these years and I'm . . . Like, hellooo?

Now, I've arranged that your photos can be sent through *to* another party, like, as an email or a text. No probs, my pleasure . . . Glad to be of service.

Yes, you *can* access that now. Er . . . well, not *right* now, like today. Sorry . . . There is, like, a forty-eight-hour delay before you can actually *use* this facility . . . Yes, well, I'm sorry, they should have expl— Which town was you in? Andover? Is that with a haitch? (*She yanks phone away from her ear.*) Are you all right? I said is that with a haitch . . . (*Yanks it again.*)

Oh dear, did you drop it? Hello? . . . Hello?

(*Off*) This geezer's gone like ape-shit. I can hear broken glass an' a really long scream . . . Wonder if he's had a fall. Er . . . hello?

(*Falteringly*) Er . . . Thank you for calling . . . er . . . This call may have been recorded for training purposes?

Hello. Kimberley-Kate speaking. How can I be of service?

IT Girl

I have this strong memory of my dear old dad sitting in front of the television watching some 'shock of the new' revelation, shaking his head and quietly murmuring, 'You can't bloody *believe* it, can you?'

At the time, I found his Luddite responses rather sweet and a bit risible. It went with his deference for authority and his fear of wine waiters and banks. Now, as I inexorably *become* him, my patronizing stance appals me.

In the old days of touring a play, I just packed up me. That meant underwear, over wear, too many shoes and a script. You should see me now. Or maybe you shouldn't.

Now I travel with cables. My laptop travels in a black bag with four wires: one fat grey one, one translucent grey one, one thick black one with integral black box and one spare one for when the thin grey one fails to work in each new location. There are two unidentified spare plugs in plastic bags in the canvas carry-all with the broken zip.

The first thing I do on arrival is plug in as many of the little Perspex things as I can find holes for. Then I spend a couple of hours pleading with desk clerks, who are hard to contact because the phone won't work when the computer is plugged in. The bills when I leave are shocking because I haven't yet grasped that while I'm ruminating on what to write, the cash till downstairs is ringing with an *Are You Being Served?* regularity.

In the old days I would come back from the show, knock back a Scotch and soda and some monkey nuts at the bar with my current cast or book a massage from the hulkiest masseur in the solarium. Nowadays, I spend the hour till midnight answering requests to send a support message to a cycling event up the Trossachs to raise money for a solar-powered computer in a Namibian college of media studies, or politely declining to be interviewed about my views on trowels by a fifteen-year-old reporter from the *Gosforth Gleaner.*

That's if I get connected. 'No,' says the receptionist when, pyjama-clad, I wander down into the lobby, 'there is no Internet connection in your room, but there is wireless connection in the drawing room if you would care to open up an account.' I ponder changing hotels. In the feverish night I write a letter to the laptop:

Dear Sheba the Toshiba,
I don't ask for much. Just e-mail and Copy, Paste and Send . . . I'm a bit bleary because I did two shows on half a scone and a Redoxon for my dinner. I don't want to argue with you. I know you have a superior intellect and 100 per cent more memory – as indeed does a pumice stone. The thing is, between you and me and the European Built-in Obsolescence Mountain, shh . . . I really hate you. I'd like you to spontaneously implode and leave me in peace with an HB pencil, a sheet of A4 and a first-class stamp.

I admit it. I fell in love with your sleek, willowy good looks, so opposite to my own lumpenness. It was purely a physical thing. I thought with the right help I could handle you but I'm sorely out of practice, and I was no good at it the first time round. I shall go to my bed, fake a headache and turn you off.

In the clear light of day, pausing only to consume a kipper in honour of Jack, who adored herrings in all their forms, I shlepp my bag of cables downstairs and continue to write in the drawing room. I am enraptured by the business scenarios going on around me. There is a florid chap by the fireplace, trashing his fellow employees over an up-and-coming vacancy and to my right a power struggle is being resoundingly lost by a gentle soul of a man whose every gesture clearly irritates the hell out of the boss woman opposite. All human life, after the manner of Ricky Gervais, is here.

'She can't cope,' says one of the by-the-fireplace males, smiling the smile of an alligator. 'She's a control freak. She's repacked my case and went mental cos I let Judy book my flights.'

I'm suddenly glad I'm in a profession where, on the whole, women have as much mouth and trousers as men.

Coincidence and synchronicity have dogged me this week. The lady who sat by me in the stunning and historic Garnethill synagogue in Glasgow on Yom Kippur, was a haematologist, who had spent four years at the Royal Marsden working with Jack's myeloma consultant.

The taxi driver who brought me back from a nourishing trip to the Burrell Collection in Pollok Park, was in the Blue Caves on the north side of Zakynthos this year at the same time as I was.

As I put on my robe to start the matinee, already thinking of the next tour date – Bath – I found myself remembering, years ago, driving down there with the late, great actress Gwen Watford. I sat down at my dressing table, recalling our last conversation, which was about our husbands, as I picked up my mail. The first letter I opened began with the sentence, 'Many years ago, I sat beside the actress Gwen Watford at a fashion show and always regretted that I never spoke to her . . . so I'm writing to you today . . .'

On Sunday night, at the Cheltenham Literary Festival I talked to Ari and her mother over the book-signing table. Ari was maybe eleven or twelve, fair and pretty and riven with cerebral palsy. Because I'm a patron, I asked her mother if they'd tried conductive education as created by the Israeli educationalist Reuven Fuerstein. The mother exhaustedly shook her head as her daughter and I exchanged a sort of communication, and they moved on. The next couple to approach the table were smiling. He knew Fuerstein's work well, because he ran an institute of conductive education in Birmingham.

Now, if I were to tell my children of these coincidences, one of them would be wide-eyed and say, 'I don't believe it – that's amaz-ing! What can the odds be on that happening?' The other would say, 'Yes, but think of the number of times it *doesn't* happen.'

Bath loves the show, James the delightful hotel clerk has man-aged, with the help of my server, to connect me and I'm off for a hazelnut latte. All's well with the World, web-wise.

West Side Glory

When the Sharks and the Jets taunt Officer Krupke with the snarling observation that 'deep down inside us there is good', it sums up all the things we seem unable to change in a civilized democracy and everything we know about deprivation in society. With immaculate lyrics by Stephen Sondheim, to a shimmering score by Leonard Bernstein, adorning a book by the great Arthur Laurents, based on a play by promising playwright William Shakespeare from an, arguably, original idea in a 1530 Italian novella by Bandello, its relevance in 2007 is particularly marked.

Gang culture is the greatest fear of parents and politicians, and the prime minister, when leader of Her Majesty's opposition, once memorably urged us to 'hug a hoodie'. *West Side Story* could be the most important musical of all time. Hugs are nice, love and attention are necessary, but it is time and money where mouths are, which are what really count.

Camila Batmanghelidjh, the founder of Kids and Company, an organization that has turned around the lives of countless rejects of society, has to spend her life fund-raising to support her charity. Other charities rely on philanthropy to raise money for musical instruments for street kids from South America and South Africa who are redeemed by playing in youth orchestras.

In the 1950s, while three complex, musical Jewish boys were getting together to write *West Side Story*, I was growing up in Hull,

where we didn't have much in the way of rebellion, but the resonance of the show came throbbing over the Humber in as visceral a
way as the sound of four lads from Liverpool would a decade later.
I can see the LP now, with its scarlet cover, and feel the excitement
of slipping it onto my Dancette *record player* (two words, imaginatively, describing exactly what it did). Over and over, I would mouth
the words and mimic the stance of the sultry star with whom I most
identified – Chita Rivera. Sallow of skin, bespectacled, buck of tooth,
I was about as Puerto Rican as Peaches Geldof but as far as I was
concerned I *was* Anita and, accordingly, I salsa'd around our newly
built extension, with its contemporary yellow plastic furniture, watching myself in the French windows and snarling, 'A boy like that
who'd kill your brother' at an imaginary Maria.

Thirty years later, playing in Neil Simon's *Lost in Yonkers* at the
Strand Theatre, I would see Ms Rivera in *The Kiss of the Spiderwoman*,
at the Shaftesbury Theatre. I was fortunate enough to meet her afterwards and was as star-struck as when I was a teenager. She was
dynamite. The injustice hit me once again. Rita Moreno was given
her role in the film. Pretty face, good dancer yes, but Chita's talent –
light years away. How could she have borne it?

In spite of the politically incorrect casting, the film of *West Side
Story* was impossible to ruin. The cast were pale shadows of their
stage counterparts and once again, the ubiquitous Marnie Nixon
sang the soundtrack for Natalie Wood, as she had done so brilliantly
for Deborah Kerr in *The King and I* and would do for Audrey
Hepburn in *My Fair Lady*. Nevertheless, the movie had a raw exu-
berance which hit you in places you barely conceded existed. It was
brash and trumpety, daring and dynamic. There were no heroes, no
villains, only victims of prejudice and poverty. I love every frame of
that film. It won ten Oscars.

But, I've never seen *West Side Story* on stage. Come to think of it,
who has? How long did it run in those heady blue remembered days
when I'd visited London only once, on a weekend excursion? Bed
and breakfast at the Cumberland Hotel, the Changing of the Guard,
Lyons tea room and nothing left in the coffers for a West End show.

In 1987, Leonard Bernstein came to Watford to see me in another
of his musicals, *Wonderful Town*. (I tell you this purely and simply to

show off.) He told the cast that he'd written the music in three weeks to pay for his new baby daughter – the young woman who was hanging on Dad's arm that night. He was leonine and dressed to the nines in leather trousers and an aquamarine macramé sweater and he burned my ears with praise. I can't remember a word of it. Three decades earlier he was a young man trying to make a living. Sometimes the time, the place, the talent and the period combine to make perfect history.

I'm left wondering why producers revive corny old shows from *On Your Toes* to *Babes in Arms* and disregard the – book-, music-, lyrics-wise – perfect musical? If ever a show held up a mirror to a damaged society and changed the thinking of its audience, *West Side Story* was it. Surely, as the song says, 'There's a Place for Us'.

I had a request recently from an American biographer of Bernstein's, asking for my permission to reprint a letter I had written to L. B. after *Wonderful Town* closed, in 1987. To my astonishment, it had been in his archive ever since. I leaped back twenty-three years to the breathless girl I used to be. 'Well, Mr Bernstein,' I had written, 'the curtain has rung down and the star is rung out!' I read it in wonder that he should have kept it all these years.

Every year, as the committee selects worthy and wonderful women for the Women of the Year Awards, I sit and marvel at the ordinary wives and mothers who decide, quite randomly one day, to get underprivileged kids off the streets and into rock choirs or cheer-leading or dance or drama and somehow manage to change the direction of their lives. What could be better than to stage *West Side Story* with real gangs? Daniel Barenboim created the West-Eastern Divan Orchestra for Israeli, Palestinian and other Arab youngsters. Would anyone like to join a woman from the north, down south in London's East End, and do the same story with *West Side*?

The Best Hundred Best List

I finally left Birmingham after four triumphant weeks, on a Saturday night, having completed two shows. I packed seven plastic bags full of greasepaint, blackcurrant teabags, computer cables and kitchen rolls into the back of the car and set off for home sweet home at around 10.30 p.m.

I arrived in London at twenty to three after an M1 road closure involving a diversion to Bedford, fifteen miles of unsigned darkness and raging hunger. While in the gridlocked jam I'd recovered four celery sticks and some Lockets from my make-up kit. They were sublime. To keep myself from the ravages of self-pity I surfed the radio stations for gentle music to froth to. Classic FM was giving me *Late Night Lisa*, a girly breathless treacle-voiced presenter who was clearly desperate to keep me awake. After 'Danse Macabre' she gave me some sort of Russian revolution job, 'Music to Sink Battleships to'. I turned to the World Service. A voice said, 'And now for the short story "The Night I Drowned".'

To all you media studies students, would-be celebs and thespians in the making this is the reality of the business there is, apparently, no business like. By the time you've reached home, the applause is no longer ringing in your ears, believe me, only the roar of the juggernauts. And I was the lucky one. The rest of the actors had been dropped at East Acton Tube and were carrying their bags and chattels down the steps of the Underground on their way to South

London to repack their sundries for an eight-week Glorious tour of the provinces.

It is an acknowledged fact that a woman who has visited Malvern, Glasgow and Bath in the space of four weeks must be in awe of stonemasons. Never was there seen such magnificent perspective, such carved and curlicued splendour. A spectrum of creams, ochre and biscuit to outrival Tom Ford's underwear drawer. All this, plus surrounding hills *and* shopping. You can't put too high a price on looking back from Great Poultney Street towards the Holbein Gallery to see tiny rows of parchment-coloured houses climbing up into the seven shades of green which hover over the tops of the buildings. Bath may have been the Big Apple crossed with the Hellfire Club to Jane Austen, but it appeared classy and cool to a tired old thespian on her last mile home.

To celebrate I spent a hedonistic afternoon at the cinema watching the latest and earthiest version of *Pride and Prejudice*. It had managed to avoid me for the eight weeks of travelling around by disappearing from each cinema schedule the minute I decided to see it. I was rather glad in the end. The place to see *P and P* is within a nib throw of where Jane Austen wrote it. For once, I didn't sit there wondering why I wasn't in it. I loved it. I laughed, cried, adored Mr Darcy – hair-do and all – admired the casting and didn't even mind the endless giggling of the girls, which had propelled my daughter out of her seat and into the nearest pub.

No matter how many times I read or watch *P and P* I'm still on the edge of my seat, worrying that something unforeseen will stop Elizabeth and Darcy (does Darcy have a *first* name? Percy? Dick? Colin?) getting together. And no kiss. No blinking kiss! Just as Miss Austen dreamed it. Just a wondrous, yearning, burning, white heat between them, which bodes so well for draughty nights at Pemberley.

Compare and contrast my viewing on the hotel TV the night before, the imaginatively named *Hundred Most Erotic Movie Moments*. I mean what next? We've had the Classic FM Bank Holiday Hundred Most Popular Requests and the Hundred Best Films Ever and the BBC viewers' Favourite Comedy Moments and, no doubt, the Hundred Favourite Meerkat Out-Takes. Everything, these days, has to be pre-digested into competition form. Never doubt that one day there will be the Hundred Best Programmes of the Best . . . Hundred Best Programmes.

I missed many of the movie clips through sundry spats with room service, the need to log on and the even greater need to take a very long bath when somebody else is going to clean round the rim; but I saw enough to convince me that the voters' idea of eroticism is very different from mine. Well, of course. Anyone who can be enticed to be interactive with a cathode-ray machine of an evening has an even sadder life than me and probably does it as a respite from voting for a cockamamie celebrity in the tired and emotional *Big Bruvver* or a Big Brenda in the contrived *X-Factor*.

Can the high point of cinema eroticism be discus-thrower-shaped Ursula Andress walking out of the sea with a big pair of conch shells in her hands? Can it really? Doesn't do a thing for me. Mind you, the interview with Ursula *today* may have put a few of the elderly male voters off their stroke. It was scary time. Joan Rivers crossed with Bardot crossed with a cake. The second most erotic moment was Jessica Rabbit, followed at number three by a scene from a movie I'd never heard of showing a stripper dancing with her foot in someone's mouth, while somebody vaguely familiar looked on. Aargh, just pipped by a hare!

Yes, *Body Heat*, *The Postman Always Rings Twice*, Sharon's snatched moment in *Basic Instincts*, Glenn's bum in the sink in *Fatal Attraction* and Demi's feat of clay in *Ghost* were all in there somewhere. Not forgetting *Last Tango in Paris*, with Marlon 'I can't believe it's not buttocks' Brando, indulging in floorplay with poor Maria Schneider, who was nineteen at the time and never recovered her dignity.

But where, I wondered, was the best sex scene ever? Donald Sutherland and Julie Christie's reconciliation lovemaking in Nic Roeg's masterly *Don't Look Now*? Best because it expressed something more than sex? It was probably going down at number sixty-nine, just behind some sophomore shagging in *Wayne's World 3*.

One definition of eroticism, which is glued to the tip of my mind's eye, was related by Gervase Phinn, but I had the advantage of already having heard it from a teacher friend up north. It was about a loutish lad in a literature class who demanded to know, to stave off more Jane Austen and Brontë, what Miss thought was the difference between erotic and kinky. The teacher, unfazed, took a deep breath and said, 'Very well, Darren, let's suppose that I were to take a long, silky ostrich feather and trace it, ever so slowly, over the whole length of your body. That would be erotic, wouldn't it?'

Darren could only enthusiastically concur, so she continued, 'If, however, I were to use the entire ostrich . . .' she paused, 'that might be construed as kinky.'

No, give me Darcy and Elizabeth's near kiss. Or any single frame from *The Unbearable Lightness of Being* or any afternoon in the salon in *The Hairdresser's Husband*. Or Clark carrying Vivien up the apples and pears in *Gone with the Wind*, growling, 'This is one night when there's only going to be two of us in the bed.'

I must confess to finding *Secretary* quite darkly erotic, though I'm not sure what that says about me. If any bloke tried to spank *me* with a heavy book I would uppercut him. Years ago, in my twenties, playing the memorable role of Second Randy Woman in a musical called *Tyger Tyger* about William Blake, I sported high black boots, PVC hot pants and a tiny knotted-under-the-bust gingham shirt and sang a raunchy song, the lyrics of which went roughly:

I'm a buxom widow,
I sleep on sheepskin with my arse out the window!

They don't write 'em like that any more . . . rest soundly on your laurels, Mr Sondheim.

Anyway, some months later, working at Stratford on *As You Like It*, I received an unexpected call from the theatre critic Kenneth Tynan, whom I'd never met, asking me to have dinner with him after the show. I was newly married, astonished and terribly flattered that he should have picked me out of the cast of players. I went along in a little jersey suit and prattled away all evening about our new Hampstead flat and how much I was longing for a baby. It was only years later when I read his spanking diaries that it occurred to me that perhaps the Master of the Queen's Slipper had taken my Second Randy Woman persona literally, and had let his imagination wander somewhat on a theme. When it comes to eroticism, I think I prefer less slap and more tickle. I guess I'm more at home with Keats' imaginative take on the 'Grecian Urn':

'Bold Lover, never, never canst thou kiss,
Though winning near the goal – yet, do not grieve;
She cannot fade, though thou hast not thy bliss,
For ever wilt thou love, and she be fair!'

I wonder what rank John Keats might achieve in the Randiest Poets Ever Competition which can only be just around Poet's Corner.

I often wonder why we don't have a word for 'genre'. People on arts programmes are always having to use the word and invariably struggle not to sound embarrassed, so that it comes out sounding like 'Jeanne' as in D'Arc. I suppose 'oeuvre' might be just as confusing on air, coming out like 'Irv' as in Irving. I've also been troubled by the over-use of the adjective 'extraordinary' in broadcasting for some years. It's not just part of our admirably evolving language, it's unimaginative. I counted twelve in as many minutes on this week's *Start the Week* from a panel of literary giants and wordsmith Andrew Marr. Film is extraordinary, actors are extraordinary, biographies and documentaries are about extraordinary people and with such easy usage, the word becomes – ordinary. Are they not being taught vocabulary as well as grammar? We had it drummed into us with the use of a ruler. Drumming and ruling have gone out of fashion.

A friend of mine was filming in a state primary school and noticed that out of fifty staff, only one was a man. On enquiring why this was the case he was told that hiring male teachers was almost impossible as there were few applicants and those they hired didn't stay the course. His take on it was that men have been marginalized in the wake of the media hysteria over child abuse and paedophilia.

Now, I can see that might be so in a secondary school. I have strong memories of the tweed-clad, middle-aged history master at my grammar school being the unwitting recipient of shards of unfettered teenage lust. But in a primary school? With absentee fathers and single parents, working mums, au pair girls – where are the male role models for these kids?

Teaching has a far higher profile these days, happily, but whatever your sex, how would you deal with the response I heard from an eight-year-old, scolded for a breach of discipline by his teacher.

'You can't talk to me like that!' he yelled. 'My mum pays your salary.'

Lydia

Lydia is a fantasy sketch about a Victorian woman in her late twenties, who has no status or rights in the world and is utterly dependent on and in fear of her drunken and irascible father. It started out as a spoof Jane Austen and ended up as a slightly sinister short story. I'm a huge fan of Austen, but the film Americanization of her in Being Jane *left me disappointed. I'll let Lydia speak for herself.*

Lydia

Papa, I am home, Papa. He must be in the parlour, Maud. Quick, the clock is striking four. Remove your bonnet. We must make ourselves tidy before tea is served.

We are home, Papa. Here, let me help you, my dear sister. I have asked Becky to serve it in the parlour at four because . . . because . . . Oh my poor heart is thudding. Tell me, Maud, is my cheek flushed?

I know. I must have more care . . . Shush, shush, my sweet sister, put your face against the glass as I do. It will cool your brow so he will never . . .

Yes, Papa! Coming, Papa!

Let us proceed – No, wait. Your sash is . . . let me . . . better. Is mine . . .? Thank you, my dear. Yes, Papa, we are! Look at the rug, my angel sister, for your eyes are so bright, he might . . .

We are – we are! We are arrived. Here we are, dearest Papa. We are at fault to tarry over our cloaks. You should not have had to rise from your familiar chair and move away from such a cosy fire. Let me . . .

OW!

Sir, I pray you, for what reason did you strike me with your Toby jug? We were indeed three minutes late, but there was such a high wind and Spreckle ran us a merry dance on the moorland.

Ow! Sweet Lord, I am very slightly scalded. No, Father, not at all. I am glad to see, indeed to feel, how pleasantly hot Becky has made the tea. No, sir . . . we most humbly beg your pardon for the lapse. It was entirely my own tardiness and not Maud's.

I do not know, sir, what my punishment should be.

You wish me to kneel down and make myself into a fireside table, Papa? For how long this time, dearest Papa?

Till Tuesday, Papa? Very well.

Please don't cry, Becky. 'Tis no hardship to be kneeling overnight . . . Kindly fill up Papa's mug with fresh tea . . . Oh dear, now you have started Maudie off. If Papa wishes to rest his tea on my bodice and . . . ugh . . . his buttered toast on my head . . .

(*Pained*) Er . . . perhaps, Becky, you might remove Papa's hobnail boots since he had decided to rest his feet on my bustle.

Maudie, don't sniffle, loved one, for that will only anger Papa more and he is beginning to rest his tired eyes, see. Quick, Becky, rescue his mug from his hand and run off to the kitchen before he . . .

Aaah . . . aargh! Papa, I pray you, no! No!

Ah, me. Pick up the pieces, Becky dear, and bring Papa more fresh tea. (*Sotto voce*) How much porter did you bring him this day? And Becky, run that hand under the cold tap or it will blister.

Do as Papa bids you, dear sister, bring him more cushions to support his back . . . No, Papa, leave her be. I beg of you, leave Maudie be. If you must take out your anger, do it to me, not to . . .

Please, Papa – Papa, our crime was merely one of tardiness. Surely you can forgive us now?

Mercy, sir, how came you by that knowledge? Whosoever would . . ?

Oh Lord, that stick is heavy and missed my head by a whisker . . . Maudie dear, remove the shards of glass from the rug post-haste.

I beseech you, Father, to believe me . . . I swear.

How could you have thought I would keep that from you? I was about to tell you during tea but you became so . . . I did not mean to deceive you, Papa. My sister and I had no intention of tarrying with Captain Wynchwood and the king's regiment. It was chance only that led us to cross Turnpike Ho at the same time as their manoeuvres and . . . Uargh! The embers from your pipe were unimaginably hot on my . . . I have indeed learned my lesson, Papa.

No, Papa. We will never speak to the good captain again. I swear on . . . On the life of my dear Papa . . . Sir, you have my word. So long as you live, dear Papa.

(*Pause*)

Ssshh, Maudie. Hark, he snores. He sleeps. He sleeps. I cannot . . . I can no longer . . .

Maudie, shush. Shush, shush, sweetheart. Listen carefully now. You must stop weeping and follow my instructions carefully and to the letter. Sshhhssh. Take the pillow you brought for his back. Take the biggest of the pillows, dear child. Yes, the tapestry brocade once so beloved of poor dear Mama. Take the pillow to Papa and do not wake him, darling child, just put the pillow over his face . . . Do as I say. Over his face . . . Yes, dear child, *over his face,* and press down with all your might. Lean on him with all your weight; I will add my own.

Dastardly, dastardly heinous ROGUE! *I say lean on him!* Good. Lean, my love, *lean. Push* and lean till every breath is squeezed from his *cruel* body. PRESS PRESS PRESS!

Aaagh. It is over, Maud. I said it is over.

Stand up, child. Take the pillow and replace it exactly where you found it on the settle. Come and finish your tea. Some cake? One slice or six? And six for me too.

Now, pass me the tea bell, Maud. I *said,* pass me the tea bell.

Becky, dear, Miss Maud and I will be going out. Yes, *now.* So fetch our mantles please and order up the phaeton. My father is sleeping, but he has given us permission to go back into Featheringham for supper. When he wakes, please inform him that we shall not be back late. Come, Maudie, put on your bonnet. And pinch your cheeks, dear. You look as if you've seen a ghost.

Mayor Culpa

One Thursday I took out a contract on the life of the then mayor of London, Ken Livingstone. If he'd washed up on the tide by Eel Pie Island – it was me; I'd confess. My defence, however, will stand up in any court in the land. The thing about the congestion charge is that despite what Ken, with his own brand of nasal congestion, talks about, it actually *causes* congestion.

From six in the evening, all round the outer zone, you can see skulking Skodas and hovering Hondas in every side street in the capital. One of them is me in Audrey, my audacious Audi. On the stroke of six we all rev up and head for the same street at the same time. Still gridlocked in Gower Street forty-five minutes before curtain up, I opened the car door, yelled g'bye to Natalie, who was driving me, and legged it into the frozen night. I was wearing a long faux-fur, a cloth hat, high-heeled boots and carrying a throat-steaming machine in a bag. As I hurtled down the road, a woman in the next car rolled down her window and called out to Natalie, 'She'll make it! I know she will!'

The reason for the jam? Thought you'd like to know – *eleven* buses one after the other. Just the eleven. All – I repeat, all, virtually empty, not one in the bus lane, and a big bendy bastard, on the yellow box, screwing up the others – totally empty! Then we wonder why audiences are thin in the West End. At least *I* was there that night. Wheezing like a canary in a coal mine, but *there*.

Taxis run smoothly in bus lanes. Cars respect bus lanes but are forced into them when turning left or when the lane is hidden by moving traffic. Bikes wibble-wobble around them. The only mode of transport which really can't be bothered with them is – yes, you've guessed it – buses.

London buses are so sure of their supreme right to use the bus lane that they feel free to use everyone else's lane too. They'll zoom along a bus lane when it's free, then dodge into the motorists lane if that looks freer. Where they really excel, though, is in stopping at bus stops to pick up and drop passengers. This they often prefer to do in the middle of the road. Pulling into the kerb by the bus stop would be much too fiddly, the driver wants the passengers on and off quickly, so lives are endangered all the way from Camberwell to Potters Bar because that extra wheel turn might just give the driver repetitive strain injury.

Meanwhile, I read that traffic wardens are being taught to be nicer to us, which won't work either because *we* hate what they do and *they* see us as commission on wheels.

Parking signs are deliberately confusing: 'Between 9.00 and 6.30 except 1 p.m. to 2 p.m.' *What?* 'No return within the hour.' *Eh?* And every ticket has a different format, depending on the area, with differing instructions about how and where to display it.

The roads are made of migraine-inducing, undulating tarmac which ruins the undercarriage of the car, the pleasure of the drive and the air we drive through. As I write there are thousands of roadworks in London, causing mayhem to road users everywhere. You have to have sat nav in-built in your skull to get to your own doorway. The road outside my terrace was sealed to traffic and coned off for a month before Christmas, then in January the whole thing was dug up again in a slightly different form, tunnels dug, roads fenced off, and it still remains so in March. The exit to the terrace is closed, and you wouldn't believe the twenty-two-point turns I perform to get in and out. Meanwhile, I swear on a stack of *A to Z*'s that *nobody* ever *works* on these sites. There's a number to call and I do. Frequently. 'Oh, s'Friday they've all gone back up north, 'aven't they?' said the operator' 'North of what?' I ask. 'North of Kracow?'

As for the potholes – how long have you got? My friend's theory is that this is the last-minute roadworks rush and a month before the elections they will disappear as magically as they appeared, in a puff of tarmac dust, leaving the traffic flowing seamlessly through the capital and the water pipes doing the same. I mean, if I want to change one pipe in my front yard, I must go through three separate council departments, the water board, cable companies. They send a letter to the council informing them that they will be digging a hole in the ground and blocking nine lanes of traffic and then send in the cones. First, though, they fasten yellow notices to lamp posts in the surrounding streets forbidding you, who pay hundreds of pounds for this very privilege, to park there.

But not straightforward yellow notices. The one which got me a sixty-pounder on a Sunday night at midnight when I'd been driving round for forty minutes trying to find a residents' space, said the following: 'Clear one space'. What the hell does that mean? Clear one space where? They seem to assume I know what they are talking about. I cleared one space . . . didn't see in the dark that the one space was a pay bay not a resident's and got a pigging ticket.

In two weeks' time I shall be getting my bus pass, which I may well eat.

On Easter Sunday I drove to my friend Lizzy's for lunch, with Diva, the beauteous Basenji, in the back seat. Going out with her alone is reminiscent of outings with two scarcely weaned babies. I have a safety belt, a basket, some chews, an assortment of squeaky toys, some treats, a lead, a shower-proof coat, hers not mine, and a black, fluffy penguin with an orange beak. Halfway up Winnington Road, she starts to make the yodel/mewing sound which masquerades as her bark and is much better than her bite, and I deduce, instinctive new mother that I am, that she wants to pee. I stop the car, climb out in ungainly fashion, via the passenger seat, and fold down the front seat with my late mother's voice ringing in my ears, 'What do you want to get a two-door car for? I hate it if someone offers me a lift in a two-door car. I always hurt my back and ladder my stockings, I'd sooner walk.' I release the dog's safety belt and put her under my arm to click the lead onto her collar and slide out of the car wedging my foot in the door to retrieve my shoulder bag. Then, dog under one arm and bag in the other I slam the car door, excruciatingly, on my thumb.

Outside of childbirth there's not much worse in the sickening pain area than a digit slammed in a car door. It goes through to your core and makes your whole body hum. As is one's wont when alone, I don't register any pain, I just stand there, on Planet Throb, feeling absurdly sorry for myself, as the thumb goes the colour of a naval uniform and a blood blister smartly forms.

My main concern is keeping Diva off the road with the retractable lead on 'go'. So we wander round the grass verges for a while, with me bent double trying to hold her collar. It soon becomes clear that peeing is the last thing on her mind. We get back in the car and I drive on, white-faced, waving a stumpy thumb in the air to keep the blood flowing until I can get to a tomato.

Yes, you've read it right, a tomato. The best thing to ease the pain from a trapped digit is a tomato – it's something to do with enzymes apparently, and I've never forgotten the tip, so the minute I got to Lizzy's I asked for one and she, in the middle of stuffing a turkey, carved out finger-sized holes in several cherry tomatoes. I sat with one on my finger, all through lunch and the rest of the afternoon.

I won't dwell on the three chummy thumb-squeezes one of my co-stars gave me the next night on stage because there may still be members of the audience who have rationalized, in their own way, Florence Foster Jenkins' sudden shriek of 'STOP! STOP! – THUMB! THUMB!' in a quiet part of act two.

Lately, I've been exercising my mind on the sad and sorry subject of Princess Diana's memorial wet patch. I don't know how many squillions have been wasted in pursuit of a place in which to be publicly maudlin, but what I'd love to know is who was the nudnik who finally said, 'Yes! The winner is a thin stretch of water-feature in the middle of a park already featuring natural water-features, as do most London parks.'

Whatever one felt about the late, iconic princess, one has to admit that she had the best nose in the world for a fund-raiser. It became her raison d'être in a bleak round of regal paraphernalia. My friend Geoff had the very best idea in the world for a *useful* memorial – one that might have actually pleased *her* – and that was to build, at probably half the cost of the concrete and designer-water job, a purpose-built hall to be used for charitable functions. In other words a place to raise money for good causes where the cause in question doesn't instantly lose around £6,000 of the profits raised on the hire of a hall in some posh London hotel. No prizes for thinking up that little earner.

On Saturday I passed a demo in the Strand outside Zimbabwe House. Drumming and dancing in the rain, a small group of people protested about repression, corruption and starvation in their once thriving and beautiful country. Zimbabwe's Mugabe is as cracked and corrupt as Iran's Isyourdinnerbad, but Africa will never merit the kind of outrage generated by the Middle East. One wonders why.

There is a deeply unsexy charity for the women of Zimbabwe, which might interest you, although it has failed to attract any media attention here, save for the always reliable *Woman's Hour*. Their only tampon factory has closed down, the farms are no longer able to produce cotton, there is a water shortage and the women of Zimbabwe cannot afford to buy towels at inflated prices. A box of tampons costs £4 and the average monthly wage is £12. This forces them to use newspaper or leaves and this leads to infections, which their partners often view with suspicion, and a lot of domestic violence ensues.

The charity 'Dignity! Period.' is being supported by actress Niamh Cusack in this country, and you can check up on www.actsa.org to find out more. They have a truck full of tampons, donated by South African women and big business, which has been held up at the border since Thursday, because customs, contrary to an earlier agreement, are demanding taxes of $10,000. The powerful union Amicus has lent Dignity! Period. several grand to get the truck through the border to the women, but there will be many fallow lunar months to follow.

Bus lanes, sore thumbs, Mayor Culpa? I tell you, girls, we just don't know we're born.

I Go to Pieces

I've promised myself I'm going to stop doing it. That was the very last time. I'm a grown woman in the dawn of my twilight and it's neither seemly, attractive, nor productive. It leaves me battered and drawn and, frankly, robs the whole event of any pleasure. I've been doing it for so many years though, maybe it's just part of my mode of rehearsal. Maybe I couldn't *open* without doing it and live to do a second show, and a third and a two hundredth.

Here's what I do: I go to pieces before my opening night.

After the successful eight-week tour of *Glorious*, with most of the faults of a new play ironed out (along with most of the leading lady) on the road, we were given a week off while the much smaller London theatre, the Duchess, was prepared for our arrival in the West End. There was no revolving stage, so the furniture would have to be moved manually and the back wall had to be sliced in half.

I used the week off to make a card of an elaborate collage of the cast and crew, to draw their faces and cut their names into neat little frames. It took enjoyable hours, many trips to PIP's the copyists and work with Pritt stick, tissue paper, relevant CDs and bottles of wine. Finally I achieved completion, i.e. I only left out six or seven key members of the company, a fact I realized hours before the first-night curtain went up. Oddly, the card looked bought, not made, and I didn't have the chutzpah to say, 'Hey, *I* did that!'

*

When exploring how far I could extend my vocal limits, I picked up a book from a shelf in my study called *Unlocking Your Voice*. I was given the book years ago by its author, Esther Salamon, a voice teacher who lived in North London. My memory of visiting her house is that it seemed psychedelic. There were the most vibrant hues everywhere: pinks and blues and golden yellows and a garden filled with enormous summer flowers, growing as if in a child's painting. Esther herself looked like an advert for a natural-health magazine. She filled her skin to the very edges, with a glorious head of white, white hair and cornflower eyes. I must have been having throat problems during the run of the musical *Wonderful Town* and she directed me to the Bel Canto way of opening the throat and adopting a 'welcoming' stance. I'd forgotten all of this until the day, almost twenty-five years later, when I found myself, once more, struggling with a raw throat and some ray of sunshine directed me back to her book, hibernating on a shelf; since when I've had no trouble at all, even when singing every night like a fox attempting to compromise a Siamese cat.

'I'd really like to thank her for that chapter,' I thought to myself a few weeks ago. 'I wonder if she's still living round the corner?' I was thumbing through the local paper as I had this thought and, two thumbs later, I saw her obituary on the page before me. I had to shake my head in wonder. If she'd had one more tip to pass on before she went to her next psychedelic garden, I'm so grateful it was me to whom she passed it.

On the Monday of last week, three days before press night, our leading man and piano accompanist, Bill Oxborough, went down with viral laryngitis. He had minimally less voice than a giraffe and we were advised he might remain voiceless for two weeks. Our slow technical rehearsal on the new stage turned into a tense rehearsal for the cast with his amazingly unruffled understudy, Michael Blore. We worked in chaos, crammed into inches of wing space when in the provinces we'd had acres. Stripping off costumes, tights flying in each other's faces, bosom padding falling into the void, hissed instructions as we tripped over new, unfriendly wires, intimately banging bums with stagehands we'd never met before but may have had to marry if things had continued that way. My dressing room turned out to be sixty-seven steps up from the stage. I was going to need the lungs of a Sherpa and the calves of a Maori prop forward. No drama school will ever mention these prerequisites to their students.

We crawled home in the dark and then back into the pub staleness of the theatre the following day for a dress rehearsal, then our first reduced-price preview. This is the time when one is allowed to make one's mistakes. Or was. For now we have the American system where the critics demand to attend a preview if their other nights are already booked up with first nights. So we have a missing actor, an unprepared theatre, Machu Picchu to mount – and, the pièce de résistance, Bob the bleeding builder in the restaurant next door.

Yes, the restaurant next door is re-opening on Monday and nothing, and I mean nothing, short of an injunction or builders without kneecaps, will stop them drilling into our back wall, all afternoon and most of the evening.

In between the dress rehearsal and the performance, as we sat in the stalls receiving our last-minute notes, I wept silent tears of exhaustion and fear. How could something as complete as the last show we played at the Bath Theatre Royal, one week earlier, the echoes of whose glorious reception were still fresh in our ears, turn into this cockamamie cock-up?

No time to ponder the metaphysical, the first-night previewers are in their seats, with their honed personality laughs. Up went the curtain and off came the drill caps.

'We have these noisy new neighbours in the next-door apartment,' I was forced to purr, 'and they are passionate about renovation.' The audience responded in kind and there was more than a hint of *Whose Line Is It Anyway?* in the air. It was a wild, hilarious evening ending with, if not a standing ovation, then certainly a crouching one.

The audience on the second night appeared to be a convention of mime artistes. The first act played to a profound silence. As I contemplated leaving before the second-act curtain-up, they changed tack, cleared their collective throat and chortled for Great Britain and the Cinque Ports. Go explain!

The third night was press night. I went to bed fearing nothing but fear itself and woke at 3 a.m. with the mother-in-law of all migraines.

I took the last-resort drugs and spent the rest of the night checking myself to see how I was.

It's a combination of stress and food that hits the jackpot. I don't know if the sauce on the goose contained monosodium glutamate but it tasted good enough to suggest it did. Chinese food is full of it. I've learned to avoid it, though I taste it in my dreams. I have murdered many a duck in pancakes with plum sauce when the pace of life was easy, and had not the slightest reaction. All I know is that, migraine-wise, I know nothing and neither do most of the experts I've consulted. They can tell you the latest drugs – one such maven examined and tested me for hours and concluded, 'You have migraine. These are the latest drugs; that'll be £180. Lovely to meet you, keep well. The door is the square thing in the wall.'

Tony Porter, the reflexologist who is used to saving my life, came over and saved me again. It is miraculous to observe someone pressing a place on your foot which makes your stomach gurgle and start to work again after a three-day lay-off. Without him, every understudy I've ever had would now be a major star.

My daughter once told me that she always knew when I had a migraine coming because I wore green clothes and my voice changed. I have noticed that people's voices express their wellbeing. On the phone, I can immediately tell if a friend is down or unwell because there is a deadness of tone which comes from trying to retain energy. This theory only breaks down when talking to people from Hull, whose dry tones tend to be as flat as the countryside in which they live, with or without an 'edache.

Flowers and more flowers, presents, kisses, hugs, stupid must-do rituals from long-forgotten pacts with the gods (not to mention the stalls), followed by the show itself. Our Boy Bill was back thanks to Hypocrates, silence and antibiotics, and the cast rose gloriously to the occasion. No one drilled, although I had a fine dentist joke up my sleeve, and the reception at the end was dreamy.

Afterwards there was a party in a Turkish restaurant with cheese sandwiches and country and western music. Florence Foster Jenkins herself could not have arranged it more crazily. Home to another night of the sleep of the just reprieved, and a morning of disbelief when the reviews were sublime.

Next time, should there be one, I'm going to be hypnotized. I shall have that nice Mr McKenna put me into a trance for the last production week and he can come and snap his fingers when they're queuing up at the box office for returns. I remember reading how the late Bob Monkhouse once bought a nightclub under hypnosis; my last publisher had his wisdom teeth out under hypnosis; how hard can it be to break a middle-aged woman of the lifelong habit of self-sabotage?

Animal Writes

I'm well on my way to becoming one of those grumpy old actresses with faces like crocodile handbags who live out their days surrounded by wagging tails and fetlocks, believing mankind to be warlike and feckless. I stayed overnight in Dorset with a dear old friend and fell in love with one of her three West Highland terriers – the one with only three feet, who thinks he has at least five. My own Diva was paralysed with fear by these tiny Westies and leapt three feet into my arms, trembling like a tumble dryer.

This week I've been appalled by the story of Mr Smith who, like his dear old dad before him, made a nice little living on the side by shooting greyhounds in the head. It seems, allegedly, that Mr Smith is the villain. The racing life of a greyhound is short, maybe two or three years, after which they must be re-housed or kept by their owner, which costs money, presumably not covered by the poor bugger's winnings.

'Oh, yes, m'dear,' says the trainer to the owner, 'Lady Grey's gone to some nice, dog-loving family in West Wittering. She's loving her retirement and the kids adore her. Your new dog's doing well, isn't he, eh?' Meanwhile, Lady Grey, fit, healthy and five years old, with maybe a tiny touch of arthritis in the knees from all that running and training and sweating and controlled dieting, is trundled over to Smith's field, where, as a gesture of thanks, she's shot in the head at close range and buried alongside the last batch. For ten quid a slug.

When the field gets full he starts all over again at the other end of the field. Makes good economic sense, doesn't it?

I don't suppose there'll be a prosecution, after all who is to blame? The shooter? His dad? The trainers – the breeders, the owners, the gamblers – the RSPCA? The government who keep quiet and pocket the copious taxes on racing? Because as sure as hell is hot, everyone's in the know, even by the sin of not *really* caring to know.

I wonder what would be the appropriate punishment for Mr Smith? For ten thousand lives? You could chain him to a kennel in all weathers and make him run a mile a night pursued by a pack of foxhounds. After a few years of that he might well request someone nice and kind puts a gun to his head and blows his brains out. I'd stump up ten quid for that.

I even knew, through a long-ago conversation with an actress who rescues greyhounds, that if you are thinking of having a dog you should have an ex-racing greyhound: a) because they are gentle and loving dogs and b) because you'll be saving them, after a pretty terrible childhood, from an even more terrible death. 'But don't they need a phenomenal amount of exercise?' I'd asked. She'd shot me a withering stare. 'Good gracious no. You let them out, they run like mad for twenty minutes and they're happy for the rest of the day.' And, I guess, for the rest of their days . . .

All over bar the shooting, I know, but the winching of the whale made a dent in my week which can only be smoothed out by committing it to Word. In the media there was an awful lot of excitation for the ex-cetacean. From first sighting of blowhole to veterinary pathologist, Big Orca/Willie/Moby made the front pages of most newspapers in most of the world, and the worst of the excruciating puns involving the word 'whale' had left the sub editors' desks by Monday. (The *Blankety Blank* cheque book and pen goes to 'The Writing Was on the Whale'.)

All this coverage – helicopters, paparazzi, zoom lenses – excludes Norway and Japan, where whales are a source of revenue not conservation. The thought of spending £100,000 to save an old salt, plainly bent on Dignitas, left these nations agog with disinterest. Few of us here minded the expense, though I might have done were I a survivor of the Hatfield train crash or an elderly patient in only the *first* stages of Alzheimer's disease.

The whole thing worried me from the moment I heard about it. It seemed like a bad omen, this massive mammal choosing the heart of London to die in. It's easy to imagine it as a metaphor for the city itself – ancient, scared, scarred, polluted, isolated yet gridlocked . . . beached. During the struggle for survival I worked out an alternative motivation for the beast. She'd wanted a weekend in London before she died. She was just a tourist, stopping by to see Chelsea now it's stopped swinging and surrendered to the rouble and maybe to take in a spot of theatre – s'posed to be the best in the world, isn't it? Maybe Sir Rhino de Bear-Giraffe would be playing somewhere.

After all, other animals seemed to figure largely in the theatre classifieds. She'd checked with the travel agent before leaving. There was *The Lion King, The Night of the Iguana, The Wild Duck, The Rat Pack* and, coming shortly, though the spelling could be improved, *Who's Afraid of Virginia Wolf?* Obviously her best bet was to head for the Prince of Wales theatre, and a front-row circle seat, with concessions, for *Mammal Mia . . .* (Stoppit, just stoPPIT! Ed. I can't, sorry, I'm on a roll. Mo.) All that remained was for her to participate in a little thespian outing. It was only when she failed to get a callback for the second auditions for *Swamalot* that she finally gave up what Edward Albee termed *The Goat*.

Years ago, a friend of mine, over dinner, handed his sweet old mum a list of words to read out as a sort of party game. I know it wasn't kind and we shouldn't have laughed but it was hilarious at the time, and in fairness she never really did know why. The assembled guests got more and more helpless as her perplexity grew. The list of words was: whale, oil, beef and hooked. Please do not try this at home.

Street Furniture

Jean is my oldest character. She has true working-class grit without a shred of self-pity about the hand life has dealt her. She is a magnet for kids, dogs, pigeons and down-and-outs. She has a fine, intelligent mind and is opinionated but not judgemental. She would have made an able councillor or politician, and has regrets but no bitterness. She has humour, loyalty and resilience.

Street Furniture

(Jean, sixty-eight, grey perm, anorak, rainhood, stockings and fur-lined boots. She's doing the crossword.)

Irony. Must be. Eight down 'more ferrous than sarcasm implies'. Oooh, he's a scallywag, this setter, isn't he? Even his lights are *mischievous*.

'Ello, boy . . . Oh you're a lovely boy, aren't you? What is he?

Oh *she*! My mistake. My mistake. Looks like a fox on a lead, I've never seen the like. Aaw . . . aren't you clever? That's a lovely paw, thank you . . . No, I 'aven't got anything for you, love – that's just a bit of bread for the heron.

What's her name? Floribunda . . . Dulcinea Jubilee out of *what*? Blimey, that's a bit of a mouthful, isn't it? Well, I'll call you Flo . . . Yes, I will, yes, I will.

Mind, I had a sister-in-law Flo and her bite *was* worse than her bark. Oh, you like having your neck rubbed, don't you? Yes, you do . . . Where's she going?

Ow Lord. She's gone in. Whaddyou wanna do that for, Flo, eh? You'll get yourself saturated; she wants to watch those swans. They're mean 'uns, you know, them swans. That's cos they stay monogamous with the same 'usband swan for life. I feel the same way meself.

Come out, why don't you? Oh, my Lord, you've shaken yourself all over them lovely suede boots of your mum's.

I hope you know the Queen can shoot you if you start with her swans. Oh, yes, she can. Ow now don't you fret . . . She'd never get a gun in that little handbag of hers. It's full of aspirins and speeches and spare crowns.

Yes . . . Aaw, look at her face . . . like a drowned ferret. Look at those frown lines. Drop of that Botox for you girl, eh? I bet that Sharon Osbourne gives it to her dogs.

(Cranes over to look at dog-owner's paper.)

I got stuck on that one. Seventeen across, but I've got it now. Ooh, no, I wouldn't consider telling you . . . Spoil my day if someone did that to me.

Aw, look at that . . . He's let that big mutt do his business all over the Italian gardens. Shame. Tut tut tut. Mucky beggar – pardon my expletive. With all them bins right there for the asking. Hideous great things. Dog poo's all they're good for, if you ask me. Oh, *don't get me started*. Look at 'em. One two three four five six ten of 'em strung across that lovely old square. White houses, lamp posts from the old days and stuck right in the porticos to the gardens, huge black plastic monstrosities, like black dogs at the gates of Hull.

Oh, street furniture they call it, do they? More like street fustilugs. You never 'eard of fustilugs? Stone me, it comes up all the time in the *FT*. Means mouldy, obsolete, but used to be common parlance for a gross obscene person, usually female.

Well, there you are. I just got one of them retentive whatsits, minds. I still got all them poems from school in me head, 'Battle of Lepanto', 'Had we but world enough and time', 'Shall I compare thee to a summer's day?' Yeah, well, I was the brainbox out of the eight of us. I could've gone on but me mum needed the wages so I left school at thirteen and went cleaning with her. Hospitals.

So, don't get me started on the streets of London.

Who? The Mayor? Mayor Culpa I call him. Me neither. I never met *anyone* who voted for him . . . His daft ideas: broken-down, bendy buses, rubbish bins the size of articulated lorries all labelled – brown glass, green glass, paper and plastic, potato peelings and underpants, Foster's lager and bubblewrap.

Recycle they say, re-blessed cycle! I done that and put it all out in a green box and it's still standing there. Three months later. Only thing taking it away is the rats. They comes more 'an once a fortnight. Reckon they took Dick Whittington's waste more often than ours. Shameful.

Watch out! What's she eating? Put it down, Flo! Drop it! Oh dear, too late . . . you'll have to catch it at the other end now.

You reckon that's what it is? The postmen? Them rubber bands all over the pavement. They're wrapping all yer post in plastic bags, right, and binding them with rubber bands what all go down yer dog's throat.

Conspicuous waste it's called. No wonder all your post offices are closing. I've yet to get over Consignia.

I don't know about you. If that whatsit – new one – worzel toff, with the platinum-hair bob, yeah, your Boris, gets off his crossbar long enough to put his fat, pink hands on our pensions we'll soon 'ave to pick 'em up at 'Arrods.

No, love, they don't expect us to live on it. Expect us to die on it more like. I'd like to see your toff Cameron live on fifty-nine quid a week when a packet of PG Tips costs a fiver.

That's a staple though, isn't it, Flo? Nothing like a nice cuppa tea.

Yeah, I should cocoa!

What do they say? 'How can you tell if a politician is lying? If he touches his cuffs he's telling the truth. If he smooths his hair he's telling the truth. But if he opens his mouth . . .' My nephew told me that and he's six! Laugh!

I think she *has*. Taken a fancy. Yeah, well, we know when we're liked, don't we, Flo?

Got what? Separation anxiety? Who has? You or the dog? You're taking her to a dog hotel? Dog hotel? How much did you say? Twenty pounds every day and a dog walker? You're having me on!

Fifteen pounds an hour? That's more than I got cleaning the hospital. A lot more. And they got five or six of 'em on leads, so that's five times fifte— Oh, I'm not going to go there. It's enervating, innit? What's it all coming to?

Tell you what. I'd look after you for nothing, wouldn't I? I'm only over there on the estate. Your mum could drop you off. It's not so bad as they write it up, honest. There's good sorts as well, that'll look out for you.

No. Well, I can understand your feelings but she'd be safe as ho— right you are. My mistake. That's all right. Just a thought. No skin off my—

(*Silence*)

Are you off then? Bye bye then, Flo. Off you go. No . . . go with your mum. She's waiting. See you again, I hope.

(*Thinks, then calls out.*)

By the by, that clue. Seventeen across. I done it earlier. Eighteen letters or 4-2-3-9. It's an anagram. It's 'care in the community'.

Doctor Who's Who

Usually my Sundays are precious to me, especially when I'm playing in the theatre six nights a week, but the chance to play a cameo role in the new and revitalized *Doctor Who* – as an alien operating as a TV announcer inside a television console the day before the coronation of Queen Elizabeth II – was unmissable.

I was to film it on my day off in the disused studio at Alexandra Palace, where television first began. It was very cold and unloved in that old building and the wind blew up my bronze chiffon Neil Cunningham party frock, made for act one of my solo theatre show, *Live and Kidding.* Yes, these days you get to bring your own clothes and do your own hair and make-up in television. I didn't care. I couldn't wait. I knew I would have to *imagine* David Tennant and Billie Piper were pursuing me to my death – that I would never in fact meet any of my fellow actors, but when you've done one-person acting in theatre, it's no sweat to imagine that you are imbibing enough earthly energy from a television audience at home in 1953 to send the entire planet skittering out of its orbit.

I was up for it . . . and not too early either since I lived in the very shadow of the Palace and had watched it burn down at least once, clutching children in my arms as they sobbed, 'Do something! Do something! Don't let it burn down, Les!' Les being the part-time fireman who lived upstairs with Ruth, our Swiss au pair, in our three-bedroomed terraced house. Those were the days.

It was so cold that the wind blew up my evening dress and rattled my pearls. I was the only actor among several technicians and I had to respond to commands like, 'OK, Maureen, could you give us fifteen seconds of having every last drop of energy sucked out of you?' I obliged gleefully. Then, 'Could you screech and cackle as you suck all the features off the children's faces, please?' It was great. I was a born alien. My kids, when small, would have thought it was just me being me after I caught them weeing in the waste paper basket.

I had virtually no voice the next evening for *Glorious*, the play I was in at the Duchess Theatre, but, fortunately, I was supposed to sound like a violently braking Harley Davidson in the Blackwall Tunnel . . . and I did! Then I forgot about it.

Nothing in my life this far has brought me more fan mail. I sign pictures of Tennant and Piper constantly and the autograph books, arms and motor-cycle helmets of some of the oddest people you'll ever see, hanging outside BBC buildings. The dress I wore is going for auction on *Cash in the Attic* and my feeling is there will be bids from all over the planet. *Doctor Who* is on all the time somewhere in the world and though it's not science, it's no fiction that there are no repeat fees for us aliens. I've always wanted to be Doctor Who. Always. It's time he was a woman, so how about a pensioner with comic timing, all her own hair and a toy boy? I wonder if there's anyone at the Beeb who knows who I am, isn't already dead and whom I haven't already offended?

Glamour, Us?

I'm embarrassed to tell you that, contrary to the line I've been shooting for some years about life in the theatre being arduous and solitary with cold baked beans from the tin and no social life save watching re-runs of *Curb Your Enthusiasm* on E4, my last fortnight has been verging on the glamorous. In truth, I bet even Sadie and Sienna have nibbled less canapés under less canopies in the last couple of weeks than I have.

It started with a phone call from novelist and Oz party girl Kathy Lette, as my family and I were walking the dog round Hampstead ponds.

'Now, don't dismiss this out of hand,' she began, at full tilt, 'because this is one you can't refuse. I know it's ridiculously short notice but you've just *got* to do it. No, don't say no till I tell you the whole thing. It's tomorrow. It's Roland Garros. The French Open. It's the Channel Tunnel at 7.30 a.m. It's PARIS. It's champagne and lunch in the Krug tent, a tennis match, dinner and a night at the Ritz. June Sarpong and Caroline Thingy and Simon . . . and Robert doodah and meee! You're a *goddess* – we need you . . .'

I finally spoke. 'Who dropped out?'

She dropped her voice to earth register. 'Ronnie Ancona.'

'That's good,' I said. 'I like her. I'd hate to be replacing a Cat or a Kelly or a Caprice . . . the disappointment to the Gallic psyche when they saw *me* could be *de trop*.'

'So *will* you come? You'd love it, it's gonna be very girly and—'

'Kathy, you know I love you and any other time – I mean – I've got a reading at the BBC on Friday morning, I haven't looked at it and my Geordie accent's as good as my Maori and—'

'You mean you just have to *read* something? So? You can read, right?'

'Yes. No, it's a sitcom *pitch.*'

'Why does a sitcom have to be pitched?'

'Why? Cos the execs can't tell by *reading* it if it's any *good*. No one will stick their necks out.'

'So, read it tonight. You'll be brilliant.'

'Kathy, I'd *love* to and I know it would do me good. But *tomorrow*? I can't . . . I absolutely . . . I . . . I. What time did you say the train goes?'

Which is how I found myself leaning over the balcony of the Krug tent, snapping Roger Federer, doing his pre-semi-final warm-up ten yards from the bubbles in my champagne, and why I now have *five* panoramic photographs of a white blur with a racquet in its hand on my mobile.

It had been a blistering hot day as we'd rattled through the English Channel on the shortly to be all French Eurostar. I'd remembered my beloved mother taking a similar trip to visit my brother in Brussels.

'Will I see the water?' she'd asked.

'I bloody hope not!' said my brother. 'But if you do – leg it.'

It still feels like a miracle to arrive at Gare du Nord, without going up in the air, and find a new land and language. Kathy changed on the train into a tiny strawberry-covered mini-suit and fruit-encrusted shades, actress Caroline, black and beautiful, changed from skin-tight jeans into skin-tight cut-off jeans, June's neckline plunged deeper than the Channel, and the blokes and I stayed in crumpled linen.

Lunch was asparagus froth, osso bucco, strawberries and rose-water ice cream. It was all sumptuous and, during it, Panos of Krug explained to me how oak-barrel storage differentiates their bubbles from rival bubbles, which are kept in stainless steel. I tried to look grateful and excise all thoughts of Jeffrey Archer and shepherd's pie from my mind.

The heat, the eager ball boys, Federer's femurs, the colour of the clay, the drama of the seventeen-year-old Czech girl Vaidišová almost trouncing her rather substantial Russian opponent, the harmonized grunting, like a cheap, Eastern-bloc porn film: *Aaagh! Wuuoff! Aaagh! Wuuouff!* – it was *glamorous*. I wanted to freeze-frame the whole day and pin it on my fridge.

As if that wasn't sybaritic enough, on Sunday I headed off, with six friends, for a week on Zakynthos, my Greek island of yesteryear. In my experience, if a holiday isn't disastrous then there's nothing to write about. Our base was a villa with sundecks and terraces around an infinity pool bordering a sea the colour of Paul Newman's eyes. It was furnished with exquisite simplicity, the walls left plastered with designs in deep blue paint to match the cornflower shutters.

Trevor and Valerie Grove leaped out of their beds at dawn, straight onto the tennis courts of the next-door Peligoni Club for two hours. Trevor cooked meals which made my myopic old eyes water. Val Hall and Josie brought their own rubber gloves. Colin brought eight books and kept to a strict routine of one book a day, and a diet of muesli, cheese and eggs. Clive arrived from Athens on a ferry and took four sweltering hours in a cab to find us. Me, I was munched by every mosquito in the Peloponnese. (Mozzies get very little Jewish food on the island and I sincerely hope I lay on their chests for days. Do mosquitoes have chests? Google calls . . .) I remained as contented as a bottle-nosed dolphin in a herring shoal. I won't go into the prickly heat except to say that on a couple of photos, I look like a Kit-Kat wrapper.

The Peligoni Club took us on a boat for grilled sardines and Sophia, my adorable friend from the year before, opened her art café for a moussaka as light as air and eleven kilos of baked lamb. Friends from last year threw *cocktail* parties for us – I mean I haven't been to a cocktail party since waspies went out of fashion – and, as the Noël Coward song says, 'I *couldn't* have liked it more!'

Reality check. I'm back. The dog came into season without me, bled on my bed, ate the stair carpet and is gated for three weeks. I reckon glamour has a quota and I've had mine for the year.

No Smoke Without Being Fired

Dree Daniel occurred to me after noticing the oddly disparate groups which now assemble outside office buildings, pubs, cafés and salons of their native cities. The pariahs, the lepers, the renegades, the misfits – what do they all have in common? People who would probably not even nod to each other in the course of a day's work, now find a subtle kinship. They are the last of the smokers. Reduced to a dense stock, like chicken soup, they huddle in doorways, blind to the death threats writ large on the front of their cigarette packets and robbed for ever of the simple reward of a fag and a drink at the same time.

No Smoke Without Being Fired

(*Outside a large, modern, glass building, a fashionable woman in her late thirties is trying to light a cigarette. The wind keeps blowing her lighter out and her cupped hands won't shield it. She wears a wrap which keeps getting in her way, but it protects her from the wind tunnel.*)

Dammit . . . Aaaargh. Bugger this for a game of cards. Sodding lighter. C'mon . . . Ah, got it, you bas— Noooo! (*Breathes out long and hard, then looks up.*)

Hello! Sorry! Hello? Yes, *you* – fellow pariah – can I have a loan of your lighter? Your lighter. Mine's died on me. Oh yah, I realize it's great *looking*! So it ruddy should, it cost as much as my parents' first pigging house, it just doesn't do the one thing in life it's supposed to do.

Like having a sodding smoke isn't hard enough these days? Jesus in 'jamas. I'm out here, like a tossing leper, freezing my tits into stalactites. And I can't even get . . .

No! Tell me my eyes deceive me. Excuse me? What is that you appear to be waving before my eyes? Matches? A box of matches? Perleez!

Oh, *forgive* me. Bryant and May matches, are they? Well, pardon my total lack of interest in designer matches, but are you fully in charge of your senses? You think you can light my cigarette in a force-ten gale with a piece of wood and some friction? Don't tell me, you have *boy scouts* in Human Resources or wherever it is you've sprung from?

The *sorting* office? Well, well, well, what strange bedfellows an edict can throw together. Edict? An edict's like when – Oh, forget it. Just light me, will you? Yes, well you may well have lit *yours* with a match but that was before we set foot in this frigging wind tunnel. Hang on.

(*She bends down and tries to inhale.*)

Impossible. I can't believe I'm even . . . Yes! Nooo! Hell's bells and buckets of armatures! I did *not* blow it out! OK. *Do* another one but it won't work I can assure . . . Sweet Jesus. I did it!

(*Deep inhale and exhale.*)

Braised bollocks, but that's good!

(*Pause*)

What language? How do you mean, mine? Well, yes, I suppose I do. Why? Doesn't everyone? Christ, *I* don't know. Why? Do you find it offensive? I'm so sorry. Perhaps there should be a separate area for *swearing* smokers. In the boiler room! Why not, for God's sake?

I'm *not* angry. I just wanted a fag, all right? All right. Now I've had one, thanks to you and Bryant and fu— er . . . May. I am sooo grateful . . . I am on bended f— *fornicating* knees. (*Touching forelock.*) Gawd bless yer, kind sir. And may all yer troubles be pressed and folded away. Sorry. Am I genu-flecting enough?

Right. Must get on. Board meeting – that's b.o.r.e.d. Bored? Please yourself. No, it was a joke, a pun. Christ, are you from the Planet Trog or something? It's like having a conversation with bloody *Tadzio*.

Oh spare me. *Tadzio.* Thomas Mann? *Death in Ven*— forget it.

Sorry. I said I'm sorry. I'm a patronizing witch. God, you're strange.

Anyway. Thanks. You saved my life. I'll get this lighter mended. Or con-demned or something. No, I only ever have *one* fag and another when I get home. With my bloody Mar— Do you always stare like that?

I just wondered if you do it on purpose because of your eyes. Well, the colour of your eyes. You must know. God, don't they have mirrors in the sorting office? Steal your soul would it if you godda glimpse of yourself?

They're not hazel, you dickbrain. Sorry, just a figure of speech – Oh lighten up, for God's sake. I called you a dickbrain, I didn't garrotte your expletive-deleted hamster. They're *beige*, for Christ's sake – no, mushroom, taupe, straw coloured – wait. Hell's bells – wait. I've got a Farrow and Ball chart in my bag. We're re-doing the atrium, Lord knows why. No one ever looks up it. Or down it for fear of spontaneous hurling. Easy way out of a press-ing appointment with a pigging pie chart.

There you are. Stand here.

(*She holds the paint chart up to his eyes.*)

There. Hardwick White! No. Pigeon? Buff? No. Smoked Trout? That's it! Smoked Trout. Very romantic. 'Darling, your eyes are like smoked trout. I could gaze into them until Graham Norton turns heterosexual.'

No one? Not one human bloody being? You amaze me.

Ooooh. Was that a smile? The boy can smile. I'm blinded by the light. Are they your own? The Hampsteads? You've got hundreds of them!

Hampstead Heath? Teeth? Keep up, keep up!

Hey. What do you think of mine? No, really? Veneers every man Jack of 'em. Cost me my Christmas bonus and hurt like fu— a lot.

Why? Good question. Why did I? I'll tell you for why, since you ask. I'll tell you precisely for why. Because Henry told me to. Henry? Your *boss* dear, and mine. Henry Leggat Junior. Sir. Mr BIG. Ralph Lauren, refractor lenses, Lexus hybrid. Probably doesn't make it into sorting that often otherwise he'd've pressured you into cosmetic bleeding dentistry. On the other hand yours don't overlap and you're probably not having unprotected intercourse with him every second Wednesday, unless there's an 'R' in the month.

No, I thought not. Not even dropping to your knees every time he crosses the threshold?

Should I? Do you really think I should? Have more self-respect? Gosh, I'd never thought of it that way . . . Well, of *course* he has a *wife*! But wives tend not to drop to their knees unless there's a Chopard diamond buried in the shag pile.

Well *I* don't know. Why do you ask?

Actually, what business is it of yours? Jesus. I only wanted a tossing light you know, not an hour in the psychiatrist's chair and ruddy trust exercises. You're not Pamela thing – Stephenage – married to the Scotch bloke who laughs at his own jokes, are you? Has anyone ever seen the two of you together?

(*She laughs sharply, then stops short.*)

Are you serious? Er . . . no, I tend *not* to do that. As a general rule. Mostly on Sundays I treat myself to a bottle of Sauvignon Blanc, a black and white Bette Davis and a bloody good cry.

Oh, you think it would work for me? A good pray? Works for you. Does it really?

You do? Homeless people. What? Every Sunday? And addicts. What, off your own back? Is that right? In a hostel. What do you get out of that then?

Yeah, well I *am* kind. In my own way. I'm sodding saintly if I want to be. I could give Mother Theresa a run for her rupees. I did the fun run for what-sits, didn't I? Cancer breasts – six miles! No, of course I don't know them *personally*. I mean, they're ill people . . .

I haven't got room for – I can't. Because my head is full of him. Yeah . . . *and* my heart. I don't believe this. Listen, you pimple-laden Jesus freak. I asked for a *light* not eternal sodding salvation, OK?

(She turns away, moves off.)

Because I *love* him.

How do you mean? You feel the same way about *who*? And this is recip-rocated is it? And this love is just for you, do you reckon? You share it with three quarters of the world. Right . . . and I mean He knows you feel this way does He? You know that?

I don't get it. You live in a shelter, you work in sorting, you don't swear or party or have sex, you love Jesus and you're in a state of joy. Just answer me one question, will you?

For the love of Jesus, *why* do you smoke?

The Archers of Umbridge

Last week I compèred an auction and ball at the King's Head pub theatre in Islington. Now the King's Head is something of a legend in showbusiness circles. It was one of the first ever fringe venues in London, transferring more than thirty productions into the West End and six to Broadway. For thirty-odd years it was run by the charismatic, Irish-American showman, Dan Crawford, on a wing and a prayer. When Islington council mysteriously withdrew the theatre's grant, money for keeping up the crumbling edifice and production standards was scarce and the constant struggle didn't exactly prolong Dan's life. I don't recall the end of a single show at the King's Head when the collecting buckets weren't out. It was an accepted ritual and gave the place a slightly evangelical feel.

Now Stephanie, Dan's widow, is fighting to raise enough money to keep the roof on and the King's Head flag unfurled. Hence the more than regular galas: 'And if we really do well and raise a fabled sum of money at tonight's auction,' I told a packed and glamorous, black-and-white-clad, house, 'we will be able to afford something we've been aching to provide, for decades, in this once and future home of great theatre. Yes – you've guessed it – new collecting buckets!'

It occurred to me that the only way to raise the serious amount of money needed to turn the unisex corridor of a dressing room into – well, something *not* resembling an abattoir's waiting room – was to have the lovely Andrew Lloyd Webber front a save this theatre TV programme called *How Do You Solve a Problem Like Arrears?*.

Actually, dahlings, I was only standing in on the night for fellow thespian Joanna Lumley, who was filming in Devon with Jennifer Saunders and couldn't get the night off. 'I have a confession to make,' I told them, realizing their disappointment that instead of the thinking man's crumpet they were getting the drinking man's bagel. 'I am not Joanna Lumley. I am truly sorry for that and indeed, I always have been. Please think of me as Joanna's body double, though in truth, she's a helluva lot rougher than I am.' Joanna is now a goddess on a pedestal, although an old soldier told me that the excrement is going to hit the fan when it transpires, as it probably will, that the Gurkhas will have to forgo a considerable pension from the British army in order to live in a flat above a chippie in Chippenham.

Back at the King's Head bar I encountered my old sparring partner, Mr Jeffrey Archer. I've bumped into jocular Jeffrey several times at other gavel-wielding functions and I have to say he's slightly grown on me.

'What are you doing tonight?' he asked me.

'Well, I'm doing the auction with you, Jeffrey,' I told him pleasantly.

'No you're not.'

'Oh.'

'We can't both do it. Either you do it or I do it. I don't mind. I do four a week, you know.'

'Right then. Jolly good. I'll just introduce you then, shall I?'

'In a moment, Mr Jeffrey Archer will take the floor. Closely followed by the walls and the windows. Here is a man whose integrity has never been questioned, indeed, it's never been mentioned.' (God bless Barry Cryer for that one.)

I have to tell you Jeffrey and sidekick, Chris Beetles, did a truly skilled, humorous and professional job, and we raised £22,000. Furthermore, bless his little wrinkly forehead (which so reminds me of the forehead of my own dear Basenji), he did allow me to do three or four bids on my own, including selling 'Tea with Joanna Lumley', which went for a thousand pounds. All I have to do now is pluck up the courage to tell Joanna that I volunteered her for it. I hope she turns up. Er . . . Barry!

Jeffrey must have taken a shine to my gavel work, because I was invited to his Christmas bash last year. Sorry, but I had to see it. It was fab. The penthouse overlooks what seems to be three sides of the Thames, if there are three sides – possibly he's had it dammed to look that way and it is very posh. The paintings remove the breath from your larynx, the Krug flows and it all works like alchemy. The great and the near-great are greeted at the lift entrance by Jeffrey and his luminous wife, then, on the dot of something or other, he announces the a cappella choir, who work magic on what you thought were jaded Xmas carols. Then he announces shepherd's pie and we queue up neatly for it, then the choir do a few more songs and he announces pudding and we get back in line, then we dwindle a bit, then we go home accompanied by a whole monster Cheddar with the name of all Jeffrey's books on its rind. It lasted ages and always raised a grin. It should have been a Cheshire.

One of the auction prizes was a masterclass with Gordon Ramsay. You know the sort of thing: 'Repeat after me, please, in broad estuary: NO, IT'S NOT AN EFFING SAUCE IT'S AN EFFING COULIS! YOU EFFING PRAT!'

Another prize was a 'West End Opening Night With a Well-Known Critic', which reminded me of the night my late mother told me, after one of my opening nights, that she'd sat next to a critic who had not come back for the second half. Intrigued, I rang the press office to ask which critic was seated in row G, seat 4, because he'd left at the interval. She phoned me back some time later to tell me the name of the critic, adding that he hadn't left in the interval, he'd merely asked to be moved to another seat because all the way through the first half the woman sitting next to him kept peering at his notes.

Hull Is Other People

After the floods of 1997, I offered my services for an evening to Kingston-upon-Hull to raise money for the rehabilitation fund. I thought they might mount an evening of cabaret and I'd do a section of it. I didn't bargain for the mindset of my dear home city. The previous night I'd attended a glittering charity evening at the Dorchester Hotel in aid of HFT, the Home Farm Trust, which takes care of adolescents with learning disabilities. I couldn't get there till after curtain down so I missed David Frost interviewing HRH Princess Anne, one of their patrons. I was to be interviewed later by Sir David, between the meal and the auction.

It was at a similar occasion for the same charity some years ago, when I had been seated next to the princess, that my mother signalled to me that her bridgework had got stuck in her lamb chop. Twice I had to excuse myself to race to the loo with Mum and screw it back in. After the second time, the princess looked at me askance and I said, 'I bet I've just done something for my mother that you've never done for yours!'

I reminded HRH about this during my interview and she nodded and grinned and clearly remembered it herself. Frost got up both of my nostrils by asking me in front of a roomful of strangers what it was like to be courting again after such a long and public marriage. I was discombobulated by his chutzpah, but, in retrospect, I suppose that's what makes him a good interviewer. As I was courting Mr

Unsuitability at the time, I didn't want to delve too deeply into what made my private life Frost's business so, uncharacteristically, I stammered, burbled, giggled a bit and generally came over coy.

When the auction came round, the prizes were seriously top-notch. There was a box at Wimbledon, a day at Lord's, vintage champagne, a holiday for two in St Kitts. I found myself bidding for a large, framed Manchester United shirt, signed by all the players. I thought my son Adam might like it on his wall. As the price rose I found myself engaged in a knock-down battle with the Royal Bank of Scotland. It was impossible to back down as all eyes were on us. Finally, I had to run to the other bidder's table and hold down his arms to prevent him raising them. All's fair in tooth and claw, I reckoned. I went home with the shirt.

Next morning, Sunday, finances severely depleted, I headed for the Hull train, working out a few jokes en route. I was met at the station by a representative of the committee who informed me in Hullspeak that we were all meeting up for a tagine on the Beverley Road. The idea of anyone having a tagine on the road I used to cycle up each day on my way to school was mood-enhancing and I asked her if the other performers would be there too. You are ahead of me – yes, I was the other performers. They'd given me an hour and would I draw the raffle? I w-w-would. I did. It was a far cry from the night before.

'The first prize,' I called out, 'is twenty pounds' worth of meat.' I wondered if it was in a string bag wrapped in greaseproof paper with blood dripping through.

The second prize is . . . three pairs of spectacle frames, never worn.

The third prize is . . . one driving lesson at Sid's School of Motoring.

The recipient of the winning ticket for the third prize took a while to come up to claim her prize – that was because she was blind.

The first gig at the Dorchester raised £100,000. The second raised about £850. From my point of view though, the second came first.

The surrealism of life continues. A friend rang to tell me about her aunt's stone setting in Liverpool. It is the Jewish tradition that a year after burial, the headstone is erected. This eminently sensible law gives the mourners time to recover and consider. Visiting the stone-mason for Jack's headstone was one of the things I'd most dreaded, but as it happened I needn't have. The lady in charge had a marvel-lously dogged dog in the office, which required a tennis ball to be thrown at his nose repeatedly. It was hilarious and, as well as getting the job done, I ended up having a really nice time.

So here was my friend, haring up to Liverpool to attend the cer-emony, only to be greeted by ashen-faced relatives who, aghast, informed her that the headstone had been put on the wrong grave. The deceased's eldest son took a sanguine angle on the whole event.

'That's Mum,' he said, 'she never did have any sense of direction.'

Apparently, the synagogue had rung the family to apologize.

'We're ever so sorry,' they'd reportedly said, 'but I'm afraid some-one in the office appears to have lost the plot.'

Pauline Buchanon

Working women always sacrifice something and modern working women sacrifice most. There is no support for a career woman, even in my business. Nowadays families live far from the places we need to be. Siblings are not numerous and kids can't play out in the street, and there is, according to Mrs Thatcher, the career girl of all time, no such thing as society, nor much community I might add. Pauline has opted out of what is safe and normal to be a ladette in a man's world. A very male world indeed, that of the stand-up comic. She is frightened by the very profession she has chosen and is as judgemental and angry as most comics tend to be. The combination of fear and rage means that her closest relationship is with a bottle. Pauline is Scots, wiry, spiky and not quite as inebriated as she'd like to be.

Pauline Buchanon

ANPIOC! Get that in your brain, girl. It's not rocket science, it's a whatsit, that's all. A thingy – prompter. What's the word? Namibia? Amoeba? Anemone? Something with an 'N' I know . . . In case I dry. Which I won't if I felt-tip the initials on my arm. Like Sarah Palin she's no mug, you know. Actually she is a mug and it's also the name of one of her kids.

Amnesia? No!

So it goes ANPIOC:

(*Jokes all told in a rapid, expressionless, just audible mumble.*)

A – is for all of us in this room. We have one thing in common: we none of us know what I'm going to say next!

N – N is for nuns and I do the nun in the bath. Knock, knock. Nun: 'Who's there?' Man: 'Blind man.' 'Oh, come in.' Man: 'Nice tits. Where do you want the blind?'

So A – N – P for – polar bear joke – Nowadays we comics can only do animal jokes cos they don't have rights.

Baby Bear to Mama Bear, 'Have I got any panda/grisly/koala in me?'

'No you're a polar bear, Bla Bla. Why do you keep asking me all these questions?'

'Cos I'm feckin freezing.'

Grisly in a pub. 'Gin and . . . . tonic, please.'

'Why the big pause?'

'Cos I'm a feckin bear!'

Anpi. Anpi. So, I stands for Irish and I do the building site one. Can you tell me the difference between a girder and a joist? Yes, Goethe wrote *Faust* and Joyce wrote *Ulysses*.

(*Knock at the door.*)

Come in! Where was I? Anpi – O – Oh, I forgot that one . . . Come in!

Three old men moaning about their memories. One says, I go upstairs then I don't know why I'm there. Second one says, I ring someone and don't know who I've rung. Third one says, my memory's as good now as it was then. Touch wood. He knocks twice on wood then looks around at door and says: Come in!

(*Knock outside.*)

Come in! (*Sotto*) C'MIN! Jeez, do you want a hand-written invitation? Oh, hi, Bazz. How's the house?

Really? Well, p'raps there'll be a few more on the door. What's the prob this time? Hole in the ozone? Swine flu pandemic? That's it! Mnemonic! I knew it began with N!

Mnemonic? How can mnemonic begin with an M? It's not m-nemonic, is it? Like 'Mnif I Ruled the World?' Harry Secombe? (*She sings in high-pitched lieder tenor.*) 'MMMnif I ruled the world . . .' Oh, forget it, you're too young to remember *Highway*. Sunday tea-time? Harry Secombe in a Gannex raincoat standing at the foot of an escalator in a shopping centre in Ilfracombe singing 'I have a friend in Jesus' with fifteen lady florists in trycil blouses.

No, I'm fine. Fine. Not nervous at all. Why, do I look it? S'all right, I've got no bronzer on, and my eyes always go small on single malt. I know I don't usually, but I'm stressed – don't tell me what I can or can't drink, Bazz, you're my manager not my mother . . . I won't. I don't get migraines any more. I had my last one when Sheryl left and I haven't had one since and I've had fifteen bars of Bournville, mature Cheddar for breakfast and enough red wine to drown a bison. It was *her*. She was a pain in the bum and it gave me a referred pain in my *head*. Anyway it's whisky – rye – and I'm not intolerant to that. I'm a wry comedienne. Geddit? Actually it was Sheryl I was intolerant to . . . of. How long have I got?

I've gotta iron that shirt yet. I've done it once but it looked worse . . . It's a crap iron. Course I had it switched on, Bazza. Oh, at the mains . . . Right. I see. No I don't want spray starch, Bazz . . . I want to go on as *me* not David Bloody Copperfield. I dunno what I'll wear with it. I'm clueless with clothes. My jeans? Why not? Look, I'm out there doing a comedy gig, you know, not pulling tarts. Big shirt, jeans, my biker boots, tartan scarf. That's cool isn't it? Cool enough for this porridge-spattered backwater anyhow. I mean, I've heard of the Fringe but this place is more like the Minge.

That's quite good. I could get that one in. Get off! That's not offensive. Not for this dump. It's a bloody compliment. Course I'm angry, Bazz, I'm a comic. I'm supposed to be angry. I'm meant to curse at bastard men and cellulite and people who have four-wheel-drive cars and breast feeding and celebrity culture. If *I* don't rail at bloody British Rail, who will?

Look, let's face it, leaving me was the best thing Sheryl could have done – for my act. Well, because I wasn't angry before but now I'm livid, bloody livid. Cos I can't *find* anything and no one knows what tea I like or gets me a massage or types out my stuff from scrumpled up Post-It notes and I bloody miss her, which of course she said I bloody would – it's infuriating! I can't even work the effing remote. I've been watching teletext for weeks.

You? You, hen, you're about as useful as a Vicks inhaler at a lung transplant. Joke. Sorry.

God, was that beginners? Oh bollocks – I can't do this – look at me I'm not dressed and I'm pissed and my face is covered in snot and, Bazz – I can't – they'll crucify me. Oh, my God, why hast thou forsaken me?

(*Long pause while she sits with her head down between knees. Then she straightens up, takes a long swig and stands.*)

That's my music, right? I'm OK. Give me that other bottle. Give it me – I'm going on – stuff iiit. I'm going to chuck out the opening jokes – can't be arsed – and the nun stuff is as old as original sin. I'm going on, Bazza. Don't stand there flapping like your mother's pinny. I'm going on. Further than I've ever been before. This is serious. Deadly serious. This is raw. This is war . . . this is death after life. Heeeres appallin' Pauline . . .

(*She parts the curtains and sways forward and onstage.*)

Tarraaaa! Good evening, lads and lasses. My name is Pauline Buchanon and last week my girlfriend – whom we shall call Sheryl – because that was her fecking name . . . left me for a mother of three wi' thread veins and an arse the size of Aberdeen.

Oh, you think that's funny, do you? Actually I found it quite cruel. We've only just had the civil partnership. We've got unwrapped hers and hers mono-grammed lavatory mats and a parrot to divide up. I'm sick as a blood orange. My heart's still banging like a groupie in a tour bus. I'm sleeping one hour in eight and my face looks like someone's stuck a pin in it and let all the air out.

What did the inflatable teacher say to the inflatable boy who'd brought a drawing pin to the inflatable school? You've let me down, you've let the school down, but worst of all, you've let yourself down. Oh, please, will someone close my joke genes down for just two seconds? You think that's a laugh, right? Anyone here ever been dumped? Feel good, did it? Yeah . . . come up here and tell us. Still laughing, are you? What's your name, hen? Marlene . . . right Marlene. Wow. OK. How's your confidence these days? What are you going to do with all that purple underwear and the black hold-ups? Why have you stopped laughing?

You should see my manager in the wings if you want a real laugh. His face has gone *barely black* and his eyes have got deficit signs popping out of them. Come on stage won't you, Bazz? Come on! Don't be a spoilsport . . . we're all letting it hang out tonight. Come on! Give him a round of applause will you, lads and lasses. I want you to put your hands together and possibly your feet for the saddest git in Ayrshire. Lads and lasses – small it up for my man-ager! Bazz Frost – gimme a B! Gimme an A! Gimme a Z! Here's Bazza!

Do you think pain is any different if you're heterosexual, *Bazz*? Why is it better to be black than gay? Cos if you're black you don't have to tell your mother. Yeah, yeah, yeah – me too, at primary school.

There's no logic to it either. She always wanted to be in showbusiness right? Woman she's shacked-up with, what does she do? Solicitor for oaths. OATHS. Like 'Till death us do part', right? 'For better and for worse.' It doesn't get any worse for fuck's sake – and that's an oath, isn't it?

And don't let anyone tell you to get a vibrator. There's nothing sadder than a woman lying on the floor, with a glass of wine, jiggling herself about in front of *Cash in the Attic*.

No logic at all. I've got your attention though, haven't I?

(*Looks into wings horrified . . . Turns to audience.*)

Oh Gawd, Bazza's trying to hang himself from the flies. Cut it out, Bazza, don't do this, Bazza, please. We didn't mean to laugh, did we? Shout out! Shout out! Tell him – you didn't mean to be cruel, you were just having a laugh. He can't hear you . . . Louder! They're sorry. They didn't mean it. They're all shouting out – get down! They're all sorry. Aren't you?

Yeah, well s'all right. I was only having you on. Bazza's in the bar with a can of McEwans. No one's hanging themselves, and of all the audiences I have ever played on this circuit, in the five corners of the globe, you have been the most recent. I was Pauline Buchanon and will be again.

Goodnight. (*Exits*)

Yes!

Be Careful What You Say In PC World

So, 'Baa baa black sheep' is no more. It's official. From now on your kids and my grandkids will be chanting 'Baa baa *rainbow* sheep', because it's less offensive that way. It's quite offensive to me that the line no longer scans and that sheep tend not to be coloured, in any sense of the word. 'Mary had a little Quorn' will no doubt be next. Still, as long as they're chanting rhymes not gangsta rap, it's a blessing.

It's strange how scraps of childhood verse wing their way to you at the first sighting of a snowdrop, as you wander, lonely as a cloud, via the fox droppings to the wheelie bin in your urban garden. The sun is hard and bright on the pruned borders and, yes, there are sugared almonds piercing the naked boughs, and fragile crocuses prising their way through the frozen lawn and a young man's fancy turns to thoughts of love, as do the thoughts of perky pensioners. As Ogden Nash had it:

De spring is sprung, de grass is riz,
I wonder where de boidies is?
The little boids is on de wing.
Ain't dat absoid?
De little wings is on de boid.

Carl Sandburg said, 'Poetry is the achievement of the synthesis of hyacinths and biscuits.' I love the sound of that line, and the thought that poems are an accompaniment to the miraculous and the mundane. So, as I step into the bath and the lines of ticker tape cross my mind, 'When their bones are picked clean and the clean bones gone, they shall have stars at elbow and foot.' Or mentally react to a bearded man with lines from a school text book:

There is laughter like the fountains in that face of all men
    feared;
It stirs the forest darkness, the darkness of his beard.

Then, I realize that everything I've ever learned is in there somewhere. My mind is like my house, with everything piled in stacks or crumpled in drawers or hoarded in suitcases, silently screaming, 'File me, for God's sake. File me or, failing that, put me in the trash!'

I keep reading articles about how to exercise the brain. Crosswords irritate me, I can't think to order. Sudoku is Sanskrit and card games are a bridge too far. I've had a bottle of Ginkgo Biloba on my bedside table since 2002, but the only mental exercise I get is figuring out how to line up the two arrows on the lid in such a way that they can be opened by a short-tempered, short-sighted human with a very average IQ.

Last week I arranged to have dinner with two different sets of people in two separate restaurants, on the same night as the producers had invited the cast out to a company meal. One of the producers said to me, 'I shouldn't say this, but I don't know how you play this part, eight times a week.' I gazed back at him with bloodshot eyes. 'No problem, love, it's a piece of polenta.'

In truth, I was exhausted by technical gremlins plaguing the show last week. A special or roving light went AWOL on Tuesday causing a hefty version of Tinkerbell to accompany me round the set of my apartment at all times. And on Saturday, when I had friends out front, all the power went for the second act and the last scene had to be played out in silent Stygian darkness followed by the kind of overhead lighting you only see in Marks & Spencer's food hall or police photographs of the peroxide phase of the late Myra Hindley.

*

Last weekend, Valerie, widow of writer Willis Hall, came to stay and we talked Jack and Willis for hours as we always do. Because we *could*. Willis could make Jack laugh over the phone like no one else. He would call during a break from writing and the relief for both men was palpable. 'I don't know what to put,' he would say, echoing the days of homework. He would leave Jack braying with laughter.

Willis would arrive from Yorkshire and insist Jack joined him at the Garrick Club for The Writers' Guild dinner. Then he would phone the club in advance and tell them that Mr Rosenthal was dining that night but didn't want the fillet steak or partridge or duck that was on the menu, but wished to have two fried eggs instead. He then, deadpan, watched Jack's astonished face as everyone was served the full fillet and he got the back end of the hen.

It's been a hard week of losses for humour. I always thought Linda Smith was my very own discovery and now I know that everyone else felt the same. John Junkin was the man behind the men who made us laugh. Today is the funeral of another good and true husband of a friend, felled by a heart attack last week. Sandy was that rare man, who was thrilled by his wife's vivacity and gave her a frame in which to sparkle. It's going to be hard.

Most of the time, these days, I think I'm OK. Over my own bereavement, I mean. Halfway back to normal, using work as grief therapy, but there are countless moments when emotion quite unreasonably overcomes me. One evening, alone, after eating a meal I'd carefully cooked for myself, I stood up and said out loud, 'Right then, love, what's for pudding?' It was the word pudding that finished me. Don't ask me why. It was the sound of his voice in that comical word. People say, have a holiday, counselling, take up Tai Chi, get into genealogy, move house . . . I should, I know, but I can't move anything, until I take his hat and coat out of the wardrobe.

Still, the puppy is Miss Congeniality. So far Diva has leaked, appropriately enough, on the faces of Mark Bolland, the prince's former aide; on Hazel Blears, looking like her name; and on a hilarious triptych of George Bush throwing a cricket ball like the biggest, daftest big girl's blouse you've ever seen. Discerning she may be, but at nine this morning when she'd chewed through the computer wires, it was the line 'out, out damned spot' which came most readily to mind. Which reminds me, I must pick up that little *rainbow* dress from the cleaners.

Once or twice during the night I surfaced to hear on the World Service, the late Alastair Cooke describing with painterly precision, the hysteria and chaos as Bobby Kennedy died on the floor of the hotel kitchens. Curiously, the next time I came to, hours later, it was to hear that Alastair Cook had just scored a century for England in Pakistan. It's a surreal world where Michael Moore is the treasury spokesman for the Lib Dems, Kate Mosse is in charge of the Orange Prize short list and Debby Reynolds is the spokesperson for all things poultry.

The joke goes:

'When I roar,' said the lion, 'the whole of the jungle trembles.'

'Well, when I growl,' said the bear, 'the whole of the forest quakes.'

'That's nothing,' says the chicken, 'when I cough, the whole world shits itself.'

Rage Roader

I'd arrived back from a wonderful holiday in Greece, feeling relaxed to the point of ancient hippiedom. Through my agent I'd learned I'd been savaged for the second time by the tiny terrier of the *Sunday Times*, A. A. (so good they named him twice) Gill, in his TV column. 'That nice Jewish actress,' was his opening line. True, but more information than was relevant.

The angry mind begins to wander in the face of injustice where there is no retribution. Should I lie in wait for him at the Ivy and throw beetroot juice over his crumpled linen? Should I send him a box of chocolates skilfully filled with Warren the rabbit's rotund droppings? Should I appeal to his editor or merely send him a list of the religion of every actress in England so that he can incorporate his prejudice into his future reviews?

Throughout the morning, there was a reef knot in my stomach. I didn't want it there. I was brown and gorgeous, dammit, and I didn't want to spend a minute of my life scowling into my driving mirror in heated conversation with an *initial*, however witty and caustic my side of the conversation was. It's hard to harness anger, except as fuel for comedy.

En route to the dry cleaner's in Hampstead, I watched a large, hot young man (in the sense of sweaty rather than 'pffweuaw!' – he was far from that, in his low-crutch shorts and well-filled T-shirt) backing into a parking slot in his four-wheel drive. Asleep in the back was a tiny child of about two. As he backed in, an elderly man stepped down from the pavement. To alert the driver, he smacked the side of the car with the flat of his hand.

Was our man in the driving seat upset? Was he shocked by the near miss? Was he concerned for the pedestrian's frailty? Was he hellfire!

His face went maroon.

'He hit my f***ing car!' He threw open the driver's door, murder in his eyes. 'Don't you touch my f***ing car, you f***ing—'

'Hey, hey, hey,' I called out. 'Cool down, will you? He's not a young man and you nearly hit him!'

'There's a f***ing zebra crossing just there,' he screamed. 'He shouldn't be in the f***ing road in the f***ing first place!'

It was the sort of situation that my late husband always swore would be the death of me.

'All right, all right. You've got a child in the car – just let it go, can't you?'

He was half in the car and half out and he didn't know who to excoriate, the jaywalker or the nosy parker. At this point another witness arrived and pointed out that the innocent party had hit the car very gently, considering it was about to make him one dimensional, but still our fat, fiery friend cursed us and the world in general and started up his motor to leave the scene of the non crime.

I watched him, cleverly jotting down his number for future reference on the back of the cleaning ticket I was about to hand in (no Precious Ramotswe me). Then I saw him re-park the car and meticulously examine the side of his vehicle for evidence of the kind of violence an elderly palm can impose on polished metal.

'Pathetic,' I said, walking away.

This was my mistake. Never play them at their own game. He swivelled and delivered his final brilliant riposte, 'Yeah, and you're f***ing pathetic as well!'

That told me.

If a young, affluent father, with a tiny child in his car, can be roaring in scatological rage at an avoidable incident like that one, what chance is there of soothing people who are nothing *but* their anger?

That ugly twisted road-rage face is one I see every day. It's one of the most common London faces. I'd probably displayed it myself when I left the house.

Later, back home, I heard the news about the London bombings from my daughter who'd been on her way into town on a bus. I was shocked, but as the day wore on I was also mortified. What was I doing nursing dented pride when this horror was going on in my own town? How could I sit watching the news when there were shattered people out there in need of help?

'The police ask that no one comes into London unless their journey is absolutely necessary,' said the newsreader.

I phoned Colin Shindler, writer and family friend, otherwise known as 'Shindler's Lift'.

'Do you think we should do something?' I asked him.

'Er . . . Yes, but . . . like what?'

'Well, we could drive down to Camden or Swiss Cottage and see if anyone walking needs a lift back up north.'

He's a nice man. He humoured me. We set off.

There was no one in the streets. We were stuck in tailback traffic going *into* town.

'There's someone!' said Colin. 'He looks like a businessman. Shall we . . .?'

'Er . . . I don't know. He looks pretty fit to me. He might have only come from Regent's Park.' We pressed on, scouring the streets for office workers with osteoporosis or young women on platform soles. No one. The streets were deserted.

We arrived at Swiss Cottage and came to a bus stop. I lowered the window. There were young people standing there.

'Does anybody need a lift up north?' I asked tentatively.

The faces were a uniform blank. Finally a young man muttered, 'But you're goin' south, missus.'

'Well, yes, but we're turning at Eton Avenue and then . . . Oh, never mind. Quick, Colin, drive off.'

I was embarrassed out of my skull as I realized that from the pedestrian's point of view we were some sort of cruising perverts. We became mildly hysterical and headed for home.

On the way we finally found two stranded souls who responded to my bleating with crazed relief. One of them had been travelling from Canary Wharf for three hours.

'This is the first act of kindness I've encountered since I came to London,' said South African Rose, who'd made it all the way from Camberwell.

'How long have you been here?' I enquired, pleased.

'Sixteen years,' she replied.

We took the girls home to Crouch End and East Finchley and I went home feeling marginally more good than I'd felt in a while. On the radio, pundits were labelling the terrorism appalling but largely the result of chronic frustration over Western aggression in the Middle East. I wondered whether a feeling of impotence gave us all a licence to kill at random if we really felt frustrated about things we couldn't change.

There is a short song of Joyce Grenfell's, which always brought the house down when I was playing my show *Re: Joyce!* in the West End of London. It's called 'Hymn' and it features a woman in church singing a hymn with gusto, who realizes, halfway through, that she's left a pan of soup alight on the gas ring.

As I entered the kitchen the smell of burnt chicken hit me like a wall. I'd been out for an hour and a half. The pottery casserole had exploded and the chicken livers were smouldering on the Amtico. I like to think that if I'd been out buying lipsticks and Crème de la Mer, there would have been no house to come home to.

Hockney Practice

I had such a treat this week. I'm still on a low simmer because of it. Jack always used to say to me, 'How is it that when I go out for a pound of sugar, I come back with a pound of sugar? You go out for a pound of sugar and you come back with a three-act play.'

It's true. On Tuesday, like thousands of you, I saw the David Hockney watercolour in the centrefold of the *Guardian*. Unlike other thousands of you, I come from the very part of East Yorkshire he immortalized, and the painting made my heart sing. The next day, Wednesday, was a two-show day, and I decided that, instead of getting my head down in my Lilliputian dressing room, I would wander over to Somerset House to see if a) the open-air ice rink had started up and b) if I could see the thirty-five other Hockneys in the exhibition.

When I arrived at the open courtyard, it was twilight and the ice was an opalescent square lit by street lamps, like a birthday cake awaiting decoration. The gallery was quietly anticipating closing time in 45 minutes and it was with real disappointment that I discovered the Hockney exhibition didn't open until the following day.

'He's down there now, as it happens, doing some radio thing,' said the helpful guide. 'Are you press, madam?'

('No, actor, but we have the same high insurance premium,' I didn't quite manage to say.)

'Erm, yes,' I lied, '*Guardian*.' It wasn't such a lie then as it is now –

and he pointed me towards the lift where I encountered Ann, a Canadian who was leaving for Toronto the next day and would die if she didn't see the Hockneys before boarding her maple leaf.

'Stick close by me,' I told her, 'I have a double first in chutzpah.'

We hung around outside during his radio interview, then slipped into the gallery and gazed at a wall of thirty-six delicate, fresh, almost youthful watercolour landscapes, individual, but somehow making up a whole, of a part of the country regularly cited in polls as the worst place to live in England. Standing in front of it was the man who begged to differ.

We were introduced, Mr Hockney and me and Ann, my dear old friend of several minutes, and to our delight, he began to tell us how he went about the paintings. How he'd observe the setting and the light he needed and, with some of the paint already mixed, complete each one in three hours. He could drive, he said, for miles along the roads round Kilham and Driffield and never encounter a soul.

On the opposite wall there played a video of the great man, in a flat cap, turning a blank page into a reflection as tender as brush strokes on rice paper by a Chinese master.

Ann and I were a bit overexcited.

'I can't believe this is *happening*,' she whispered to me. 'I just want to ring up all my friends.'

I, too, had made the journey to Salt Mills to marvel at his early draughtsmanship and had seen both flesh and water through new eyes during his Beverly Hills phase and I fear I behaved a bit like a drama student granted ten minutes with Elenora Duse.

'So, when the script comes through to you, Madame Duse, do you mark your own part first in highlighter or do you read the play as a whole?'

Hockney seemed unfazed by our bobby soxer devotion.

'The thing is,' he said, chattily, 'you have to know in your head exactly where all the white parts are before you start. You see the dew drops on the sheaf of wheat – there? Well *that's* where I had to start.' He put on his trademark fedora and stood up. 'I'm just going outside now for a cigarette.'

I said bon voyage to Ann at the door and raced back to the theatre. I was so excited that I said my first two lines in reverse. On Saturday, when Victoria Wood and family came to the Duchess, I whisked them straight across the road, giving them no time to discuss the play, stood them in front of the ice rink, now a Breughel of tentative, scarlet-cheeked skaters, plied them with hot mulled wine and blagged them into the Hockneys. As we say up north, it were a right treat.

Visiting the Francis Kyle gallery for a preview of Portuguese and Cuban paintings by Paol Webb, I was introduced to an Italian gentleman, name of Mauritzio, who had just completed a solo trip across the Channel. Nothing unusual about that you might say and you'd be right, except Mauritzio did the trip by car. Amphibian car. Custom-made by Mauritzio. The trip took him six hours. We could only communicate in French, my Italian being confined to one aria from *La Traviata* and *gelati molti tutti frutti lollipop* – so, in truth, it may have taken 106 hours – but I've seen the DVD and, *mon Dieu*, I fail to understand why such a phenomenal achievement failed to reach the front pages when Prince Charles's seven boiled eggs and President Musharraf's lucrative book deal with Simon & Schuster so piercingly did.

The whole experience turned me into an art groupie. I'd got a taste for it. I wanted Monet to show me his lilies, Pablo to be inspired by my pony tail and Vincent to pop in for an Elastoplast.

My wish would be answered at a charity do at the Royal Festival Hall, where I met the curator of the Hayward Gallery's Anthony Gormley exhibition and learned that the man himself was doing a conducted tour the following morning at eight. Now, normally, I don't get up for less than two croissants and a box of Dorset muesli thrown in, but the following morning I was wearing mascara before the cock crowed and out and about with actor David Horovitch in tow, with the other yawners on the Northern line.

It was splendid. Gormley was down to earth and hearty. Why would he not be, just because he's achieved greatness in his own lifetime? One exhibit was a room full of fog, which gave many of the guests claustrophobia but made me feel snug and cosy, like staying in with a cold while a blizzard uproots your garden.

I must point out that part of his oeuvre were the bronze statues of himself, naked, which, during the time of the show, had been placed in unusual positions all over London, rather as, a few years ago, cows were displayed and currently miniature elephants. (I was promised a cow to paint but it never came. Which was really a shame cos I was going to put my cow in a velvet smoking jacket, a cravat and a cigarette holder and call it Noël Cowherd.) There was one of Gormley's statues on the roof of the Savoy Hotel and several jauntily adorning the City landscape. There was also one standing proud, very proud, as you would if you were generously endowed, on Waterloo bridge. I wish I had a falling Euro for the number of helpless, giggling young women I saw in one hour, giving bronze Ant a handshake in a place that wasn't his hand.

I met Mr Gormley himself in a room of life-sized bronze men, vaguely Cubist but cast in his own mould. I could just see him, hovering behind himselves. I told him that the room reminded me of a maze and that what I really wanted to do was glide through it from one corner to the other, singing, 'Must you dance every dance with the same fortunate man?' He liked the idea very much and joined me from his own corner. We met in the middle. It was a piece of performance art and both of us wished the camera had captured it.

It's not easy to get up and go to exhibitions and galleries, I'm the first to admit, but even a bad one can be provocative and a good one – like Hockney's, Gormley's or the mischievous Anish Kapoor show at the Royal Academy where a cannon fired red wax at a wall and a wax train moved imperceptibly from one gallery to the next – can fill one with inspiration. At the recent showing of quilts at the V&A, where there was one massive quilt of great delicacy which was stitched by women prisoners on their way to a penal colony in Tasmania, said more and made you feel more, in a ten-inch square, than ten history lessons on our colonial past from the Simon Schama brigade.

There is a joke about a famous painting hanging in a Scottish gallery of three naked black men sitting on a wall, one of whom has a pink penis. The experts give their opinions of the meaning of the painter. The art critic of *The Times* says it is an allegory of the colonization of the black man by the white and the black man's need to behave like a white man in a white world. The second critic argues that it is the white man's fear that he is inferior in his sexuality to the black man. The third critic disagrees. To him, the painting represents the de-sexualization of the black men by the in-your-face post-feminist women.

An insignificant little man in a tweed cap and muffler has been listening to their debate.

'Excuse me,' he says, 'I couldn't help overhearing your heated discussion and, well, I'm the artist so maybe I can tell you what the painting is actually meant to be.'

The three men cannot wait to see which of them is proved right and beg the painter to put them out of their misery.

'Well, none of you are right, as it happens,' he tells them modestly. 'As a matter of fact, it's a representational painting of three Scottish coal miners having a midday break and one of them went home for lunch.'

Art at Sea

My monologues include some women who don't necessarily possess the talent for the work they do. The first is Sheila who cruises the world on budget liners, teaching watercolour painting to the passengers. She is in her late fifties, plump, red-haired – always definitive when performed on radio – and long ago gave up on her own ability to sell her work except postcard-sized at sea. She is affable and warm, but without self-awareness or any sense of humour whatsoever.

Art at Sea

Lay them the other way, William, will you, love? Sideways. And weight them down with the palettes, will you, in case it gets squally? Lovely.

Hello! Hello! Welcome, please sit anywhere. My name's Sheila, I'm your tutor for the duration of the voyage and I'll explain everything in situ when there's a full complement.

Willy here is my amanuensis and what I can only describe as husband at sea . . . (*Huge laugh*.) And your names are? Maeve and Norah – lovely, and have any of you painted in watercolour before?

Oh dear, oh dear, well . . . Norah, you mustn't let that put you off. Every teacher has their own methodology, although I must say, that was a bit – final, wasn't it? I try to be more encouraging than that. It's the coming that's important, not the performance I always say.

Oh, was that funny? That's good.

Hello! Hello . . . do come and join us. Yes, anywhere you like. I'll explain everything in situ when we've got the full complement. Now, Angela and Bente, you were here yesterday . . . meet Mavis and er – your friend. Sorry, I've forgotten already – it's my age, I must do more Sedaka. Sorry . . . yes, of course, Norah. No, that's perfectly tickety boo if you just want to watch – although you might feel inspired to join in when you – well. (*Huge laugh*.) You're right . . . it *will* be a bit like watching paint dry.

Yes, the bar is open. Er, no, not for me, not a tequila at this time. But thank you for the thought.

I shall have to have my wits about me with your friend around . . . er – Mavis – Oooh, what a lovely pinny, Mavis, and fancy you having the foresight to bring it. Oh it's cruised before has it? Thirty-one? My word you *are* an old sea dog. No . . . that's just a turn of phrase, I really didn't mean to be personal. Here, have a Kleenex. I'm so sorry. Ah, now, here's Norah with the tequilas. Such a pretty shade of cobalt blue those umbrellas and against the cherries . . .

Now, where was I?

Hello! Hello, how ravishing – our first male member. Super. Oh, now Norah's got a fit of the giggles again. Oh, golly, it's infectious . . . you're all at it. What's your name, sir? No, we're on first name terms today, Mr Richards . . . Everard? Well, my word. You're my first ever Everard . . . take a pew. I'm glad of another man on board. Do say hello to my Willy. Oh, more laughter in court. What larks! Oh, you're not going already are you, Everard? Won't you come back and join the ladies? They're a heck of a jolly crowd.

Oh well, changed his mind, never mind, here's another candidate. Hellooo! Can you get the wheelchair past the easels? Oh, that's the ticket. Everybody will you give a big welcome to . . . Your name is? Connie – meet Mavis and . . . sorry, you are Connie's helper? No, her sister . . . Felicia. That's a pretty name and I know I shall have trouble remembering it. Oh, well I'm sure William can do the honours. Can you balance that board all right? Oh, sorry. Yes, I can see you *can* manage. Sorry, I didn't mean to imply . . .

So. Looking at the big hand I can see we should be kicking off cos we've only got an hour before deck quoits on the main and the lecture on manatees in the Gemini lounge. So, now, if you're all sitting comfortably – and if you're old enough to remember that expression then you must be a baby boomer like myself and weren't we the lucky ones with all that free milk and cod liver oil and rock and roll?

What pill, Norah? Oh, I see – THE pill. (*Pause*) Er . . . comfortably . . . then, I shall begin.

We are moving paint around paper. I'll repeat that. We are moving paint around paper.

What do I mean by that? By that, I mean that watercolour paint is different from oil or acrylic or any other medium you may have used because it dries VERY QUICKLY. Therefore your effects have to be made VERY QUICKLY.

Now look at the painting I've done of this bowl of cherries. We've got a bit of a cherry theme today, ladies. I've used only cadmium red and water and I've done six cherries in various depths of paint. Now dip in your number two brushes and try to capture that immediacy with one cherry.

Using cadmium red only and push the paint across the paper to the very edges of the cherries. Push! Push! Push!

Has who ever been a midwife? Me? How do you . . .? Oh, I get it. (*Huge laugh.*) Oh, your friend is very droll, Mavis – MIND YOUR ELBOW, Norah! Oops-a-daisy.

Will, dear, Will, dear . . . could you get the cloth, love, and help Mavis mop up the water? Thank you. Oh, Norah, you are going to join us. Oh, I see, another tequila. Well why not? You're on holiday.

Oops – it's getting a bit choppy out there. Look, you can see all the spume – ooh la la. Willy, can you help Norah back onto her barstool? And, Will, another plastic beaker of water for Mabel – sorry – Mavis. Ooh my brain. I shall get a transplant when we get to Florida. (*Huge laugh.*)

Tilt your boards, ladies, to move the paint around. Lovely. Now. Attention, ladies. Who among you has got a dry cherry?

Ooh dear, she's off again. William, help her back up. She is a cheerful soul, your friend, isn't she? That's awfully good er . . . dear. You see how Connie has, by moving her wet cherry around, captured that lovely pellucid quality.

Now then, where were we? Oh yes. Now, with William's help, we'll all put aside our cherries and start on the big peonies I picked up in port.

Dear me . . . Almost anything seems to set her off, doesn't it?

I want you to notice the tiny vermilion tips and the glistening moisture on your peonies and use a – I'm sorry, how do you mean, Norah?

Do I get jealous . . . of what? Do I have peonies envy? Erm, no, I don't think I do at all, dear. I mean there are so many lovely herbaceous flowers – one can't really compare like with like.

Oh, dear me. Mavanwy – er, thank you, William. *Mavis* dear, do you think perhaps your friend might like a lie down in the cabin? She could have cracked a rib with all that rolling around you know.

So. The peon— the flowers in the vase – are you already to dip in your fine-pointed sable hairs and have a crack? Off you go then . . . remember the more water you put in the paler the – now that's a lovely choice of flesh pink, Fellacia . . . wha . . . where . . . where is she going? Bente? Mavis? LADIES? Where are you – have I missed something?

LAND AHOY IS IT?

How very peculiar. William – Will, everyone seems to be running off looking for Fellacia . . . And only Connie lingers . . .

Do you think it could have been something I said?

Rivet, Rivet

It was the World Service which informed me that scientists have discovered ultrasonic communication in the male Concave-Eared Torrent Frog. This Chinese tree frog has evolved a way of making himself audible to other males over the roar of flowing water. The birdlike sound is two octaves higher than the call of a bat. To make and receive this sound, parts of the ear have adapted, so the bones of the middle ear must be shorter and lighter in weight.

I sat bolt upright in my bed. How did the scientist find this out? Was he strolling past the frog's tree, whistling 'It's a wonderful world', with the universe's most powerful microphone sticking out of his tote bag, when the concave-eared one happened to emit a territorial squeak to one of his like-eared buddies? Or did he capture the frogs, and experiment on their little hairy sensory cells in the discomfort of his own laboratory? This discovery, like all discoveries, was waiting to be found and will, one day, perhaps lead to astonishing steps forward in the fields of tinnitus. There is no progress without some pain. Back there in her spotless tree though, perhaps Mrs Concave-Eared Frog is having a quiet chunter to herself.

'Yeah, all right for some, innit? He's out there propping up a branch with the lads, putting the world to rights in voices only a scientist can hear, and here am I stuck up here with the kids, no mate and no bloody voice to complain with if I had!'

Incidentally, I'm thinking of getting on to the Kennel Club about my barkless dog of the Congo. Last week, when the chap from the shoe shop across the road popped round with some copper inner-soles for me to try on, Diva barked. I have a witness. It could be described as a yelp but it was definitely two octaves short of her customary Jimmy Savile yodel and in Concave-Eared Frog circles it was virtually Ivan Ribroff. (Or Paul Robeson, if you haven't heard of the Russian bass baritone with eight octaves.)

Which is not to say that I would wish my divine Diva to be unwittingly experimented on in the service of medical progress. We know it is inhumane, but so far no one seems to be able to come up with a better solution. If we reduce living creatures to mere groups of mutable cells, then we deny them the very thing which makes them alive. A soul, I suppose.

I cannot bring myself to think about the advances made via Nazi experimentation on what they regarded as inhuman species, nor about the desperation which leads people to sell their kidneys, carry heroin internally across borders or, as we horrifically witnessed last week, volunteer for trials of untested drugs in order to buy their mum a holiday.

Yet, it seems that these monoclonal antibodies, such as the one tested for use on MS and leukaemia at Northwick Park, are proving hugely beneficial across a whole range of incurable diseases. They have to go on being tested. Even Thalidomide, the drug with the most infamous of side effects, is now used to fight myeloma.

'But what will happen to Dod's arms?' my sensible, thirty-odd-year-old daughter had wailed when told that her dad was going to be put on a course of Thalidomide. Actually he had no side effects from the drug; it just didn't work. For many myeloma sufferers though, it is keeping them alive.

One more thought. Like many of you, I am riveted to *Planet Earth*, the BBC's miraculous David Attenborough series, but troubled by the slow-motion close-ups of, as it were, dog eating dog. The snow leopard sinking its teeth into a tiny antelope's rump sending it to an agonizing death in a glacial pool, and the crocodile snapping the neck of an antlered stag, who had been having a quiet clubby drink with mates at a watering hole, were hard to take, and questionable in their lingering detail.

'It took the creature an hour to die,' intoned Sir David, in his occasionally uncomfortable voiceover, as we tuned out all our sensibilities to watch the proud creature thrashing about in agony. Man and beast have, I realize, the same fierce instinct for survival, whatever ethics are involved or ignored. God and mammal, God and mammal.

Napoleon's Extraction

So, the Christmas season is over again. The cards recycled, the refuse men tipped, the candle wax dug out of the menorah, the earrings exchanged for the kitchen clock, the case on wheels deposited on a station platform and the inflatable beds deflated. As are we all.

It's all as far away as ever, bar the shouting in print.

'Best book/film/play/installation/survivor of Simon Cowell of the year! Best overarm-bowling ballroom dancer of the decade! Most memorable celebrity cock-up of the century!'

My most memorable exchange was shouted over a shoulder by a cab driver taking me to an interview. The dialogue was so precise that I haven't changed a word of it. It was crafted by a lifetime of throwing nuggets over that same shoulder and it was one of a thousand moments when I wanted my late husband by my side to revel in it with me.

'Funniest trip I ever had to make – now you'll like this one.'

(Then straight into what they call 'the footballer's tense', as in, 'So I've spotted Giggsy on the wing an' to be fair to him he's put in a peach of a pass to me an' I've just been fortunate enough to get me 'ead on it.)

'So I've got a call on me wireless,' he continued, 'an' 'e says, "Ere, I've got one for you." And I've said, "Oh yeah" and 'e's said, "Yeah, you're gonna like this one. I want you to go to this address in Kensington, pick up Napoleon's tooth and take it to Swindon for auction." So I've said, "You what?" an' 'e's said, "You 'eard. Napoleon's tooth. An' I 'ope you're insured cos it's worth eight thousand nicker." So I've said, "Thass all right then, innit, cos my bloody car's insured for firty farsand."

'Anyways, I picks up this thing an' I slings it in the back seat . . . yeah well, leave it out, I didn't want that little French bleeder sittin' up in the front wi' me – he gave us enough trouble at Waterloo didn't 'e?'

'Well, we did beat him,' I've managed to say.

'Well, yeah. Still, I'll tell you somefin'. You gotta 'and it to his *dentist*, 'aven't you? 'E shoves that tooth to one side, an' 'e says, "I'll 'ave that and I'll keep 'old of it till someone invents eBay."'

He paused for a moment's reflection. 'Still, whatever, I'm glad the little git suffered a bit of pain.'

When I'd stopped laughing long enough to recover my powers of speech I asked, somewhat predictably, 'How did they know it was really Napoleon's tooth?'

'Oh no,' he fixed me a baleful . . . 'It *was* 'is. It was verified like. It was definitely 'is 'ampstead!'

And I was off again. Helpless.

'Anyhow,' he continued, revving up for the perfectly honed punch line, 'I took it to Swindon and when I gets back to the depot they got a new nickname for me, haven't they? They're only callin' me the bleedin' Tooth Fairy.'

I was a very happy woman when I got out of that cab.

To say he made my day is to say, well, you know my day, right? Well, like . . . he like, well, *made* it. Know what I mean?

Ready When You Are, Lord Reith

My late husband, Jack, used to point out that in the early days of television it was quite possible to walk into the office of a senior producer at Granada or the BBC and throw a fresh idea across the table and be told, 'Go on then, lad, go away and write it.' You were commissioned. If it succeeded, you got a pat on the back, and if it failed you were given a slightly gentler pat on the back and told to do better next time.

A couple of weeks ago I did a reading with three other distinguished actors for a pilot sitcom at the Beeb. A *reading* for one. In the old days, they would have polished the script until it shone like a good deed in a watershed world, then cast it, rehearsed it for a couple of weeks then wheeled in the audience and shot it.

Give or take the vagaries of the warm-up man ('Ey, I saw that Wendy Craig's dressing room on me way down 'ere. At least I think it was Wendy Craig's. It had her initials on the door.' Ba boom.) it was generally all right on the night. The judgement whether to proceed to a series or not comes later. Now the actors rehearse for a morning with a director, then thirty or forty chairs are laid out and in come a crowd of secretaries having a bit of a skive off of a Friday afternoon and one or two producers, who meet and greet, and off you go – you and the script, auditioning together. There was a rumour circulating that there was in attendance the actual titular head of genre commissioning. We were seriously overexcited about that one, me and the wonderful actress Selina Cadell. I'm not sure what genre we would have fitted into with our pilot. Genre-lization, probably.

We keep saying television is not what it was. But what is it other than a reflection of the times that we live in and, like everything else, it has to change. I know that, but I must have been very angry on Jack's behalf when I wrote the following:

Anyone who is driving through the streets of London on Boxing Day this year should beware. When I leave the Duchess Theatre, after giving my Florence Foster Jenkins in the play *Glorious*, I will not stop for the mandatory chit chat, nor to remove my make-up. Instead, I will be racing home at a certifiable speed, to be greeted by one or both of the kids, mug of tea in hand, at the door, with the television pre-warmed and at 11.15 p.m., we will sit in front of it to watch Jack's last televised drama, *Ready When You Are, Mr McGill*.

Despite the advent of video recorders, it mattered a lot to Jack to experience his programmes at the same time as they were aired. Out of respect to him, it is important to us to do the same.

For me, this moment represents poignancy, as well as celebration. Though made in 2002, Sky Television, who professed to be delighted with the finished product, held on to it for a year before showing it at ungodly hours to the audience to whom Jack devoted his career. *Mr McGill* is a satire on the mechanics of making a TV drama; it was Jack's swan song and his final message is an apt one. In it, he sends up modern-day television – a medium he believed to be run by those obsessed with ratings and hooking the viewers over several nights of the week. Single-play commissioning has been replaced by serials and driven by star vehicles (especially ambulance and police vehicles) which are often underpowered or due for an MOT. *Mr McGill* makes this point beautifully, with the quiet observation and naturalism for which Jack was best known.

Though grateful that his programme is at last being shown at all and on a good night like Boxing Night, I can't help but find it sad that the man who penned *Bar Mitzvah Boy*, *Eskimo Day*, 200 early episodes of *Coronation Street*, co-wrote the Hollywood film *Yentl* with Barbra Streisand and created the TV series *London's Burning*, should be relegated to an eleven o'clock slot at night – what we used to call the graveyard shift – a year after the film was ready for transmission.

Perhaps the powers that be thought that a play was an old-fashioned concept, not sexy enough to win good enough ratings. Maybe they distrusted a drama which gives a hearty two-finger salute to the current commissioning policies of their drama departments.

But the way that *McGill* was treated greatly upset Jack. Professionally, his last decade was often awkward and frustrating. Gone were the days when he could approach an editor with an idea and say, this is what I want to write, and be given the freedom to do it. When he died he did not know if or when *McGill* would be aired. And although I am glad that his name is now being honoured, it has obviously been an irritation that it was not aired sooner. Many people felt he deserved a televised season of his plays to commemorate him after his death.

Jack was asked to remake his 1976, Mike Newell-directed version of *Mr McGill* by the successful independent production company Working Title Films in 2002. Although he had already been diagnosed with 'smouldering' myeloma, the rare blood cancer that, two years later, would take his life, he relished the opportunity to update and reconsider his earlier play. He had undergone treatment some months before and he was in remission, which could last for up to twenty years, we were told.

So he attacked *McGill* with characteristic and renewed vigour. The latter-day version stars Sir Tom Courtenay as the eponymous Mr McGill, an extra on a TV police drama, who has only one line to say. Amanda Holden sends herself up beautifully as TV star Amanda Holden, Stephen Mangan plays the unloved writer and Stephen Moore the smarmy TV executive. The director, played with eccentric brio by Bill Nighy, takes out all his frustrations for the day, and, probably, for his whole life, on the extra, the one person who can't fight back, the hapless Mr McGill.

Few great writers go 'gently into this good night' – they usually have a moment in which they want to say something important before they die. We saw Dennis Potter's wry rant; we heard much from Harold Pinter and Simon Gray when they were both fighting cancer; Alan Ayckbourn has just completed his seventy-first play, after recovering from a severe stroke; Alan Plater was doing rewrites almost to the day he died, and Alan Bennett is in triumphant remission. I think that *Mr McGill* was Jack's last shout.

Jack made dramas about real people, yet ironically, nowadays, people think life is not real unless it's corroborated by the media. We have lost touch with what reality is. Our soaps are so full of murder and mayhem they have ceased to reflect our lives. They reflect life as reflected in the *Sun*. TV was always *for* the people, now it is *by* the people too.

Commissioning editors want people screwing in jacuzzis, plays written by people who don't know what a past participle is. I was asked to appear in *Celebrity Midwife*. I think we are seconds away from televised celebrity shagging. Will we soon be able to watch two experts who are experts in having sex? Will there be a panel of judges who will watch WAGS and their boyfriends at it, saying, 'That was really bad form when you went for her tits first'? Since the beginning of time, drama has been responsible for illuminating society, but these days, I see no illumination in putting a camera in toilets in the jungle.

Interestingly enough, if you talk to an actor contemplating doing a stint in the celeb jungle or celeb *Big Brother*, they will be doing it for two reasons. First, to turn their career around after years of being in a stereotypical rut, and second to make real money, which they can't do playing Falstaff in a twelve-week tour of the Hebrides in *Henry IV Part Two*. Inevitably, it does turn their careers around. For a couple of months. The *Graham Norton Show*, *Big Breakfast*, turning the lights on in Stoke Newington . . . Then what? The rut beckons once again just as it does for the non-celebrities, the real folk. Where are the first *Big Brother* survivors now?

An artist's spirit, even one as indomitable as Jack's, is easily depleted and I think that, although he took it all in his stride, during his last few years, literally and metaphorically, he limped.

That is not to say that his energy or enthusiasm for life was diminished.

Though in remission, he worked a full twelve-hour day on the *Mr McGill* set during the summer of 2002. His adrenalin was pumping; he was invigorated. He was in at dawn, first at the catering van, last to leave the editing suite at dusk. He didn't have to do that, but that was Jack. He was a Virgo, a perfectionist, and a much loved man. Sir Tom Courtenay said that playing McGill was the best experience in his forty-odd years in the business.

Shortly after filming finished, however, Jack had a relapse, from which he never recovered. During the succeeding years, when he was slowly losing his battle against myeloma, he loved TV nights and so did I. We were never more tender than on those leisurely evenings when we just ate the most delicious food I could make, drank fresh vegetable and fruit juice and watched *Curb Your Enthusiasm* on some extraterrestrial channel.

Depending on the state of his health, he slept in the dining room on a special hospital bed, which we could adjust to ease his current pain. It was hard to leave him, harder to get to sleep without his shoulder beneath my cheek. 'Do you want to lay on my chest, darl?' 'Might. Might not.' Like most long-married couples we had our own peculiar little rituals. In the last months, I would read him Alexander McCall Smith's *The No. 1 Ladies' Detective Agency* in a rubbish Botswana accent and he absolutely adored it. Couldn't wait for the next chapter. Roared with laughter.

People ask me whether, because it was his last work, *Mr McGill* holds a special resonance with me. Whether, because he worked on it when ill, it is particularly painful. As with his other plays, he reworked *Mr McGill* from his desk in the dining room, and he would just get on with it. Afterwards, he'd come out and make salmon fish-cakes or wander up the street for what he called a 'reality coffee' or a bar of Ritter chocolate.

McGill is just a play, but a play in 2005 is a rare thing. And as ever, Jack's last one was about the people who are regarded as failures in life. But Jack didn't regard *anyone* as a failure. Every man had a story to tell. His plays often gave a voice to the voiceless – the dustbinmen, the firemen, the cab drivers – not that he would ever have claimed this for himself. He had little self-regard, but a lot of self-respect. *McGill* was a last roar, and even if it only comes out as a whisper, I wanted that whisper to be heard. His twenty-year remission lasted just over three months.

When Jack died, the country lost a playwright of soul and I lost a soul mate. That's a hard thing to replace, but it's an experience that is happening every day to a butcher and a postman. Grief, as Katherine Whitehorn recently wrote, is a strange country in which one is a refugee who has to learn all the Laws. And that's the truth. You can either go down on the funeral pyre or you can force yourself back into life. I did that, with Amy, by finishing his autobiography, and by championing *Mr McGill*'s cause. Like the butcher and the polo player, who have memories and photographs, I have an archive of Jack's work.

There was no evening dedicated to Jack's 250-odd screenplays on national TV, although the BBC played three of his works on BBC4, to which almost no one, in those days, had access. ITV have issued their own DVD of his complete works for them. I hoped to persuade the BBC to do the same with the Bafta-award-winning *Bar Mitzvah Boy*, *Spend Spend Spend*, *Bye Bye Baby*, Emmy winner *The Evacuees*, *Wide-Eyed and Legless*, *Eskimo Days* and its companion piece, *Cold Enough For Snow*. Time slipped by. Ready when they are.

Then in 2008, at the Chanukkah party of Chief Rabbi Lord Jonathan Sacks, I brought him and Elaine, his wife, the *Jack Rosenthal at ITV* DVD and he asked if there wasn't a similar one at the BBC. In the hearing of Alan Yentob, I told him that the BBC had no interest in putting out such an item and indeed, felt there would be no market for it. Alan was surprised to hear this and promised to look into it for me. Every so often I would drop him a line reminding him, but heard nothing.

In March 2009 at the Jewish film festival, there was a showing of the Coen Brothers' new take on their Judaism, via the myth of Job, *A Serious Man*. It was a serious and rather bleak take on Judaism in the fifties in America, with wry laughs, of course, but generally showing a club you might not badger anyone to let you join. Its climax involved a bar mitzvah and therefore the organizers followed the film with a thirty-three-year-old print of Jack's *Bar Mitzvah Boy*.

The first film made you squirm a bit in your chair with embarrassment, the second made you fall off it with laughter. The lines were dazzling, relevant and performed by a beautiful ensemble cast of Maria Charles, Cyril Shaps, Adrienne Posta and Jonathan Lynn. The irony was *affectionate*, from script to direction.

During my post-*Bar Mitzvah Boy* talk, I mentioned the BBC would not be publishing Jack's work. Later a friend, songwriter Geoff Morrow, approached me to ask if I would let him try to put out a few feelers with a mind to selling it commercially. Having nothing to lose I thanked him and agreed.

One week later we had a deal with Acorn Films to publish *Jack at the Beeb*. The Beeb and Jack's agent had come on board and it will be issued in January 2011. It doesn't matter who made it happen, because Geoff and I are ecstatic that in March 2011 justice may soon be seen to be done – and cleaned up too in high definition.

Ninety-Nine, Not Out

When Elsbeth Juda and I arrived in Skibbereen, Ireland, in 2004, for the sixtieth birthday party of a mutual friend, it was after a gruelling, delayed flight, a reroute through Dublin, a wait for a second plane to Cork, much airport hiking and a car journey. When asked whether she would prefer to have tea or take a rest, she replied, no, she would like to take a walk round the lough which, at seven o'clock at night, to my horror, we did. At the time Elsbeth was a mere ninety-three years old.

Last year, on 16 April in her ninety-*eighth* year, she was busy curating her first exhibition of photo journalism from 1946 to 1965, spanning her time at the magazine *Ambassador*, for the gallery L'Equipment des Arts in New Quebec Street. When we met there, she was dressed as usual in the finest of linen slacks and crisp white shirt and a cashmere sweater. Her short white hair framed the softest, cleanest skin ever to grace a woman of half her age. Her dazzling black and white photos were stacked against the walls and she took me on a quick tour of an epoch, remembering not only every famous name from Norman Parkinson to Graham Sutherland, but also their wives, the models and even the factory managers she captured in Bradford's textile mills. The pictures, meant to express the superior nature of British products to a global market, are never victims of product placement, managing instead to convey wit as well as worth and a myriad of detail. She was dismissive of the importance of her work. 'It's just a job lot,' and is quietly worrying that the frames are perhaps too prominent for the delicacy of the photos.

Her extraordinary memory was well trained. The eldest of two daughters, with two more brothers at home, she was picked out by her stern and distant father as the brains of the family as early as the age of four. Julius Goldstein was a German Jew – in that order – former cavalry officer, then professor of philosophy in Darmschtadt, a job his mother-in-law called 'breadless art'. He insisted that his daughter present him with a piece of work, either a poem, piece of prose or artwork, outside of her school work, every day at 4.30 p.m. in his office and insisted that at school she took Spanish instead of art because 'the child has no visual sense'. Every summer she was sent, alone, for the whole holiday, to stay with one of his grand former pupils, to learn perfect English.

'I remember travelling for sixteen hours by train to some large country house. I arrived at four thirty to be told by a butler, "Go to your room. A bell will ring at six to change into evening clothes and a second bell will summon you to dinner at seven." I was so hungry. I wasn't even offered a cup of tea. I had only one dress, an orange and white child's crêpe de Chine, all crumpled up in my trunk. I came downstairs when the bell rang and sat shivering at table where they served something with rice. I took one spoonful and spat it out over my one dress. It was curry. I was sent back to my room without so much as an apple.'

She remembers that when she went home and her brothers and sisters surrounded her jumping up and down with glee she was summoned to her father's office to be told, 'I want you to know that I'm just as happy to see you as your brothers and sister.' She ran from his study, fearing he would see her cry. It was the kindest thing he had ever said to her.

Aged seven, Elsbeth threw a snowball at fourteen-year-old Hans Juda who responded by putting her over his knee in mock anger. 'If I ever marry anyone, it will be him,' was her immediate reaction and fourteen years later she replied by telegram to his proposal of marriage. 'Confirm. Oui.' In her own words, she had been waiting fourteen years for this letter. Elsbeth was working as a secretary in Paris and her worldly, handsome, sporting, six-foot-four-inch beau was studying economics, law and music in Berlin. The week before the wedding there were seven dress shirts in his laundry. 'Well, darling,' he told her, pre-empting the life she could look forward to, 'I had to take out all my girlfriends for dinner, didn't I?' They lived in an enclave of ultra-modern flats, surrounded by artists and musicians in the Berlin of Isherwood and Auden with all its cool, liberal freedoms. Religion played no part in their lives. 'When you're called Juda,' Hans said, 'you never have to explain anything.'

Friday night, however, was known as sex night. 'Silence in this brothel!' Hans would yell out of the window. 'I'm married!'

In the thirties, while Hans was out working at the *Berliner* newspaper, the SS stormed the building with bayonets and began burning books. 'Books burn slowly,' muses Elsbeth, 'they were still burning when he came home.' Hans was on a list of intellectuals due to be interrogated and, tipped off by an undersecretary of the interior – 'Leave now! Tonight!' – they left for England with two cases, one of clothes, one of books, plus Hans' precious violin.

From 1934 to 1963, they founded and worked on the British trade magazine *Ambassador*, promoting the best of British textiles and fancy goods abroad. Elsbeth learned her trade from Lucia Moholy, the ex-wife of Laszlo Moholy-Nagy of the Bauhaus movement, and developed all her photographs in the bath at their small apartment. She became the renowned 'Jay' when her boss, Captain Richard Everett, failed to turn up for a photo shoot for an important client, the furrier Reveillon, and she improvised well enough to poach his job for the next thirty years. Her inventiveness was legendary. She would set off by train with model Barbara Goalen, arrive at a mill and drape her subject in enough rolls of fabric to create a stunning display of model, product and grimy environment. She would charm the waspish Norman Parkinson into placid camaraderie and jolly Churchill out of his sulks over Graham Sutherland's hated portrait. She started British Fortnight at rival stores Lord and Taylor and Neiman Marcus in New York. And everywhere she made and kept her friends. It is her gift. She once met the actor Julian Glover, then playing Furtwängler in Ronald Harwood's *Taking Sides*, in a lift and was able to tell him that she was at the concert portrayed in the play. An actor's wish fulfilment. At ninety-eight she had her first London exhibition in a gallery and almost sold out.

The ten years after Hans died of a brain tumour were a wilderness, which she emerged from only with the lifeline of art and her passion for music. Her light and beautifully intricate collages were exhibited all over Europe and hang now in her airy eyrie of a flat in Fulham, marked by small red dots to indicate who receives them when she goes. She visits the Wigmore Hall three times a week, does Pilates on two days a week, was the oldest recipient of a hip replacement at ninety-six and still leaves her flat and stands at the bus stop daily to visit the Royal Academy or the National Gallery – depending on which bus comes first. Once there, she studies one item only for the whole morning. She is my total role model on how to grow old in a child-like manner and to know her is to love her.

One day, I noticed a collage of a psychiatrist with a patient lying on an old-fashioned couch. I asked her to tell me about it.

'Oh, that,' she said, smiling puckishly. 'That was my homage to Freud, who saved my life.'

'Freud saved your life?' I swallowed. 'Freud, as in Sigmund Freud?'

'But of course. I was a screaming baby and my father insisted my mother put me outside on the second balcony so he would not be disturbed. Freud came to the house and asked why the child was screaming – he was of course a medical doctor too – and took a look at me and told my parents that I was starving.

'My father was affronted. He pointed to my elder brother running about and said, "This child has been fed by the same mother and look at him. The child is just misbehaving."

'Still, Herr Freud tested my mother's milk and found that it was water. A wet nurse was engaged for me and – voilà – ninety-eight years later, thanks to Freud, I am still here.'

Luke Warm Tickets

There are many reasons to go to the theatre, several of which occurred to me after a full house last Saturday night and the kind of reception usually reserved for rugby squads bringing home the World Cup or the late Sir John Mills getting up onto a podium to receive something from Sir Richard Attenborough that is too heavy for either of them to lift.

It had been a *Glorious* performance to a brilliantly perceptive audience. It matters. The audience dictates how the show proceeds and in so doing, takes on the character of one human being. Sometimes, at the outset, there are stragglers who hang back from laughing, in a less than full balcony, but after a while they all come together and then the sensation is like riding a superb horse over a familiar course, holding her back at certain jumps and urging her forward at others, always with the other riders and spectators in mind. (Why I chose that particular simile is a mystery since the only time I've ever been on a horse was in 1966, outside my parents' terraced house in Hull, when a horse-mad school friend brought her chestnut round and I climbed up one side and fell down the other.)

It just feels like the most relaxed yet most complex coordination imaginable. Quite often, and invariably on the front row, i.e. two feet from the actors, there will be a stony-faced man, with crossed arms and a thunderous brow, surrounded by shrieking, hooting, body-popping punters. It must be dreadful being them, I always think. I've been that misery many times, gazing round, bewildered, in the midst of mass hysteria at a play which the critics have vouchsafed was the funniest night out since Touchstone first wowed 'em in the Pit with the mustard and pancakes speech . . . What's wrong with me, I'd be thinking, that I've developed a humour bypass?

There are, sadly, other reasons not to go to the theatre. I noticed an article in a London paper where a young woman was sent off to do seven days of cultural visits in the capital city, and not one of those visits was to a theatre. People have got into the habit of one anniversary splurge a year. It's that no man's land after Christmas, let's say, when you're stuck with the odd relative still here so a block of six tickets is booked for the *Lion King* and off you all go, on the Northern line or in a hired people carrier to a matinee and then to a pizza parlour. It costs a lot, you know, but it's *done* now and the kids and the in-laws will all remember the elephant walking down the aisles and you can tick off theatregoing for another year.

'Did you enjoy it, darling?' I once asked my mother, after an armanaleg of an expedition, involving SAS-style organization. 'Mmmm, yes, it was . . . good,' she said, with qualification implicit in the very removal of her rain hood. 'I mean it was a *musical*, you know. Far-fetched.'

Someone wrote to me at the Duchess this week, saying what pleasure Florence Foster Jenkins' hilarious optimism had given them. They were theatregoers from the early years of their marriage and always came to London for a cultural splash every year. This year, she wrote, with the train and the tickets and the *administration fee* on the tickets, plus the programme, drinks and meal, it had cost them £500. My blood pressure rose and a vein started throbbing in my temple. Thank God they enjoyed the show.

What exactly is the administration cost of booking a theatre seat, I'd like to know, and why should it differ from booking a hair appointment or a restaurant? They just pick up a phone and consult a seating plan, don't they? Can someone enlighten me here? I mean box-office staff were always knowledgeable and helpful and one or two, back in the sixties, were the ears and eyes of the whole outfit. Now their skill is relegated to face to face booking in theatres which largely have no walk-past trade, and all telephone bookings are transferred to ticket agencies or on line ticketing. Then the would-be purchaser endures the wretched 'If you want to waste twenty minutes and only get through to a Dalek, press two' ordeal and, more often than not, will be told there are no seats available for the show of your choice.

And here's the rub. The major agencies allocate a few seats to each subsidiary agency, so when they tell you, 'There are no seats available for *Glorious* or the *Blue Men Group*, but we do have seats for *Phantom of the Opera* or *Stomp*', they are, at best, distorting the truth. I've had friends tell me they couldn't get into our show when the house was only three-quarters full. Some of the ticket agencies are owned by the theatre owners themselves, which in itself is worth investigating perhaps, said she, looking nervously over one shoulder. Meanwhile the buildings are archaic, the seats maim you, the toilets are vintage and few – a throwback to Edwardian times when women didn't have bladders – as for the views backstage, well, there are very few open days in London theatres you'll notice.

At least Cameron Macintosh puts as much back as a theatre owner as he puts in as a producer and his recent renovations are monuments for future theatregoers' pleasure. For some it's just bricks and mortar on the outside, whatever tosh it takes to keep it open on the inside, and slap the inflation on the programmes and ice-cream bills.

(This week M. L. takes a pop at theatres and TV. Next week, sadly, she signs on at Job Seekers.)

Dinah

Dinah is very good at her job. She is a waitress in a small Yorkshire tea-room and she knows and loves her customers, works on automatic pilot but without remoteness and has a total obsession with a fifties pop singer not a million miles from Sir Cliff Richard. After years of looking after her husband, mother and brother, Dinah feels she deserves the bit of magic that seeing and hearing her hero brings. She also believes the relationship is equally important to him. All her customers know about her abiding love and she is not hurt at all by their ribbing. This was the very first monologue I wrote and I'm very fond of Dinah.

Dinah

(A small steamy café. Dinah is leaning on the wall by the till. Behind her is a kitchen hatch and a counter with glass-covered cakes and pies. She's writing out a bill.)

Oh, I'll be outside all right. I'll be outside that theatre by hook or crook, fallen arches or no fallen arches notwithstanding. Well *(She chortles.), with* standing if you like . . . *(Examines shoe.)* I've been on me feet that long . . . busy? You must be joking, it's chef's new menu and the hailstones, it's like first day o' Arrods sales in 'ere today. I'm on me uppers.

Coming, Mr Milner . . . No the twenty p's for the extra toast. Oh, well listen, bring it in when you've picked up your benefit, we're not goin' anywhere. Right you are, Mrs Pritchard, and the same for Jennifer . . . with a pot of breakfast and a Diet . . . lovely. She looks nice in that little pink fleece; suits you.

(Into hatch, top of voice.)

Two sos, Tom, double mush, double e. Fried b, one with, one without. Gareth, pot o' b and a Diet Coke.'

(Resumes)

Oh, I'm goin' all right, talk about wild horses. I never miss one of his concerts – well, they're gigs now, aren't they? I have trouble keeping up, me. I never miss one. He couldn't manage without me. Forty years, man and boy, give or take the odd hiccup like in Leeds, on his last tour, when I missed him at City of Varieties on account I'd had me bunion booked and they'd suddenly sent for me.

Oh, thank you, love, that's very nice of you, you didn't need . . .

Then they wrote sayin' they'd a bunion backlog, so they put me off. Then – an' you'll never believe this – it turns out the cancellation was a cock-up in admin and they brought my bunion forward to that night. Same night! I could have kicked 'em in admissions; it would 'ave been worth the agony but they wouldn't take 'no', an' I showed 'em me front-stalls tickets and everything.

Well, it was more important to *me*. Oh, go on – say it – what do I want to go gallivanting off to pop concerts for at my time of life? Following him round five corners of the world . . . I've heard it all before. Our Martin says I want me head examining and he's not wrong – but . . .

Look, I don't smoke and I don't drink. I've no kids driving me mad for trainers with gas in their heels and I don't like abroad because me ankles come up in departures, so why should I begrudge meself, eh? I'm not harming no one, am I? There's no embargo.

All right for you, Mr Bennett? Right you are. Brown or ketchup, I forget?

I was that choked when I missed him that one time with me op. I've never got right since. I think about it every night that dawns. It was the February. Power cuts. Pipes frozen on all t' wards. We was nithered. But all I could think of was him doing the show without me . . . all through me pre-med, I was watchin' it happen in me mind's eye, like I was one of them flies on the wallpaper documentaries on Channel Four. Him arriving at the stage door in his white Bentley and all the fans cheerin' and givin' him bunches of old-fashioned roses and him signing programmes for all the regulars – Sonny Boy with his red toupee and his one tooth and Soft Norman, bless him, with his mam and Myra and the twins all the way from Ilfracombe on a coach. Course some of 'em have dropped out over the years and got James Blunt all over their iPods – an' all of a sudden, I could see him, plain as day lookin' up and sayin', 'Where's Dinah then? Dinah not here? Blimey!' he says. 'Can't do a gig without my lucky mascot, can we?'

An' when I come out from under me general, I could hear a voice singing 'Bachelor Boy' and it wasn't him – it were me! And staff were all collapsed laughin', but not me. I was panickin'. I was dead certain that summat had gone wrong in the second act when he does that reggae version of 'Bachelor Boy' with all them lasers. I was never so sure of anything in me life. I kept tryin' to get off the trolley while they were wheelin' it. They thought I was delirious. They kept pushin' me back, but it wasn't me foot. I never gave a thought to me foot, I never even had a painkiller. They all thought I was dead stoic.

No, it was *him* I was havin' the upsetment over. Me heart was banging like a drum and in the end I got the nurse – the *nice* one – to wheel the phone up to the bed, so's I could phone Eileen and make sure it went off all right. (*Pause*) She said it went perfect. Like greased clockwork. Start to finish. 'Living Doll' stopped the show. Yes. So I was worrying for nothing really. I was relieved it had gone smooth for him. For his sake. He's got to be balanced see . . . Libra . . . and he's got it rising an' all.

Still . . . shows you. He got by without me . . . his lucky mascot. Great . . .

She couldn't talk much, Eileen. She'd had a goujon by mistake in Leeds in all the kerfuffle and forgotten her fish allergy. She was blown up like a puff adder an' her lips went numb. Still they'd had a whale of a time. She said everyone was on their feet.

Except me, of course. The silly beggars had only operated on the wrong foot, hadn't they? I were in a splint till Whitsun. I'm still limping. He'll think I'm Long John Ruddy Silver when he sees me . . . all I need is the African Grey. I'll be there though, come rain or shine, even if I have to crawl up Market Street on me hands and knees with me tote bag in me teeth. I'll be there.

(*Sings*) I'd walk a million miles for one of his smiles . . .

I would though. It's the only time I feel, you know, alive like. When I'm watchin' him. He knows that. Deep down . . . doesn't crack on but he knows all right.

(*She's in a reverie.*)

I love him. Always have . . . He's a marvellous artiste.

(*Snaps out of it.*)

Sorry? Oh yes, chuck. Barbara, can you give number four an ALLACART . . . and I think Mr Bennett's ready for his pudding. What's it to be, love? There's kiwi crumble, rice p or chef's tisamiru? (*sic*) Right you are. Condensed or evap? Lovely choice, you won't regret it.

(*Through hatch.*)

One rice p with e. And a decaff Nescaff for Alan.

(*Resumes*)

No problem. You what, Mr Bennett? OK coming up.

Yes, course it is. Have you not seen him in here before? Never! He comes every Thursday, half past six, regular as clockwise. Oh, he's a lovely man. YEESS! Course he's the same one – the play writer. You've seen him. You have. He's often on. With the Fair Isle jumper and the little owl glasses and his hair all cut round like a pudding. We take no notice. Speak as you find. That's why he comes, I reckon. He's no bother. Right as rain. He's a bachelor . . . I've often wondered if he might have a soft spot for Cliff, hisself . . . I might ask him one day while he's settling up. He's very ordinary. Just sits there with his little notebook. Scribbling away. Shopping lists I shouldn't wonder. He's very polite, lovely tipper, but, you know, keeps himself to himself, never says much. He's in his own little world. Oh we've had 'em all in here with him, from America and everything. Sheriff of Nottingham . . . all of 'em. That Hyacinth Bucket's been in . . . she had the haddock. She's ever so ordinary.

Mind you, he's clever. Got his finger right on the pulse – very popular. Still, you can't help wonderin' where he gets all his *ideas* from.

Mugger All

As the tall, confrontational man in the beanie hat approached me on my way to my car, I affected a puzzled, reproving look and scurried off. Even my back gave me away. 'Sucker,' it said, as my conscience hectored me from within, 'it's the price of the sodding latte in your hand. Of *course* he'll spend it on lager – what's that to you?' I turned round and caught his eye. He'd already started to lumber towards me and as he took my pound coins I swear there was a look of bemused pity on his face.

Our local *Big Issue* seller is a rangy, ex-alcoholic Scotsman who operates from outside Marks & Spencer's in all weathers. Or did. He seems to have dropped off some kind of wagon though he assures me he's not drinking, just homeless and unable to afford to buy the copies. In the old days, when my daughter was at Manchester University, he used to tell me how she was getting on. It seemed she'd tell *him* what she kept from us.

'She's getting more i' the swing of it noo, Maureen,' he'd say, 'mekkin' a few friends . . . but, you know, that first term she was terrible lonely.'

He looks so ill and bronchial now, crouched up on the doorstep of the pub that used to be a church. (Is there a name for such an establishment? The Holy Sclerosis? The Pig and Stigmata?) Anyway, I gave him a note and mumbled something about spending it on a hostel before moving on to spend ludicrous amounts on posh biscuits with an unnecessary layer of paper between them and chutneys with chintzy covers.

He was smoking as I returned with my laden shopping bags. Before I could open my mouth he called out, 'I didnae buy this, Maureen. I rolled it meself.' Gulp. I hurried home, probably feeling more hopeless than he did.

Last week a Portuguese girl found me round the back of the Aldwych. She was very smartly dressed and neat with a face quivering with despair.

'I am cold and hungry . . . I have no money. I cannot ring my father. I want to go home . . . the agency take all money and send me to bad job. Many people in house . . . no one listen to me when I talk . . .' Now, I rate myself a pretty good judge of bad acting and this wasn't. Besides, she was the same age as my daughter. I took her to the café next door to the Duchess Theatre, got her some tea, gave her some money to phone her dad and made her write down the address where she had temporary lodgings till Thursday. For some insane reason I got her a ticket to watch the show – at least to be in the warm – although what she must have made of a bewigged and padded me, bobbing around the stage like a Subuteo player and warbling appallingly I will never know. I will *really* never know because the address she gave me said Number 34, Finsbury Park. Not much chance of any mail finding that address. Only afterwards did it occur to me that she could have telephoned her father on a reverse-charge call.

The well-dressed mugger is a new phenomenon. Outside Jo Hansford's Mayfair salon I was once pleasantly relieved of a tenner by a man in pinstripes carrying a briefcase telling me in Treasury tones that he'd been mugged of everything including his mobile. I actually gave this creep his train fare to Guildford and an *address* to which he could return the money! I know, I *know*! Mugged and burgled in a single day and no one but my dumb self to blame. Two hours later, with a head full of expensive highlights, I turned the street corner and saw him at it again! I couldn't believe my eyes. Not two hundred yards from where he'd fleeced me. I started hollering like the cast of *Braveheart*, 'Thief! Mugger! Don't give him a penny! Don't let him fool you – you bastard! How bloody dare you. Give her that money back *now*! Or I'll . . . Come *back*!' His latest prey and I stood there sheepishly as he legged it down the road and probably into a taxi back to Guildford or Herne Hill or wherever he kept his Jermyn Street wardrobe and his Mulberry luggage.

The beggar as metaphor, the holy man, the seer who is never a doer, is a powerful one in our religious and philosophical mythology. In the late Carol Shields' triumphant last novel, *Unless*, there is a painful cloud hanging over a family's comfortable existence. One of their three daughters has dropped out of college and is sitting on a Toronto street corner, begging, wearing a sign around her neck saying 'Goodness'. There is a political and feminist rationale for her odd behaviour, but generally, with down and outs, one's first thoughts are seldom, 'How did he/she *get* to that state?'

I have trouble with this. I know that I must buy the *Big Issue* even if I already have one at home. I know I must listen to the care in the community case who asks me for the price of a sandwich, because I *am* the community. I must stand, with a rapt look on my face, listening to the Brazilian nose flautist, before dropping the right amount of coins into his embroidered hat. I know all this. The trouble is they know it too. They can see me coming a block away, trailing my middle-class heart on my warm woollen sleeve, my wrist dripping gilt.

On the subject of profligacy, as we sort of were, I went into town to buy a baby present and came back with two paintings, a coat and some pyjamas. The reason for buying the paintings was straightforward: I love artist John Fisher's paintings of writers' rooms. I couldn't decide between two and had a blinding flash of Jack saying, 'What's the matter with you? You work like a dog! Treat yourself, for heaven's sake. If you like them – have 'em.' This from a man who, when I suggested once, in Italy, that he bought himself some shoes, looked at me and said in all seriousness, 'But I've got shoes, love – a black pair and a brown pair.'

The reasons for buying the jim-jams and the coat were straightforward too. The Italian owners were so incredibly friendly and nice over the baby present that I would have bought the floor, shelves, changing room and her granddaughter if I could. Shopping in this small boutique was a pure delight. On my way back to the theatre I thought I'd continue the pleasure by having a penne in Pasta Brown's restaurant. It was 5.45 p.m. and the large room was 80 per cent empty. I sat at a table for four – actually two tables pushed together – and took out my magazine. The waitress asked me would I mind moving to a table for two, which I did but the lighting was so bad that I moved again to a well-lit table for four. The waitress refused to serve me.

'But you're empty!' I bleated.

'In ten minutes we'll be full,' she replied.

'But, I'm here *now* and in twenty minutes I'll be gone,' I spluttered.

She removed the cutlery from my table and, growling and muttering, I left for the welcoming noodles of Wagamama where a woman alone is not treated like a noodle.

De-Scent of a Woman

Speculation is rife about women and body image in the wake of J. K. Rowling's great potter forward into the body politic arena and the sharp response from those who know her work well enough to jump out from the bushes shouting, 'Morpugnocenti was thin and bony and Valderee-Voldera was large and square, so yah boo sucks and I wish I had her money and then I could afford to be a size ten with a posh husband.'

She's right, of course, about the skinny, celebrity role models 'whose only function in the world appears to be supporting the trade in over-priced handbags and rat-sized dogs'. Never mind the clothes, you need only look at the mannequins in shop windows to feel obese. Mannequins never used to have protruding rib cages and nipples which point to the ceiling, did they?

Of course, household names are not supposed to have opinions. They are supposed to entertain when they get the chance, show up at the school fete for as long as they're still on the telly, flash a leg at the entrance to the Ukip Euro-Quip of the Year Award and be gracious and, above all, grateful when a posse of hyperactive photographers call out, 'Maureen! Maureen! Over *here*, Maureen! Maureen, look at me, Maureen! Up here, Maureen! Down here, Maureen . . .'

Seriously, you've got to see the camera wielders at a do to believe it. They have a pack mentality. They've learned the 'snapper's chant' from the original brigade of paparazzi and they're sticking to it, despite the fact that we're all familiar enough with the routine to do the smiles, looks and leg flashing in our sleep but still, they persist. 'Maureen! This way! That way! Show us yer 'anbag!' Honestly, Jack used to stand in agony, with a rictus grin, doing his level best to disappear up his own dinner jacket. I've seen Gerald Scarfe do exactly the same routine when they're hollering, 'Jane, Jane, over 'ere, Jane. Can you tell us who made your velvet shrug?'

The last time I ran the flashbulb circuit was, believe it or not, at the *Oldie* lunch. It was bizarre. There was more white hair than at a sheep shearers' convention. The smell of Fiery Jack and Dentifrice was pleasantly rampant. John Mortimer was being hauled up the steps of Simpson's in The Strand in a wheelchair, Barry Cryer was telling the one about the genie and the map of the Middle East, Beryl Bainbridge was having a quiet fag behind the potted plants, Walter Wolfgang, ninety-three (the ancient protester so kindly evicted from last year's Labour Conference), was blinking warily into the straining waistcoat of editor-in-chief Richard Ingrams, and, lo and behold, the Nikonoclasts are screaming at the guests as though we were Scarlett Johansson and Angelina and Brad in Agent Provocateur thongs. Force of habit, I suppose.

One of the reasons we have opinions is because journalists keep asking us what they are. So we make sure we've got some and duly churn them out, only to find them picked over and ridiculed by other columnists who have read the opinions and found them wanting. On the issue of skinny role models, well I'm afraid it was always thus and will be even thus-er, as long as very creative and largely male designers are, fashionwise, they who must be obeyed.

What would the point be for them, if they created a style which looked good on all women? What would happen the following season? Pack up and move on to a new career in plumbing, eh boys? That's why the ubiquitous jeans are a double-edged (and this year – sawn off) sword. A pair of jeans could last your average macho cowboy maybe ten years or more, and they spend their days roping steer and breaking in stallions as opposed to slurping lattes and picking up Tallulah from BabYoga in a Hummer.

For some reason though, women love themselves in jeans. So

jeans have to evolve every season. Stretch, embroidered, flared, studded, cropped, pouchy and so low slung that your natural hair colour is revealed. If it were up to me, I'd have denim discontinued except, possibly, as a boy's name or a bicycle-seat cover.

On the other hand, I do have a magic moment in my dressing room each night when I bend over backwards in front of a long mirror to straighten my seamed stockings and see upside down through my legs a strange, inhuman and terrifying sight. It's just legs – from a different angle but don't ever do it. It's an alien, a mess of potage, or, as Les Dawson might have said, 'She took off her clothes revealing a torso that put one in mind of a three-day tripe convention.'

Model Habits

The next character is a young model. She's twenty, pretty, blank-faced until her face is painted on and then she really can do it. She knows her time on the catwalk is limited. Sadly, so is her intelligence, although she's street-smart. She's sharp, ignorant and she's been around. She's probably estranged from her family and has a serious eating problem. She's called Sharon but has amended it to Shirrin which she reckons is smarter. She's probably right. Her end could be terrible but on the other hand, she could just be saved . . .

Model Habits

'No thanks. Not for me thanks, I couldn't. What is it? No, don't tell me –
I don't wanna know . . . could you just move it away, please? Thanks. I'll
have a coffee though if there is one. A latte thanks – a skinny latte, no
sugar, thanks. No, sorry, make that an espresso, will you? A double
espresso, right?

(*Sotto*) And hold the biscuit thing OK? You know, on the side. Sorry.
Thanks . . .

Ow! That was my bloody head. Ow. That actually hurt quite a lot. Yeah, I
know I have to suffer to be – yeah, right, but I've only got the one head –
I'd quite like to leave some scalp on it if it's all right with you . . .

Have you got a thingy, you know, like a bin or something what I can put my
gum in, it's manky. I've been chewing it since breakfast and it's gone rigid . . .
sorry. Thanks.

My God, what *is* that? I can't wear that. Oh please. It weighs four tons. No,
honest I can't hold it up. My neck can't take it. I've only got a little neck . . .
Look – it'll get an S bend in it now.

Mitchell! I'm not wearing it. I can't! Not AND WALK! And pull the scowly
faces and do the spot turns. With these Manolos as well. Platform soles a
foot deep and a deckchair on my head. Thanks I don't th—

Oww! You did that on purpose didn't you, you barcode?

No thanks, what are they? No, I don't do bread, I'm allergic, it gives me
IBS yeah, that's right. Irritable bum syndrome. I asked for a black coffee
about a year ago though . . . could someone chase it up? I'm just sooo
tired.

Oooh, I love this track, it was the last one I danced to at the end of last
night . . . (*Half sings.*) *Everything you la in a la to the left. In the la-la that's my
stuff.* On my own. Well, with my gay boys. Why? Least they know how to
enjoy themselves, innit?

No. Garth and the others was all stuffing their faces in the restaurant up
top. I'd had some at teatime, hadn't I? S'not cos I didn't wanna eat, Dee. I

don't know what they're talking about either. The bloody Zeitgeist! Footsie index, Enron, 'ave you seen it? Is he a tosser or not? Oh spare me, like I care. All bloody tossers if you ask me.

Oww! Dakota! You can't just pluck 'em out like that. You know they're actually attached to me . . . and in quite a sensitive place. No, I'm serious, Dee, that really hurt . . . It's not like they would have shown. Them shorts come up high at the butt but they don't show your pubes . . . Oww! Look it's all red. I'm gonna have to explain that!

Oooh, I like this top. What size is it? Can I keep it? Oh go on, ask Rocco, pleeze. Tell him I'll eat purple sprouting broccoli if he lets me keep it. Well, who's going to get into it 'cept me, Dakota? It's a size four or something. Pleeze . . . Oh God, thanks. I'm insane about them pintucks . . . and if I just wear nipple tape instead of a bra he'll have it off me before I've buttoned it up – he gets a bit insistent if he's on one, Garth does.

What? Where? It's not! It's not. It's just a bruise where I walked into the thingy – swingin' egg-chair. It is! You've got an horrible twisted mind, Dee. I'm off it completely . . . Yeah well, it was just a one-off, OK? I'm never getting into that again . . . I know . . . I know I promised . . . I'm clean, Dee. It was the bathroom door, like I said, honest.

No! Take 'em *away!* Sorry. Thanks, but I'm not hungry . . . Anyway, I don't do meat on ethnic grounds. (*Sotto*) She *knows* that – how many times! Just give me that bit of cucumber then . . . mmmmm . . . no more . . . because I don't! It's got no calories, yeah, but it's full of water and I don't wanna pee on the catwalk if it's all right with you. Because . . . Look, Dee, you're not my mum all right? I've had one of those and all she wanted was for me to be as fat as she is, and that's why I haven't clocked her for three years, all right?

Let me look . . . Shit man, that's me . . . I look wicked. How long have I got? Is Amelia on, then Erin, then me? Are we smiling? Are you sure my arms don't look bingo-wing? (*She sways and almost loses her balance.*) Whoops. Sorry. Thanks, no, I'm fine just got a bit giddy for a min— Has anyone got a Red Bull? Quick pass it over . . . that's better. Let me look again.

(*To herself*) Shirrin Smith you are the best fucking model in this fucking show . . . so get on there and sell it. Go girl go! Hips forward, shoulders back and . . . concentrate, man, think. (*She starts to walk the elongated walk.*) Roast chicken, roast spuds, fried-egg sandwiches, mustard pickle, French fries, ketchup, Heinz baked beans, Dairylea triangles, white-bread toast, Horlicks, apple crumble, Mum's custard, Mum's rice pudding, Mum!

Brought Up By a Guardian

It was the *Guardian* annual party and I hadn't a thing to wear. Other than, that is, the nine hundred perfectly suitable outfits in my wardrobe. I had been walking past a white dress for some days, in a shop in which I have a twenty-three-year-old *broiges,* i.e. I don't speak to them and they don't speak to me . . . neither of us can remember why. This dress, however, had my name on it and clearly I would have to swallow my pride and put my money where my mouth wasn't.

So, I hovered, dashed in, had a lovely chat, bought it in black – white may be the new black but it's not hip to have 40 inch hips and I didn't want to turn up looking like an inverted Cornetto – and waited till I got home to try it on.

Once German Georg the dog sitter had arrived at 6.45 p.m. – I know, I should be leaving her alone but I wanted to wait till her season was over and wean her into being on her own gradually. The day before I'd explained to her that I'd be gone for one hour only, settled her in her basket with a tasty bone, said goodbye and sauntered elaborately out of the door, to listen, hunched over the letterbox, for 5 or 6 minutes.

When the kids were small, as I went to rehearsals, Amy had perfected the knack of hurling herself at the windows with her mouth in an Edvard Munch rictus, which gave me heartburn for the whole day. Au pairs told me she cut it out the minute I turned the corner and went back to terrorizing her brother; but once again, I was thankful not to hear that pitiful and piercing Basenji yodel following me down to the patisserie café, where I intended to sit out the hour over scrambled eggs and smoked salmon. When I returned Diva was ecstatic – leaping and fawning and licking and bounding. She'd been awfully good, I assured her, as I patted and stroked her. 'Who's my best girl? Who's a big brave grown-up girl?'

Yes, she'd peed on the newspaper provided. 'Good girl! Good girl,' I cooed and got the dustpan and broom. It was, after all, my fault entirely that I'd left a carrier bag on the hall chair with a red feather boa inside it. Well, a *late* red feather boa. I surveyed the poultry slaughterhouse before me more in sorrow than in anger. It was a start.

So, on the evening of the party, leaving her downstairs with Uncle Georg and a liver snack, I went upstairs to slap on some concealer, confident that the dress would do the rest. It was a humid day to be wearing an all-in-one foundation garment but Dolce and Gabbana stretch cotton takes no prisoners and a visible pantie line and dolcelatte thighs were out of the question, so trussed and bound I attempted to slide seamlessly into the dress. The dress had other ideas.

For the next ten minutes woman and dress were locked in battle like muntjac and musk ox. I got it over my head and as I rolled down the dress the foundation garment rose to meet it. I started again, got the dress down to my middle and found my head was in the arm hole. I took it off again and replaced my head in the right hole, then tried a twisting action, hips going one way and chest the other. My face was a glazed crimson and my hair had collapsed. This was no way to start an evening of tinkling crystal and gentle badinage.

Still, I would not be beaten by something which once grew on a bush. I persevered and beat the damn thing into submission, smoothed it, arranged it around the protuberances it was meant to enhance and immediately needed the loo. I'm sensitive to the fact that you may be having your breakfast so I'll skip the bit where dress and foundation garment are bunched into a sort of spandex boa constrictor and cut to the arrival at the garden square in town.

I parked conveniently near Montague Place, the party being off

Montague Street, and wobbled my way over the grass on soil-piercing heels to the smallish throng of people. I was surprised on two counts: no one came to greet me and offer a drop of wine and the guests were extremely grungily dressed . . . It took a while to realize that flashing my dazzling dress at a group of students having a quiet drink in the grounds of University College was perhaps not the same as sampling the olive tapenade and mojitos at the *Guardian* summer party. By the time I found the right party, with the help of a German coach driver parked outside the British Museum, my heels were deep in mud, my dress was actually hurting me and I'd lost whatever access I'd had to my guardian angel.

Cut From the Same Cloth

The kids laughed at me this week when I mentioned the word moygashel. They'd never heard of it and accused me of making it up. I told them it was one of the words bandied about in my childhood home all the time. My father was in tailoring so there was a frequent backdrop of phrases like, 'Well, of course 'e's going potshop! He ordered it in cavalry twill and when it came in – workshop had done it in *gabardine*. No, we've none left . . . unless we do it in barathea and hope he won't notice the difference.'

My mother was also a rampant materialist. Rare was the day when she didn't have a swatch-based decision to make before sundown, concerning a choice between the moire with the gimped edging or the doupion with the slight water mark that wouldn't show, or the grosgrain with the slub trim – I mean this is for real – which needed a second opinion from seven other people, *now*, because Mrs Cockerill could only fit her in next week so all three fabrics are standing by on apro.

They didn't even know that apro was approval, meaning if it's not right you could take it back. Everything in our house had started its existence on apro. We had a puppy once on apro. It lasted not quite all of a day after a spot of territorial leakage onto one piece of the three-piece suite. Tragically, this disregard for the sanctity of uncut moquette drove the wee beast back into the none too welcoming arms of the seaman who'd foisted it on my father, as part payment on a navy nap coat.

At the obsolescence of words like weft
I feel quite personally bereft.
Soon there'll be no such word as cambric
To pep-up and pepper a couplet iambic.
Who wouldn't bemoan the loss of a stanza
Mentioning worsted and tulle and organza?
Candlewick, bouclé and burlap and baize,
Will – voile – disappear by the end of our days.

I could go on, I'm having such fun, but I realize I'm the only person who is, so I'll stop and let the great Thomas Pynchon have the last, grave word: 'He opens her closet, and in moonlight reflected from the mirror finds a crowded maze of satins, taffeta, lawn and pongee, dark fur collars and trimming, buttons, sashes, passementerie, soft, confusing, womanly tunnel-systems that must stretch back for miles – he could be lost inside of half a minute . . . lace glimmers, eyelets wink, a crepe scarf brushes his face . . .'

In the end, as in the beginning, were the words, just the words . . .

JR's Last Act

In 2007, at the behest of blessed producer Bruce Hyman, Amy adapted Jack's autobiography, *By Jack Rosenthal*, for Radio 4 where it ran for four episodes and was twice repeated within the space of a year. We gathered the usual suspects and added Rebecca Front as Jack's mother and Pat Phoenix, and actors Tracy-Ann Oberman, Stephen Mangan and even the producer's eight-year-old twins, Aggie and Nou. I was allowed to direct. At the time I wrote: 'When Radio 4 commissioned a four-part adaptation of his posthumous autobiography, *By Jack Rosenthal*, no one could accuse Jack's family of failing to put the "tis" in nepotism.' It was a family affair. Amy Rosenthal adapted it, Adam contributed to the script and recording, friends queued up to take part and I divided my time between playing myself in the book and directing the assembled players while seasoned radio producer Dirk Maggs took care, thank the Lord, of the whole technical thingy-whatsit. It was a labour of love for Above the Title productions, led from the helm by Bruce, who loved Jack as much as the rest of us.

Jack wrote through chemotherapy, stem-cell therapy and some of the most intrusive treatments imaginable. It was a lifeline. Then one day he stopped. 'No one's going to want to read this,' he said. Of all the bleak diagnoses, that was the most chilling. For Jack not to write was for the monsoon to flow upwards to the clouds.

For once he was wrong. Thousands of people have read his book and our public readings have sold out. When Bruce asked Amy to adapt it I feared for her. For me, finishing his account of the last ten years had been a ritual cleansing. It hurt, but it was a good pain. For Amy, still coming to terms with losing her father, it could have been too personal – too much responsibility. In fact, she took the baton and sprinted.

(My hairdresser Jo Handsford, recently widowed, had given me a tip based on her own daughter. 'Everyone worries and frets over how *you* are,' she told me, 'and no one expects the children to need the same support.' It was true. How many times had I heard the solicitous words, 'How's your mum doing?' answered reassuringly by my kids. Few people added 'and how are you faring, without your best friend?')

There was work to be done. Casting an actor to play Jack was . . . challenging. To capture his warmth, his reserve and his deadpan humour alongside his very particular speech rhythms would require a great mimic as well as a great actor. Stephen Mangan, of *Green Wing*, had already played the put-upon writer in Jack's *Ready When You Are, Mr McGill*, and was in his adaptation of Kingsley Amis's *Lucky Jim*. He was neither northern, nor Jewish, nor working class, but from the first reading he knew his voice, his wry melancholy and his timing. He even learned to breathe like Jack. Amy spoke for us all when she said, 'He feels like Dod.' After that the rest of the casting fell magically into place.

We spent a week recording in Hammersmith. The sun shone and the cast sat outside and sipped sodas and swapped anecdotes between takes. I skipped between the sound desk for notes and the studio for my own bits of the recording, which I didn't listen to on the grounds that I'd want to re-record them. Whoever liked the sound of their own voice?

I described my dad to George Layton, who was playing him, and Jack's mother, Lakey, and agent, Peggy Ramsay, to Rebecca Front. Amy Shindler, Brenda in the *Archers*, played Jack's ex-girlfriend and first wife, and her father, Colin, took on a range of Mancunian voices. Lord Puttnam dropped by to play himself in a scene where he told Jack off for spending too much time doing domestic stuff at the expense of his career. He wanted to improvise the scene rather than stick to Jack's script. Who was I to argue with him? He tried a couple of times then, just before leaving, reluctantly returned to Jack's dialogue. We got it on tape. If ever I felt Jack's hand on the proceedings, it was at that moment.

On the final day, sipping champagne in the courtyard after finishing episode four, we were awash with emotion. Our reduced family tree had sprouted new branches and we didn't want them to bend and sever. It had been, we all agreed, the happiest job ever.

My linking voiceovers covering Jack's illness and death were emotionally hazardous, but, with the time restrictions, I got through them more easily than expected. Months later, on tour in Birmingham with Martha Josie and the Chinese Elvis, I sat in an NCP car park and listened to an episode. Although the programme was without sentimentality, when Max Bruch's violin concerto played behind what sounded exactly like Jack's voice, and I began to talk to him, I was overcome with emotion. But not for long. It was full of wit and compassion and sheer bloody wonder at the eccentricity of his fellow man. It was dazzling. It was Jack.

N.B. The CD was withdrawn from the market because of music copyright problems. On 19 June, sitting in my tiny study with publisher Jeremy Robson, I told him about this. 'I'm going to find a way to solve this and re-record other music . . . if it kills me,' I said, and as I said it, the sound from the kitchen radio swelled up to the strains of Maxim Vengerov playing Bruch's heart out in the violin concerto. I looked out of the window, up at the clouds and said, 'I know, love, I know. I intend to get it re-edited.' I do, Jacko. I do.

Fan Tango

Faced with Camden Market, with its pierced and gothic populace, or a bustling country market place, my mother would frequently say, 'It's another world, isn't it?' What she meant was, 'Here's a community with its own customs and costumes with whom I have absolutely nothing in common.' The inference was that their deviation from her norm makes them quaint but *fools to themselves*.

So her voice was in my inner ear when I pitched up last week at a tango hall in Tufnell Park. I love to watch good tango and some years ago, at the Aldwych Theatre, during *Tango Argentino*, I think I actually levitated. In the past I had a tango-obsessed acupuncturist – I guess it's exactly the kind of divertissement which takes away the tension after making tiny holes in the meridians of slightly below-par strangers – but I've never really contemplated doing it myself.

On this occasion, I'd been to see an exhibition of paintings in a Crouch End jewellery gallery – I do jet-set when I can – and Philip Hood, the artist, is a tango aficionado. So there we were, nibbling the minutiae and admiring the art, when someone said, 'Are you coming to tango after?'

So, fuelled by grilled sardines and in the wrong shoes for anything save making sound effects on gravel, I found myself climbing the stairs of a crepuscular North London pub, into the most glamorous dive in the whole wide world and Shangri-La. It was a triumph of mood over matter, dark enough for lumpy plaster to look Gaudí not gaudy, a masterclass tango movie flickering on one wall and a DJ mixing sensuous *bandoneon* music on the other.

On a floor more densely packed than my sardines were dedicated dancers of all shapes, sizes, abilities and ages. It seems that tango talent improves with age, like Stilton. Every dance is a story told, the storytellers impassively expressing emotion through stylized movements of their bodies. I sat transfixed and prayed, 'Please don't anyone ask me to dance.' Fortunately, I was looking so gormless, my prayers were answered.

There were men in their seventies with shirts straining across their paunches hovering darkly over drop-deadpan gorgeous girls, often of Asian extraction, in slashed skirts, their gleaming heads glued to their partners', like silhouettes, mere appendages to their men. The males are in total control and the dance likes it that way. They bend, they sway, they speak an unspoken language whispered from the shoulder to the hip. Under the table my sneakers began, furtively, to mark out the steps. Left, two three, step slide cross, seven eight . . . how in hell does she *know* he's going to suddenly turn her body sharp left like that?

Back in the Ballroom of Desire, one tall, skeletal refugee from *un film de Pedro Almodóvar*, wearing a beret pulled down rakishly over one eye, moved seamlessly across the floor with his blonde partner. He possessed only one arm but his shoulder was doubly expressive to make up for his loss. Then there was Joan, wispy and blonde, of uncertain age, dancing every dance with high-octane verve. 'I started a year ago,' she said, beaming, 'and I go four nights a week now!' 'Yeah,' said her daughter, 'I've lost my babysitter to a Latin beat.'

Over there – no, over there – snaked the acupuncturist, clearly in his element. I thought about saying hello, but it was a long time ago and I didn't want to needle him.

By now, Philip was covering the floor like mercury, his shoulders enveloping Joan's, his centre of gravity low and smooth. I did a hasty shlurry round the floor myself, head down, bum out, with my friend Trevor, and thought for a moment, I might just be getting the hang of it. But then when Philip led me, *Celebrity Gooseberry*, onto the floor, I completely lost it. 'Ooops – sorry – Oh! My fault . . . Oh shit . . .' I was sixteen again, at the B'nai Brith Social, permed, Truform girdled and stiff petticoated, clutching a Vimto and a packet of Smith's crisps with a twist of blue-wrapped salt. I may have to feel the fear and do it anyway. I've paid for the shoes, I've got the shawl . . . It might be a totally different world, but how hard can it be to stop it and get on?

Barkless Up the Wrong Tree

Diva the Basenji has been in the doghouse, big time. It started with a birthday party – her first ever invitation:

> Please come to the gate of Friary Park next Tuesday to celebrate my first birthday. There will be a walk with owners, and drinks and fun afterwards at my house.
> Love Simba.

Simba is a handsome Weimaraner we'd met in the park. Now she, her owner Judy, her friends and seven hounds in various stages of sociability were waiting at the gate. There was much barking and wagging with anticipation; the dogs were pretty excited too.

We walked in a stately straggle across the park and back, talking canine, and at each end of the park Judy gave each dog a sausage. I foresaw trouble right away. Diva has a sensitive stomach and the scavenging tactics of a coyote. Back at the party house Judy flung treats all over the garden and, while the other dogs sniffed each other, Diva deftly hoovered them all up. She compounded this crime by opening the handbag of one of the guests and gobbling her dog treats. Her farewell present was a leathery bone which she unwrapped in the back seat and downed in the six minutes it took to drive home.

That night I went to the theatre. I was lucky. For most of the evening Diva projectile-spurted from both ends. Natalie, angel in the attic, dealt with the carpets, the paintwork and the small brown pig. I starved Diva for twenty-four hours. She responded by dumping in the bathroom. This went on for some days. I got crosser, she got naughtier. My new leather handbag with the front pouch for passport and phone, £80, took the brunt. It now has no front pouch.

Sunday in the park with Diva dawned. I took her for a nice long walk. There was a summer fete in the park. I wandered round the stalls, eating a maple syrup crêpe, and followed a sign saying 'Dog Show'. It was the real thing. Anxious owners, portly judges, rosettes for Best in Show and bags of luxury dried food for the winners. I sat down, charmed, with Diva to watch the merry beasts go through their paces.

Suddenly there was a tap on my shoulder. 'Are you entering her?'

'Pardon?'

'In the prettiest dog section?'

'Er . . . no, I'm not.'

'What about the smartest puppy?'

'Well . . . no, I'm happy just to w—'

'Tell you what. How would you like to judge the best rescued dog section?'

'Er . . . Would I have to feel their – bobbly bits?'

'Nooo. Just choose the saddest story. Go on, they'd love it.'

Which is how I came to spend my Sunday pinning a rosette on a lurcher rescued from a JCB. On Monday Diva and I started training school. It's either that or I'm *looking* for a JCB.

All the books told me that Basenjis are very cat-like, meaning they are hard to train, very clean, hate water and seldom come when called. They refuse to do anything twice that they've learned, occasionally eat fruit and have been known to climb trees. They were bred from the pharaoh hound to hunt lions – hence their absence of a bark, and despite the absence of lions in Ealing, where she was born. Like Rolf Harris, some of them occasionally yodel.

I'm thinking of reporting her to the Trade Descriptions people. For a start she's learned to bark. Not often, but enough. She's also learned to whinge *before* she is accidentally stood on. She is, according to the Dog Hotel owner, Maria, 'the cleberest dog I eber met'. Maria is Spanish and loves dogs more than life itself. Sadly, Diva blew her good will when she learned how to open the door at Maria's home and ate through her computer leads and a smart leather bag belonging to her daughter. More in sorrow than in anger, Maria was forced to ban her, pop-star like, from the hotel.

She *is* cat-like in that she bears a hefty grudge. If Natalie goes away for a weekend, the dog rewards her by pooing in her room. If I take her to Guido's overnight, she upchucks on his stair carpet. This is understandable behaviour in a puppy but less attractive in a four-year-old. If left alone, she will tear up plastic bags into tiny pieces, drag her bottom on my Annie Phillips rug and destroy small Persian prayer mats.

Adam once took her for a walk while I was away, and she crouched over by the bus stop in Praed Street and started contractions. Clearly, she was having difficulty passing something, so Adam bent down by her side and saw, to his amazement, a pair of my white(!) Sloggi pants emerge painfully and slowly out of her. As he guided them into a plastic bag, the people at the bus stop stared open-mouthed. 'I felt like a conjurer,' he said.

Then there is the duck. The duck is her special toy. It is yellow, fluffy, one-legged and almost as big as Diva. When denied human food, or refused human expeditions, she sweeps out of the scene of the betrayal, into the guest room where the duck lives, stalking back minutes later, paws tapping with studied casualness on the floor, straight past the perpetrator of the oversight. She then lies down, duck stuffed hugely in mouth, with her back to you. It is very funny. If you go round to look at her she avoids your eyes but her body language says 'Don't try to get round me', as she turns back the other way. When offered a treat with the words 'Well, what are you going to do for it?', she takes the shortest route to success: aware that the speediest trick is to turn round in a circle to the command of 'clock', she now revolves disdainfully before the word 'clock' is uttered, to get the treat sooner.

She likes Shreddies for breakfast, meat and couscous or rice for dinner, a slice of fresh coconut at any time of day, a nice cup of tea and, oh, lettuce at any time. She's in the advanced class at agility, going round the course, through the silk tunnel, up the A-frame and over the see-saw in excellent time. She can count to five, find a mark and lie on it, give you a high-five, distinguish shoulder, arm, knees, and right and left; and she puts two reluctant paws on your back if you sit down and say 'On the bus!' She lies down, fully stretched out, to feign sleep, weaves through legs on command, and her cutest trick is to go into her cage, staring forlornly at the shut door, listening intently to the story of the poor lonely dog who was left alone in the dog home at Christmas time. Only when it gets to the part about the family coming to take the poor doggy home does she burst free from the cage and run round like a loony.

She howls joyously like a coyote when my kids come round on a Friday night, sometimes as many as five times, especially for Adam, whom she reveres on the grounds that he generally ignores her. When we go out walking, I have to inform enquiring strangers about every twenty yards, 'No, she's not a fox, she's a basenji – the barkless dog of the Congo.' She is fearless of dogs three times her size and has a penchant for snarling at small white bichon frises on leads. Her optimism about catching pigeons and squirrels, in spite of years of evidence to the contrary, is eternal. She likes chicken-flavoured toothpaste, eating rubber bands in the street and frisking with an ice cube like a Viennese show horse. Yes, we've anthropomorphized her every habit and we are wrong to do so but we, too, are old dogs and can't be taught new tricks now. In short, Jackie Collins-like, the bitch has mastery of us all.

The other day, in the park, a Swedish woman stopped me to ask if Diva was really a Basenji.

'I have never seen one off the lead before,' she told me. 'I used to have one myself and we could never let her go, because she would not have returned.'

I tried, but failed, not to look smug.

'Oh, she always comes back,' I told her. 'She's pretty well trained really.'

The next day Nats rang me from Hampstead Heath, five miles of woodland, lakes and grassy park in North London, where she regularly walks Diva. She was sobbing. Diva had been missing for an hour and a half. Nats had been running, shouting for her and giving every stranger she met her mobile number. She had called Amy, who lives nearby, and they were combing the area.

The next time she rang me, Diva was back safe and sound. I asked her what had happened. Diva had played with a greyhound in the wood; the greyhound came back and Diva didn't. After searching everywhere on their usual trail, she tried the car park, where a woman told her that she'd seen a small tan and white dog near Marks & Spencers. Nats ran there like a maniac screaming for Diva at the top of her lungs. Suddenly she saw a small tan and white, foxlike creature, straining to reach her, firmly held on a leash, by the local vet.

It seemed that Diva had crossed and re-crossed the busy road near the car park, tried Marks & Spencer (where she sometimes went with Amy, food shopping), and then run to the place they often retired to for a latte and some froth on a stick – Starbucks. A doctor from the Royal Free Hospital kidney department, seeing the dog in a state of panic, closed the door and rang the vet. And when Diva finally heard Nats's voice she began dragging the vet in her direction.

The problem is that though she can do all those complicated tricks, she's just not hot on 'Diva, come!' when she's sniffed a duck or a squirrel. She's hysterical if left in the house alone, or even if one of us gets out of the car to go into a shop or pay for petrol. She sets up a pathetic high-pitched whimpering and flails around until the alarm goes off. Guido says a dog should know it's a dog. He loves her, but he does say a dog that can come when called is slightly preferable to one that can give you a high-five.

I'm not sure how to proceed from here. Keep screaming 'Diva, come!' at the horizon? Call in a dog whisperer? Or just email Starbucks and see if they're looking for a new advertising campaign?

Bette, Baseball Mom

Bette is an American baseball mom who has been in England for more years than she ever envisioned when her husband was posted here, and has never acclimatized. She drinks a little too regularly because she can't decide whether it would be worse to stick with her errant husband or to return home an army wife without a husband. She stopped liking herself a long time ago. With no apologies to Sarah Palin.

Bette, Baseball Mom

(*American women in England at inaugural meeting of the American Women in England Society. Dyed hair severely pulled back in sharp bow, crisp shirt and slacks – over made-up with a mirthless laugh.*)

I'm *fine* to do it, Shirley. I'm fine. No problem, honey . . . Is this the mike? Has someone moved this mi— For Pete's sake I had it all set up . . . J . . . No one can hear a word I'm saying and I can't shift this motherf***er.

Who can hear? Oh, *you* can? Shit. Oh, pardon me I thought it was mute. Ha! I'm so sorry . . . Jeez . . . inauspicious start.

Well, hi there, ladies, or should I say *how do you do* and welcome to past and present members of AWE – American Women in England. Welcome to this, our inaugural meeting of the year 2009, and may I, first and foremost, sincerely thank Mrs Treena Perskowitz for the use of her beautiful mock-Tudor home . . . Treena is grateful to you all for removing your Ferragamos – aren't these white carpets delicious? And I certainly hope we can figure out whose drizzle-boots are whose before we brave this *endless* downpour.

Thanks are also due, as ever, to the ladies of the AWE committee for the fabulous eggplant canapés and the neat selection of coffee cakes – and *perlees* let me assure you that Dorothy's homemade sloe gin, culled from local hedgerows – is for raffle purposes only. Mind, it's got me through many a long evening listening to fascinating lectures on carriage clocks and topiary!

Seriously though, we meet, as most of you know, on a bi-weekly basis and our purpose is to inform and entertain you new recruits as you adjust to this adorable but oftentimes confusing English way of life. This is *quite* a welcoming country, once you get to know its inhabitants and they can be as warm and hospitable as we are back home – once they have decided what class you are.

Oscar Wilde said, of course, 'We are two countries DIVIDED by the same language' and it's kinda true. I mean when I first arrived and went to London, I asked some tweedy guy by the subway for directions and he *said*, with his goddam pipe in his mouth, he *said*, 'Go about a *furlong* down the road and turn left.'

A furlong!

It's Anglo Saxon. Google it, honey.

Which is, of course, the primary reason why we, of AWE, formed this fabulous overseas club to er . . . what's the word? It's on the tip of my tongue. To . . . no, DON'T put words in my mouth, Peggy – to *acclimatize* – you to all this . . . politeness – formality – No, it's not *arrogance by any other name*, it's . . . just a very indirect way of saying what you mean. You gotta unravel it like your grandmother's quilt.

This is my *seventeenth* year of what started out as a two-year stint. *Seventeen years*. Ha! Why, my two boys are as English as Colonel Blimp. They take a baaath for Pete's sake and go to the *loo* and know what a lorry is. I don't know how we're ever going to get them Americanized when we leave, in two hundred and thirty-four days' time . . . roughly.

If we leave, that is. I've had so many false alarms now that I more or less leave the cases permanently packed and live out of crates. Burt and Burt Junior do love it here, cricket, soccer, Simpson's on the Strand and, Foster, well, he has a girl here . . . local. Very. Who has him by the . . . Where was I?

It's my good fortune that Burt understands my reluctance to assimilate, and do all the social rounds – formal do's. He totally gets it – and of course, Miss Bunting, his secretary, gets it too. Regularly it seems. I'm cool with that.

Except on Thanksgiving. I gotta draw the line. Not to spend Thanksgiving . . . with . . . us. And me with an entire turkey rammed in the stupid English stove that won't accommodate a frigging blue jay! Cranberry sauce bubbling, chestnuts roasting. Pumpkin pie. *With an actual pumpkin* I drove twenty-three miles to get . . . on the *wrong* side of the road!

What is it Nancy? You look shocked.

Think you can do an inaugural better than I can? Like to see you try, Nancy dear, after seventeen years waiting for you to make one intelligent remark that didn't involve peanut brittle, I would relish the thought.

One. I had *one*. And it was 90 per cent frigging tonic!

Ladies of AWE, I apologize if I have shocked you.

Hey, though! Aren't we in the military? We're s'posed to *believe* in Shock and AWE? Ha!

All I really wanna say is, your time here is your own – lots of it – so while you're *here*, in the jolly old *UK*, put your feet up, watch crap movies, eat good old US of A candy and have a damn good cry. If things get really bad, insult the Queen. Tell 'em you witnessed Prince Philip murder Lady Di in the tunnel – worse still, put the milk in *after* the tea. You'll be persona non gratis all over the village before you can say Boston Tea Party.

Yeah. (*Pause*) Helloooo?

Has something happened to this damn microphone?

One two, three. X, Y, zee.

Should have saved my breath to set fire to my porridge – NO, my *oatmeal*? Any questions? Aw . . .

Ha! Leave me be. I like it under the piano. S'cozy. (*Sings*) I'm a Yanky doodle dandy. Yankee doodleguy am I . . .

Are there any questions? Good. Cos there are sure in hell no *answers*.

Gotta go dead-head my rhododendrons. (*Sings*) Born on the fourth of Julyyyy.

Thank you and have a fffff . . . rightfully nice da . . . life. (*Sotto*) Suckers.

As the former courtesan, Mme. Armfeldt in Trevor Nunn's production of *A Little Night Music*, my haughtiness and demeanour says it all.

Backstage however, an actress with a little time on her hands gets more naughty and demeaning.

The voice which made Tallulah Bankhead incontinent. As Florence Foster Jenkins (*Murder on the high C's*) in Peter Quilter's *Glorious*.

Florence in full flight ... and not at all camp. Josie Kidd looks on in ... awe?

Nightly, I died in the wings.

Ladies of Letters; at the funeral of 'our' lover Bill, Irene turns into the Twilight Crone.

Anne Reid and me, in one of our gentler moments, flashing teeth and tits.

The 'Glamour shot' I sent to the *Telegraph* critic who wasn't convinced I could play a courtesan.

Little enlarge ... Sandi Toksvig and me at the Woman of the Year line up.

M.L. and a young friend also at W.O.Y. Elsbeth Juda at ninety-eight.

'And the winner isn't ...'

After first working together 42 years ago, I give Michael Palin a prize at the Edinburgh Festival ... for doing quite well in his chosen career.

Ever seen a dog with a trunk? Diva in a hole on the heath.

Warren philosophizing in the courtyard, 'Froggit, Froggit . . .'

I know it's a back-stabbing business but it's been good to me. Guido took this shot in a park in Bath.

He likes Siberia, Mongolia and the Antarctic. I, basically, like Paddington.

Stephen Mangan plays Jack and Jack looks on, as Bill Nighy and Sally Phillips do the play within the play. Sky TV's *Ready When You are, Mr McGill*.

Josie Kidd, Val Hall and I on the island of Zakyntos, show it's possible to walk on water.

A dogmatic relationship – Nats and her leader.

Three for the road. The last picture we have of the late great Zelma.

Me looking happy on Brooklyn Bridge – as it turned out I wasn't.

Jack and I in black and white mode – in slickness and in health.

Amy and I go down the 'plug' promoting *The Horse is Stable but the Gibbon's in Decline*.

Yes Ministering to the Hospice. Trevor Bentham's portrait of his partner Sir Nigel Hawthorne.

Sporting Chance

Four years ago, I stuck my not inconsiderable neck out to predict that Italy would win the World Cup, not on the grounds that they played the best football, but because, dramatically speaking, with a corruption case on a massive scale back home in Italy, their win would stand as a metaphor for the whole beautiful game itself. Or perhaps just for its *ugliness*. Taken to the very limits of greed and referee manipulation, media hysteria, manager mania, swearing, stamping and post-goal snarling into camera, the very professionalism of the sport has turned into that other game, the world's oldest profession. Everyone is screwing everyone for the most they can get.

Perhaps a lesson could be learned. Salaries could drop a touch, less reverence for boys just out of higher education and managers with fingers in too many pies. The revenge of Sven on the British and its media has been final. Not that I haven't enjoyed what I've seen of the coverage. Italy and Germany was a nail-biting match and no film maker could have chosen a more moving track than 'You'll Never Walk Alone' sung in German at the bitte end. Sometimes though I just have to turn down the commentary and watch in silence. Similarly with the tennis – commentators seem to be obsessed by detail.

'This girl has a big, big serve although she's very small for a tennis player.'

'She is *tiny*, I know, but she covers the court.'

'I wonder how tall she actually is.'

'Oh about five foot four is what I'm hearing, well, that is short . . .'

'Yes, very petite indeed.'

There was one day when the buzzword was *early*.

'She's hitting these balls much earlier, you'll notice. She's really looked at her game and is earlier to reach the shots . . .'

'Yes, much earlier than last year.'

I sort of know what they're saying, but hell, the ball bounces and they hit it when they reach it, don't they? And if they get there late it hits a ballboy. I actually thought my ears were playing silly buggers with me when the Chinese player was snapping at the heels of Kim Clijsters and the commentator cheerily mentioned there was a lot of nip 'n' tuck in the game.

I like it when they go wildly over the top, praising one player over his opponent – *unstoppable* – *making mincemeat* – the way he's playing, the Czech player hasn't got a cat in hell's chance – then, suddenly, the game shifts, as games do, and they have to back-track hopelessly. 'Well, he *was* playing a blistering game, but you know tennis, mate – ah – yes, he's taken the set. Well, it was always on the cards.' Matchless prose.

The Vuvuzela World Cup 2010 has been and gone, leaving behind remorse, financial upheaval and one referee who couldn't, or wouldn't get out of the way. With hindsight, of course, we now understand where Wayne Rooney's missing energy was going. Wimbledon came and went and predictably, one grunting Williams sister got a big shiny plate. The only unpredictable thing was that the sun shone every day on the new rain cover roof. Meanwhile the last remaining amateurs, the women's hockey, football, cricket and rugby, have been living examples of what the term Sportsmanship actually means: thrilling play, modesty, hard graft and ultimate success. Naturally, we are only allowed to see these exceptional role models playing their fabulous games in thirty-second round-up clips. Latterly, the term 'it's not cricket' has become more Pakistani than English. I fear, like the forthcoming elections for the new Labour leader, we'll be sorry to see no Balls. Last word to the Vuvuzela . . . zzzzzzzzzzzz.

The King's Ears

Last Sunday night, in 80 degree heat, nineteen women in evening gowns, a saxophonist and a singer played fifty parts in a rehearsed reading of Clare Boothe Luce's *The Women* in front of eighty punters, to raise money for the King's Head Theatre, Islington. Between us we must have shed enough water to put the hose-pipe ban into remission.

When the King's Head says a rehearsed reading, one of those words isn't strictly accurate. I was to direct it in a day and on the Friday prior, my leading lady had pulled out due to the twin problems of a sick child and a sponsored swim. Only a few of the others were free to come to my place on the Saturday for a brief read through and I had no dog sitter. There was a bubble of panic in my windpipe when I awoke to face the heat of the day. Singer Anna Bergman flew in from New York and made the mistake of ringing to say hi. My response was, 'Have you brought a little black dress?'

Clare Boothe Luce wrote the play in 1936 and George Cukor filmed it in 1939, with Norma Shearer, Roz Russell and Joan Crawford. The dialogue crackles and spits and, unlike most women's writing today, the women are not much more admirable than the men. It's *Sex in the City* with the sex off-stage. Clare Boothe Luce was the managing editor of *Vanity Fair*, a Republican senator, ambassador to Italy under Eisenhower, the wife of a media tycoon, a mother and a prolific and successful playwright. She may well have been the first *juggler*.

We performed the reading in the manner of a 1930s radio recording, with old-fashioned mikes, all actors on stage throughout, gliding into mike for each of the twelve scenes. Except for the principals, the actors played several roles and one, Vicky Simon, proved invaluable at providing sound effects in full view, ranging from slaps and thuds in a fight scene to day-old baby howls and dripping water. Some sort of showbiz magic kicked in and, in spite of the steady waving of fans and papers all over the house – it looked, surreally, like a nail-drying convention – the audience's laughter and applause said it all.

As for me, I played every part, missed a heartbeat at every pause, mothered and puffed with pride when my chicks took flight and was so bushed at the end of it that I put my head on the dinner table and went to sleep. Acting is easier. Of course, if this were a real show, while the girls were sweating all over again the following night, as director I'd be in the Ivy, up to my pearl choker in Sauvignon and home for an early bath, on 10 per cent. Nice work if you can get it.

Dead Pirate Sketch

Well, I missed the Queen's birthday party. It was a blow but I took it on the chin. The calls had been going on for months. David Wood, Woody to his friends, was writing the play and I was to be a witch. I've witched for Woody before in *The Meg and Mog Show* and my children, then under ten, informed me that I'd never been nicer at home than when I was on that stage, every night and twice on Thursdays in enormous hobnails, singing 'I Got a Spell Right' and cackling.

To be frank, I am a bit of a witch already, in that I very often know what people are going to say next, which makes me look a bit of a smart-arse. I do cackle and make up terrible rhymes and I'm always there with a remedy even when one isn't required. In short, I told Woody I was up for the task as long as it didn't involve being excessively airborne and I didn't have to turn any regal persons into stick insects.

The weeks went by and nothing *by appointment* came through, save a reminder to book for a scale and polish, so I put it down to over-booking or Julie Walters being available and said yes to the twenty-sixth Winchester Writers' Conference at the university on the same weekend. Almost immediately, I received an email from the palace, asking me to be a pirate . . . nice, except it was addressed to Jerry Hall. Now, I know a lot of people do compare me to Jerry Hall and, let's face it, she'd have been a cracking little Beattie in those ads. But I reckoned if I'd got hers then she'd probably got mine and indeed a request followed for me to turn up at Angel's, the costumiers on an industrial estate in Hendon, where I was fitted into a fetching cutpurse, tricorn, kerchief and studded boots. I practised a few desultory 'Ah Aarrrs' (Q. 'Why are pirates called pirates? A. Because they Aarrr!'), and went home to await the call. A couple of weeks later it came.

'I'm terribly sorry to tell you this, but for reasons beyond our control, we've lost the lake.'

'Er . . . right . . . Sooo are you telling me . . . no pirates?'

'I'm really sorry.'

'It's OK,' I said. 'Honestly. I've got to be in Winchester on the Friday and Saturday so rehearsals would be difficult, no sweat.'

The following Tuesday, before the big day, I was planning my plenary address to the conference – let me rephrase that – I was looking up *plenary* in the dictionary to see what might be expected of me. I finally got to *plenary*: adj., full; complete; attended by all members. Oh, right then, I'll just do it fuller then, when the phone rang.

Would I rejoin the palace regiment as Ronnie Corbett's sidekick, someone, presumably non piratical, who was looking for the Queen's handbag? Now, I know my place. Clearly Julie Walters had got a better gig. I explained about Winchester and plenary addresses and that I'd now also got a memorial walk on Sunday morning for a friend, which left roughly one hour for me to rehearse the sidekick role and even with Trevor Nunn at the helm, I couldn't quite guarantee my utter brilliance. Before I could say, 'Alison Steadman?' they'd moved on.

Seemingly, actual chaos *reigned* when they chucked writer Woody out and brought jolly good Julian Fellowes in. Still, it all seems to have gone well on the afternoon, but if the party had been at Holyrood House you could almost have called it a writer's typical Holyrood horror story.

Meanwhile, in Winchester, I was luxuriating in the splendour of a bistro 'otel which, to the bewilderment of Barbara, the superb organizer of the festival, had no record of my being booked in there. Kindly, they awarded me the sumptuous Courvoisier suite, and I collapsed onto smart minimalism and contemplated the claw-foot bath, placed, not in the bathroom but slap up against the fireplace. Honeymoon capers . . . oh poo.

The address went well, albeit at nine in the morning – *you* try being sharp, witty and plenary at that hour – and the audience was delightful, particularly the speaker from the floor who said Winchester was marvellous because, I quote: 'I've always wanted to write really badly.' The great film writer Leslie Gilliat was honoured and the dean of the university was billed to come but didn't. Perhaps he, too, got a better gig. Thrillingly, in his place, was Professor Joy Carter, the first female vice chancellor at Winchester for 166 years, who gave a witty, perfectly formed address and looked stunning in a vibrant purple suit.

Incidentally, after my recent travels, I'm thinking of instituting a small award for the most audible railway tannoy system. The Tube and Waterloo need not apply. They sound like a foreign dignitary with emphysema drowning in fish glue. I wonder why there are not crowds of lost tourists all over England. Winchester's announcements were as clear as a cathedral bell. Give them a year's supply of port, a stack of lemons and a vat of manuka honey.

Back home for my own birthday and one of my nicest presents was a certificate from a friend to say I've sponsored a yak in Tibet. I've got my own yak! It's called Mo, which is Tibetan for 'predictive technique'. Hmm. I could have used that for my plenary. Anyway, the money raised goes to flood relief and a better life for the nomadic Tibetan people, and God and the Chinese know they need one. Mo came with a certificate, a photo (she's gorgeous and her blood can reach oxygen saturation on a high plateau) and a poem:

As a friend to the children commend me the yak,
You will find it exactly the thing;
It will carry and fetch, you can ride on its back
You can lead it around on a string.

So tell your papa where a yak can be got,
And if he is awfully rich
He will buy you the creature, or else he will not;
I cannot be very sure which.

If you fancy one for your birthday, and you don't have to be awfully rich at all, check out www.tibet-foundation.org/att or 0207 930 6001.

Meanwhile my apologies to the other birthday girl. I was there in spirit . . . Ah Aarrr! Wonder if there's a pirate video . . .

A Practically Perfect Day

Friday was a perfect day. It was cold, so I rolled over and slept until *Woman's Hour*. Then, over a porridge pancake, I read all round the *Guardian*, leaving my own page till last, and grimaced only once, which, round these parts, constitutes wild approval. Then I read the centrefold of the *Racing Post*.

'I know you've probably cancelled your subscription for the *Post*,' said my country friend Linda, archly, 'so I thought you might like to read this.' I liked to read it *inordinately*. There, in David Dashforth's column – 'My Wish(ful Thinking) List for 2006' – sandwiched between thoughts of banded stakes races and Jockey Club penalties, was a highlighted sentence which became the highlight of my morning: 'I hope ITV repeats that Jack Rosenthal drama *Ready When You Are, Mr McGill* with Tom Courtenay and Bill Nighy, which they broadcast late on Boxing Day, and was excellent. I don't suppose they will.' (I've just asked them. They're not going to.) David, I thought, you're a scholar and a prince, but it was hard enough getting them to show it in the first place. I added David's thoughts to the thick pile of *Mr McGill* plaudits which Working Title's PR firm had sent me after its showing, sighed a deep sigh and filed it all away. Closure.

Then a friend came round who works as a personal driver. He showed me the new business cards he'd just had printed. 'You might want to have them redone,' I suggested gingerly, 'unless you want to have people think that a vegetable is going to drive them to Heathrow. "Professional Chauffleur"? Sounds a bit cheesy doesn't it?' I was still laughing ten minutes later over my fried egg with *very* crispy edges on two slices of soda-bread toast with mug of builder's tea. Both my cup and my yolk ranneth over.

The afternoon saw me dealing with so much correspondence, some dating back to last October, that I was virtually in a state of grace. I rang my daughter, always glad to be wrenched away from her lap-top, and suggested a power-less walk on Hampstead Heath, where we met up with another friend, Astrid, and, by common consent, turned our blue noses towards Café Mozart for coffee, grilled haloumi cheese and polenta cake.

Driving back I stopped in Hampstead High Street to try on a pair of trousers, and I was *genuinely* surprised when the size fourteen wouldn't zip up. Well, they're obviously cutting trousers differently this year, I mused, popping another Werther's toffee into my mouth. Pleated fronts, which nicely house the stomach, are bound to come back into fashion next spring . . . I'll buy my trousers then. Size 12, obviously.

That night at the Duchess Theatre something wonderful happened. The play was elevated onto another plane entirely. We've always had the most appreciative, if not the fullest houses in town. That week though, we'd had some of what I like to call 'Westminster Bridge audiences' as in 'Dear God, the very houses seem asleep.'

Ten West End shows are closing this week. Charles Kennedy was not the only case of dead man walking. 'There's no one in town, Maureen,' said Jack, the jeweller, as he showed me some earrings at his Covent Garden stall. 'It's your mayor, innit? He's turned this place into Deadwood City.'

I lit my Friday candles in a dressing room surrounded by limp flowers and throat sweets. It can't be right, I know, but it works for me. Janie Booth, who plays my Mexican maid and is about as Jewish as Nicholas Soames, always pops in to wish me 'Good Shabbos'. On this Friday though, for whatever reason, there was an electrifying buzz coming through before curtain up, and the numbers were surprisingly high for a sub-zero January evening. Every laugh was as clean as a bell note and some new ones chimed in from the brightest audience we'd had since we left the provinces and came into the sated, over-rated West End.

The next two hours passed like a dream. In act two, when the curtain rose on two rows of hanging silver birds representing the 'Ball of the Skylarks', a mobile phone went off sharply, in a quiet moment. The phone tone was a trilling bird song.

'Dorothy, my dear,' I cried, 'how clever of you to make the skylarks sing as well as fly.' Several ad-libs later, with the audience baying for more, we really began to fly until curtain down and the most incredible cries of 'Bravo' and 'More' you've ever heard outside La Scala, Milan. I reckon that's a tidge more fun than stopping the show, admonishing the cringing, ringing culprit and re-starting the scene.

Sometimes it's only me who feels this exhilarated after a show. One night, years ago, when I was a fledgling performer with high ideals and low income, I took my bows with tears coursing down my cheeks, thinking, 'This is what it's all about! This is why I came into the business! This is – this is *Art*!' and as I turned to leave the stage my rather more prosaic co-star whispered, 'How much do you pay in car insurance?'

This Friday, though, it was the same for everyone, backstage, onstage and out front. We stood there hugging each other for a long time, just very glad, in spite of everything, leaking roofs, flooded stage doors, creeping exhaustion, endless stairs, effing congestion charge, malign parking attendants, petering out publicity, Tube strikes, late-night buses, coughs, colds, *bird* flu in *Turkey*, to be just bloody privileged to be in the job we're in.

I arrived home in time to see the last hour of *Annie Hall* which was enough to remind me of the brilliance of the first hour. 'Feels like old times,' sang Diane Keaton in a way that all singers should emulate, with the words her priority, and the glow I felt continued, assisted by a corn on the cob with unsalted butter, a pot of couscous and a small clinking Scotch . . .

I'm sorry if this all sounds like I've swallowed several chapters of *The Road Less Travelled*. I'll be better in the next chapter. With the decimation of good men in fell strokes, right now, I'm just counting my blessings.

Driving Miss Maisie

The next woman is a divorcee. She's coming up to forty and is tired of being defined by her single-mother status and being brave. She's at the end of her tether but doesn't quite have the courage to change things for the better. From childhood she's always been the peacemaker. When she married Bryan, she knew he was tricky but he became so much more mellow as their relationship progressed and she believed he would settle when the baby came. He didn't. In fact he became more childish than ever. She hates conflict, always has and just wants some peace. As she speaks to her ex-husband, she grows in confidence and ability.

Driving Miss Maisie

Hello, Bryan, good to see you. Been away? You look tanned – no, I didn't mean to pry . . . of course you're entitled. Look, I really don't want to get off on the wrong foot . . . thanks for coming, I know April's your busy time of year . . . so I'll crack on . . .

Er . . . How is work? No, of course, time *is* money . . . mmm. (*Sotto*) Always was – No, nothing I was just . . . er . . . so . . . I am. I *am* getting to the point . . .

Look, I've never asked you to be a hands-on father, have I? Yes, of course financially you've been more than generous with her skiing and ortho-dontics and I'm grateful for that . . . *and* of course how you kept it up through the Lloyds thing. I mean we both understood how tight things were for you.

And I don't want to go back on the school thing, Bryan, I really don't, because it makes both of us see red and I don't want to rake up the past – not today. What's done is done and in many ways the comprehensive has been good for Maisie.

Well, it's certainly made her more confident and, well, she doesn't have any lack of assertiveness now, that's for sure – au contraire actually – all that prep-school prissiness has . . . Of course she was miserable for the first term and I really had to force her some mornings out of the door and there were lots of scenes – No, I'm not complaining . . . I spoke several times to the head about bullying and, well, she was right, in the end it did find its own equilibrium and certainly they never bothered her again after the big fight and I do want to say thanks for paying for the jaw wiring – it would have been years on the NHS.

No, she does capoeira and kick boxing, and weight-lifting so I don't suppose anyone would start with her now. She's grown so tall and so tough. Then there's her language of course. She's not exactly *expletive deleted* is she?

Oh surely, Bryan, you must have noticed on weekend visits. She doesn't do it at your place? Oh, that's interesting. No, that's good . . . that's very good. Clearly she feels free to be absolutely herself with me but holds back a bit with you and Mariella . . . Good . . . Good.

Because, it isn't her fault entirely, well, I don't blame her. It's peer-group pressure. Her friends – I mean they all do it all the time – it's just another adjective. In fact it's in place of adjectives, which is my problem with it. Effing suffices. Effing good dinner. Effing bad effing film. Effin' crap eff last night.

Oh, yes and that's the other thing, Bryan. Maisie is sexually active now. I mean actively active. In case you didn't know we've been effed by Gareth for a few weeks and then he was just an effing w.a.n.k.e.r. and then she and Will were doing quite a bit of outside effing which was better for me – er – noise-wise, but frightened the Wednesday gardener into a state of effing paralysis.

Erm . . . what else might you find relevant to what I'm about to say?

Oh well, of course, the E. No, Bryan, I don't mean the time she spends on the computer, I mean the E tabs – Ecstasy tabs – tabs . . . for going out clubbing on Thursdays and mew mew or whatever it's called on Saturdays. Apparently they all do it and it's perfectly harmless . . . er, plant fertilizer . . . and within her pocket-money budget, just so long as she doesn't have any lunch . . . and I know you're going to blame me, Bryan, but I'm exhausted with being called a dickhead and worse, and hearing the door shudder on its hinges and the rap or rather – rape – music thud through the rafters and the phone start and the pacing and the snarling at top volume so I know just what sort of a four-letter-word I am and, well . . . somewhere in that anguished and malevolent spitting adolescent is our beautiful, kind, loving, gentle daughter and, well . . . that's why I'm – that's why – I'm giving her to you.

Bryan. You have her. It's your turn.

You deal with claims. Of one kind or another.

I'm handing her over to you in the hope that you can – reclaim her.

So. Here's her stuff. She can pick up what else she wants later. School gets out at four. Hide the car or she'll lose respect. Bye for now.

Tell Maisie I love her and I've changed the locks.

Ooer – there's a space . . . Yippee.

(*Long pause. The section which follows is optional.*)

OK, Maisie. We're here, Maisie. Maisie! Take them out. The ear things, darling. Take them out. Daddy won't like it . . . I said, Daddy won't . . .

Oh, what the hell, leave them in, it's not my worry any more.

OK, M, let's go. Come on . . . You remember what I promised? You can buy a DVD in Smiths first, while I have this little talk with Dad, OK? It's not an effing big suitcase, darling – it looks that way because . . . because I put . . . because I put a rug of Dad's in there he wanted. Yes. That's it. A rug.

You do like seeing him, Maisie. You do. No, Mariella won't be there today and please don't call her that . . . she can't help it and it's cruel to mention it. Yes, she does . . . she loves having you for weekends, darling. She'd like to have you more often – she told – yes, she did – yes, she did. Oh stop it, Maisie! There's the shop. Go in.

I need to think. I just need to think ahead . . .

How did it start?

'Oh, hello, Bryan, good to see you. You look tanned – been away?'

Freedom Past

Everything reminds me of a joke. Here is a golden oldie, an apartheid-era joke about Desmond Tutu and Willem de Klerk having private talks. They are in a small boat, in the centre of a lake, with the world's press camped round the shore line, training telephoto lenses on them. Suddenly, a gust of wind blows de Klerk's hat into the water and without a word, Tutu gets out of the boat, walks across the water, picks up the hat, walks back and returns it to de Klerk.

The next day, the headline on every front page reads, 'Desmond Tutu Cannot Swim!'

Last week, the archbishop wrote an impassioned plea for the world to take heed of the appalling situation in Darfur. It began, 'Here is an inconvenient fact about Africa: our genocides tend to happen away from television cameras.'

He went on to chronicle the million people who died in Rwanda in 1994 – the two million dead in southern Sudan in the past two decades, the four million murdered in the Democratic Republic of Congo since 1994. Just the four *million*. People.

In Darfur, he told us, where 300,000 people have been killed and two million ethnically cleansed, women and children are raped and tortured daily. There is cholera in the refugee camps and, in spite of the ceasefire, the Janjaweed militias have stepped up their brutal attacks on civilians and aid workers.

Why is it taking so long to send a UN force to Darfur? After only thirty days of the Israel/Hizbollah war, the UN sent in peacekeepers. After all, Darfur is, in the words of the UN, the worst humanitarian crisis in the world.

Well, it could be to do with the fact that it's a civil war or it could be the vast oil wealth in the Sudan, or it could just be, as Tutu implied, that it's a long way away and no one in either the media or the public really gives a flying frisbee. In 2004, Sudan, whilst ethnically cleaning Darfur, was elected to the UN.

I wonder if the *shocked and disgusted* letter, demanding immediate cessation of alleged warmongering in Israel, and the return of all refugees, the hopping-mad, round-robin rant sent to the *Telegraph* from the great and the good – the Pilgers, Bergers and Chomskys – has got lost in the post. Maybe it has fallen foul of the new barcoding system on the Internet. Maybe it's lying in a sorting office somewhere, victim of mailbag robberies in Kensington, Mayfair and Central Park South . . . at any rate, let us not hold our collective breaths.

I find myself backed into a corner frequently, defending Israel. All I ask for Israel is a level playing field, like that of any other democracy. There are, after all, 43 Catholic countries and 50 Muslim ones . . . so, although Jews make up 0.5 per cent of the world's population (there are only 240,000 of us in England), there could be an argument for allowing the existence in the world of one Jewish state.

The historian Andrew Roberts succinctly told us recently that, in its 62 years of existence, Israel has been attacked repeatedly from its fifth day and has been constantly on the front line for terrorism. It is the size of Wales, and has only seven million citizens. England has nine times the population of Israel. So, just imagine for a moment if it were *us* being attacked on a daily basis, if 36,000 rockets were to be shafted into Dover and Portsmouth and parts of Surrey from Calais, would we be morally right to respond? *How* would we respond? How *proportionately* right would we get it?

We went to war in the Falklands, 6,000 miles away, because of a *proposed* invasion. Civilians *and* soldiers died. Our hasty response to 7th July was the senseless death of a Brazilian electrician on holiday in London. In 2006, Hizbollah fired 4,000 Katyusha rockets, killing 43 civilians. Or look at it this way: our Queen has visited 129 countries, including 14 Arab countries, during her long reign. Guess where, in its 62 years of (unless you are a radical Islamist) legitimacy, she has *never* visited? Or even this way: Gibraltar defended itself for three years against Spanish invasion and received the George Cross for bravery from the UK. And to my knowledge, no visiting Gibraltarian official or academic has been banned from these shores.

If I were to cite the human genocides and civil rights failures in the world today: the Congo using kidnapped child soldiers and child rape on its own people; Burma's murderous Junta; Rwanda or Darfur's history of appalling human rights; the ethnic cleansing of the Romany people in the former Balkans; China's execution record of 500 a year and their persecution of the Falun Gong at home and Tibet; I could go on – and I do, I *know* – I would be accused by the anti-Zionists as employing what they call, 'Whataboutism'. Well, yes. What about condemning them?

There are 22 human rights abuses listed against Israel at the UN. In the last 30 years 15 per cent of UN time has been taken up condemning Israel. I can't find on the Internet any resolution condemning Russia for Chechnya, or China for Tibet, or the Sudan for Darfur. In fact, Russia and China vetoed a resolution for human rights abuse against Burma. Still, you can bet your ass that film maker Ken Loach – who vetoed an Israeli film maker, a fellow *artists'* trip to the Edinburgh festival last year – would be honoured to sit next to a Chinese film maker *and* eat their supermarket noodles.

Consider the worldwide condemnation at the building of a wall, which has since reduced suicide bombings by 85%. Remember, when Israel set up a tent in post-quake Haiti and performed miracles of surgery and altruism in the midst of chaos, Baroness Jenny Tonge stood up in the House and effectively accused the Israeli medics of *organ harvesting* and *body part snatching*. It was one step away from the Protocols of the elders of Zion and the blood libel. The whip was removed from her by Clegg but not her position as a Lib Dem minister. It's not hard to get the picture.

When Israeli commandos boarded the fifth flotilla, after four previous, peaceful boardings, to be met by iron bars and the throwing overboard of soldiers, William Hague's knees jerked into action and he condemned Israel forcefully. Since the video has shown the truth of the attack on the soldiers by Turkish militants pretending to be charity workers, he has not said a word of retraction. The pattern is reiterated and reiterated. Add to this the world's total ignorance of the extent and variety of Israel's multi-coalition government which virtually paralyses any decision-making, well, we've had a few weeks of it and most liberals are squirming in their seats. I have to keep defending Israel because, frankly, this particular playing field is about as level as the Andes.

I sometimes envisage a Hitchcock-like film-noir scenario where thousands and thousands of birds are gathering on wires around Wapping. More and more arrive, as the sky darkens and the sound-track swells with the furore of squawks and trills juxtaposed against the hammer of printing presses. Finally, the camera pans onto a hierarchy of black crows, perched on a telecommunications satellite, and as the cacophony fades into the background, we hear one mean, beady-looking crow say to another, 'It's OK. The Middle East business is dead and buried. If we move fast we can get the bird flu epidemic back on the front pages before football bungs and the Thai coup take over. Get some of the real sickies onto the roof of DEFRA *now*, and the rest of you – start coughing.'

One Day At A Time

Strangers and friends often ask me how I fit in so much in a day, and my answer is that I don't do any housework, I hardly cook these days, and I don't exercise or shop for clothes except under threat of a public airing. Only this week, I took part in a superb compilation of sixty years of *Woman's Hour* for an October broadcast. One of the items Jenni Murray had culled from a wartime programme was instructions on how to knit your own stair carpet. Here's a day in the life from last week, which sort of sums up what I *do* do.

I'm in old gabardine shorts and unfashionable trainers. My hair has not recovered from being slept on and reveals bits of scalp around upswept whirls. The dog is pulling me, which hurts my back. When I get to the top of the hill, I see a disabled man, middle aged, black, in a woolly hat, in a wheelchair, attempting to manoeuvre himself, sideways, down the steep hill to the bus stop.

'Er . . . can I help you?' I enquire.

He replies by punching the air with a fist. I take that to be an affirmative.

'Did you want to go to the bus stop?'

He punches the air again. So I link the lead to the wheelchair and start pushing him forward. I've gone less than a yard when the dog chooses, slowly and deliberately, to evacuate her bowels. I need to look carefully at this because the night before she has eaten my pyjamas. I went to put them on and where there had been inside leg there was air. It proves impossible not to wheel the chair through the mess. By now there was a small group of young men at the bus stop watching my struggle.

'Nice one, Maureen,' yelled one of them kindly. 'Nice gesture, that . . .'

He's grinning, but clearly has no intention of lending a hand. I deposit my passenger at the bus stop and, swivelling Diva, much against her will, head back up the hill to remove the offensive pile, which now has a track running through it. Ten minutes later I'm home, fifteen minutes after that I'm showered, and twenty-five after that I'm having a latte with Katherine Kent at the Wallace Collection Café.

The Duchess of Kent teaches music at an estate school in East Hull. East Hull was dead rough, even in my day, in the fifties. She is passionate about her pupils. We fall into rhapsodic mode. We both love Hull and abhor its label of England's worst place to live. She runs a charity which picks out musically gifted kids from poor backgrounds and ensures they receive proper training. On the way back I muse: 'Why don't pundits just leave Hull alone/They're just mad cos we've got our own phone/We don't need their pity in this ancient city/We're twinned with Sierra Leone!'

I decide to try out my new Freedom pass, on a bus. I flash it at the driver who hoots and says, 'You're that woman off the adverts, aren't you?' I mutter that I suppose I am and sit down on the crowded bus to read the marriage diary of the erstwhile Mrs Mark Thatcher. I'm riveted. If ever there was an argument in favour of Nature over Nurture then those Thatcher twins are it. Carol is such a geezer and Mark's turned out to be someone you'd – well, turn out. At some point deep in, I hear a voice calling, 'Ology! Ology!' Grimly, I look up. The bus has stopped, and the driver is now shouting, 'Your stop, Missus Ology!'

Not for the first time that day, as I leap off the bus, I'm grateful for not just my Freedom pass but for freedom itself.

Twelve Things I've Never Done

Appeared in *The Bill*
Shaved my legs
Slept in a tent
Taken out a patent
Visited Ikea
Watched *Extras* or *The West Wing*
Built anything
Scrubbed a floor
Tried fishing, bird watching, circus skills or an extreme sport
Learned a language or an instrument fluently
Read Dostoevsky (unlike Pete Doherty)
Taken cocaine (ditto)

Twelve Things I've Done

Appeared in *Doctor Who*
Toured Ethiopia
Learned and forgotten golf and flamenco
Spent over 300 evenings with Hugh Jackman
Cooked brisket in sweet and sour sauce
Been serenaded by a fake Elvis in a white Cadillac in Las
    Vegas
Got all shook up in the Los Angeles earthquake
Had an extraordinary healing
Had my hair turned green by Roman Polanski's Parisian
    hairdresser
Shared a bench on stage with the great Paul Scofield
Inadvertently thrown a small boiled potato across the 1834
    room at Buckingham Palace
Made a cake shaped like Joan Collins with jellies for breasts

Two large jolly people stopped me at the farmers' market yesterday and asked me, in ribald tones, if I've found the new man I'm looking for yet.

'We read all about it in the paper.' They nudge-nudge-wink – and wink at me.

Here's the conundrum. Do I explain that in an interview the *new man* question comes at the end of nineteen *book-related* questions and is casually answered by, 'Well, of course, if someone came along,' and obviously the headline 'Maureen's Desperate Man-Hunt!' is down to the hyperactivity of the sub editor? 'Any grandchildren yet, Maureen?' asked the charming journalist. 'No, I can't wait,' quoth I, hugging the dog. Front page (cue sub editor), '"I wish I were pregnant!" moans Lipman.' Or, is it better just to make growling tiger noises, paw the air and move on pleasantly to the organic sun-dried tomato stall? Guess.

Today is a perfect day. Crisp, quite cold with a blue sky and bright shafts of sunlight. I'd like to be out in it, breathing it in and watching out for the first leaves turning to my favourite russet colours. Instead I'm sitting at the computer, wearing clothes which are too skimpy for the sudden chill, with a thudding migraine, the result of eating too much, too quickly after a fast day. The Day of Atonement. The food at my friend Judith's was of such bounty that, I swear, the mahogany table was bent like a Uri Geller spoon. So, unlike the rest of my tribe, today, I'm still atoning. Everything was irresistible – so I didn't. It is a wistful time of year, though, I always feel it and part of the Yom Kippur sermon remains in my drugged mind, the part about never turning a blind eye to injustice, whether or not it affects one personally.

In the meantime, THINGS TO DO:

Be quiet. Be very, very quiet.

Shock and Law

I'm having a hard time this week with shock and awe. Scientists have created luminous pigs. Designer pigs with teeth, trotters and organs that glow in the dark with a greenish light. Apparently this will either shed light on stem-cell research, in a way which is as yet unfathomable to me, or it will just create a line of bacon which is green before its sell-by date.

Then there is the East Anglian corduroy ban. Train operators at Lowestoft and Great Yarmouth have imposed a dress code for cabbies which excludes cords, jeans and trainers. Now, as I've said before, I'm a fan of denim and corduroy only on cowboys and sofa beds, but if I were in a cab all day, even seated on one of those beaded antimacassars favoured by your modern driver, then these fabrics, plus comfortable footwear, are precisely what I would leave home in at 5.30 a.m. Either the train operators should issue the cabbies with a smart uniform designed by Mr Boateng or Mr P. Smith, or they should mind their own business, which is to make the timetable workable, the staff – rather like denim – serviceable and the tannoy system sound less like Professor Stanley Unwin crossed with a rapper with sinusitis.

The hiring of known sex offenders in schools is shocking, but I suspect is only the tip of the iceberg that has been sailing inexorably towards us for many years. Unfortunately people with a paedophile problem will be attracted to a profession which brings them into contact with kids. Most schools had a weirdo member of staff in them, even in my day, who was either a sadist or a touchy-feely nerd. I'm not condoning this, nor the blind eye turned by Miss Kelly over the hiring of those with police records, but I can't help thinking that somebody up there, at the Min of Ed, doesn't like our Ruthie any more. (Membership of Opus Dei doesn't go down well with all those millions of *Da Vinci Code* readers.) So they've shopped her and will soon be shipping her to Tyburn.

Remembering the last paedophilia round-up when crowds of turbulent 'gloved-up' *Sun* readers mounted a full-scale demo outside the house of a local paediatrician, how long can it be before kindly, bachelor buffers in mortar boards and corduroys will be named, shamed and put in the stocks and any master caught in possession of a copy of *National Geographic* will be ducked in the village ponds of Gordon's new, flag-flying England until he drowns, confesses on *Richard and Judy*, or volunteers for the *Big Brother* house?

It is so easy to mesmerize a crowd into one frame of mind. We do it every night, on stage. Four hundred disparate punters from all walks of life and corners of this sceptred isle with individual tastes and troubles, all sit down at the same time and within, say, 15 minutes, they are all responding like one homogenized hybrid. Dictators do it, even risible ones like Mussolini and Amin. Hypnotists know they can do it, so they take great pains to do it only for good. But good, of course, is subjective. I watched Derren Brown's *The Heist* last week, where he persuaded thirteen law-abiding people first to shoplift, for the kick of it, and then incited three of them to use a toy gun to hold up a security van and steal thousands of pounds. He did this by use of the most subliminal of image reinforcement and a cocktail of adrenalin and willingness to obey the voice of authority. Only one of the candidates refused to do it. His parents must have been bursting out of their genes with pride.

On *Start the Week*, one of the guests bemoaned his own faintheartedness when confronted by the blatant anti-Semitism of a group of Germans and Russians on a steamer ship entering New York. 'Here's Synagogue City' was their opening gambit and it got worse. He put down his glass and left the bar. I know that feeling well. Like remorse it's a bad companion and like a kipper it keeps coming back at you.

I still burn behind the ears because I failed to protect a fellow actor over dinner, when he was quite horribly verbally abused by the man who, at the time, was employing us. In fairness, it wasn't just me. The whole cast, including a few well known 'protesters', was silent. No food, before or since, has ever tasted more acrid. I'm left wondering whether the chap on Derren's *Heist* who failed to rob the security van would have done the decent thing.

When to let fly though and at whom, is a daunting conundrum. I once took a stand against being asked to get back into costume to resume a technical rehearsal, after being released to go home. This was at eleven o'clock at night.

'Sorry. I'm taking my cast home,' I heard my voice say to the astonished stage manager. And I did. Did I sleep that night? No, I didn't. Have I been asked to work for the same management again? No, I haven't. Would I do it again? Probably.

I'm troubled by the release from prison of the man who gunned down the last Pope. Won't he be taken out immediately by Italy's equivalent of Jack Ruby, before he can spill the borlotti beans to the highest bidder for a belting bonanza? My friend Rodney sent me a humorous email the other day – and let's face it, it's not every day one can say *that* – comparing the years 1981 and 2005. Both years saw Prince Charles get married, Liverpool win the European Cup, Australia lose the Ashes, and both saw the death of the Pope. The conclusion was that the next time Prince Charles gets married, some-one should warn the Pope.

At this time, Lord Lloyd Webber was conducting a national, tel-evised, year-long search for the actress/singer to lead his production of *The Sound of Music*. There are twenty-six pages of casting directors' particulars in *Contacts* (the UK entertainment handbook), most of them scrabbling around for a chance to cast something. Anything. At a conservative estimate, there are 572 legitimate training centres for actors. This is without going into university drama departments and centres for media studies. All those gifted people and their agents are pounding the pavements for auditions. The profession is, as ever, 80 per cent unemployed. Q. Was the Lord doing it not his way but the 'reality way' for the fame, the kudos or the money? Answers in a plain brown envelope stuffed with laundered euros please.

It's 2010 and he's doing it again. Lord Webber of Symington has fallen deeply in love with his own reflection in high definition. He's given us Connie and Jodie and now he's finding his inner friend of Dorothy. Like sugar and the mobile phone, it's addictive and very bad for your health.

Midge Darke

Midge Darke came about because I found myself thinking about women to whom sex is very mundane or casual, like flossing or removing hard skin from their feet, so that the act has no emotional content. I think that some dancers and athletes often have this attitude and, possibly, people who witness danger at close quarters. This led me to consider a profession where a female is superior to a group of males in a very male world such as the armed forces.

   If a woman, who is trained to be hard and is battle-scarred and world weary, encounters her own softness and vulnerability, it could be demeaning for her and, possibly, quite threatening. Midge Darke is on automatic pilot as she trains her young squaddies, until today, when she finds she has to go back into battle mode to win back control.

Midge Darke

At. Ease. Gentlemen. Please be seated. Mobile phones mute and your full attention, please.

Your first lecture is on firearms. I am Midge Darke your senior commander. You will address me, at all times, as ma'am.

Your weapons are on the table before you. Do not touch them without my instruction.

These, Cadets, are the ultimate deterrents. It is my sincere hope that if you have to use them it will be as a last resort. However, if you do so, it is imperative you know precisely – and I cannot stress that word too strongly – precisely – *how* to use them. They are killing machines. But they take instructions from your brain and it is your brain and your rational mind that issues those instructions.

(As opposed to the part of your body that you generally think with.)

Rational minds, gentlemen. A rational mind. One that, at all times, remains unhindered by prejudice, passion, revenge or the heat of the moment.

This weapon is to be used for the defence of yourself or your colleagues and/or attacking an enemy.

Yes, Private Holroyd . . . *and* if you are ordered to use it by a senior commander. Thank you, Holroyd, for reminding me that not everything goes without saying.

(That boy is a card-carrying bedknob if ever I met one.)

Relax, Holroyd, and you. You. Second row – Willett. Release that tension. Get up man . . . Shake out your body . . . to the floor. Anyone else holding tension in their fingers, fists, jaws . . . Let it go. Let go . . . Thank you.

Now, using your dominant hand, please pick up the rifle and hold it with your trigger finger flat against the butt and the weight of the rifle against your abdomen. Like so – and with the utmost concentration.

(Innocent faces. Expressionless. Keen. Want to please. And you . . . Flanagan, Private S.)

Are you part of this gathering, Private Flanagan?

(Black *and* Irish – great. I'm in trouble. *Big* trouble.)

Well that's a comfort to us all, Private.

(He's giving away nothing. Not even a half smile. Just flexing those big baker's hands. But this morning. Before dawn. On my hard, hairy army-issue blanket you traced the outline of my breast as delicately as if you were a brush and I were Chinese porcelain.)

What did I just say, Flanagan? Mmm? What was the last thing I just said?

'With utmost concentration' . . . Good. You *are* up and about, then?

Is that funny? Holroyd? Is it? Get up, wipe the smirk off your face and name the parts of this rifle. Don't worry, lad, I've got all day. I'm on nights. (*Pause*)

Can someone help Private Holroyd to remember the word butt?

(God it's hot in here I'm sweating like a . . . Down, down Irish boy. Just because you rode me like a bronco and made me bite my fist . . .)

Off your ass, Flanagan, and on your feet and *you* take that rifle apart. Now. Tell me each part as you dismantle . . .

Is it the cock? A bit on the *stiff side*? And why do you suppose that might be? A bit old and dry? That's your opinion is it?

I see. And how do you propose to fix that, lad?

With lubrication. (Jesus, I'm drowning here.)

(*Pause*)

Right. Clearly this gives all you soldiers cause for amusement.

(Flanagan you will *not* do this to me.)

(*Pause*)

On your feet. On your feet, men.

Raise your rifles above your heads – two hands! Attenshun!

As all but Holroyd obviously know, Private Flanagan spent this morning in my room. Now . . . one or two of you may not have heard the reason why I called Flanagan to my room. SO. Because, I am in a good mood today, I shall tell you. I ordered Private Flanagan to my room at 0500 hours this morning, right, and instructed him to have intercourse with me because – at the time, right – I was attempting to cook a four-minute egg and – tragically – my egg timer had broken.

Silence!

Stop that mewing, Holroyd. You're on a charge! STOPP-ITT!

Right, I shall go outside for a cigarette now. I may have two. Remain exactly as you are till I return. Attention!

Open that door for a lady officer, Flanagan.

NO . . . I did NOT say put down your rifle! Haven't you got anything else you can open a door with?

AS YOU WERE THEN! I'll do it myself.

I usually do.

Drying Up

I'm wandering in the night in search of hot milk and cinnamon, muttering self-hypnosis mantras.

'You will return to bed, Maureen, and be asleep by two a.m. You will sleep for eight hours solid. You will not wake at five for the "Market Report for Farmers", have a headache or wipe the hard disk in your head containing your lines. You will wake refreshed and write the thing whose deadline passed last week easily and fluently.'

Back into bed and the World Service informs me that David Irvine will be appealing ('Not to me,' I chunter). Surprisingly, perhaps, I don't want the rabid old revisionist in jail, where he will become a martyr and the focus of neo-Nazi fervour and funds which surely was his strategy in returning to Austria, in full knowledge of the country's Holocaust denial law. He'll be out on appeal before you can say Yankel Robinson, back in the public eye, and in demand again after years in the wilderness where he belongs.

Now I'm wide awake and foaming, along with my hot milk. The next day I read at least four opinion pieces and six assorted letters on the subject in the same paper. My porridge comes back at me. It's Wednesday, how will I get through a two-show day? Plus an after-show discussion with the audience, thoughtfully arranged on a matinee day for maximum angst.

The fear that I'll forget my lines, through tiredness, has always been with me ever since I dried, stone dead, one night in 1976 in

Shaw's *Candida* at the Albery Theatre. The kids were small. Adam was a baby, and his sister had reacted to his arrival as Dennis Skinner might react to winning a time-share holiday for two in Ibiza with Tony Blair. Overnight, our sweet pussy cat turned into a vampire bat. The broken nights left me pale and sweaty and the evening job suffered. Actor Simon Jones and I started off the play with a long, expositionary scene. On this occasion, I came on stage, opened my mouth and absolutely nothing came out. For the whole scene. In vain did Simon try to crowbar words into my clenched mouth, 'Mmm . . . I suppose you're going to say, that Mrs Morell is er . . . I mean, surely you can't expect Marchbanks to stay – I mean . . .' It was inventive but useless.

This was no ordinary dry, where a Shavian ad-lib could jerk you back to the plot. This was a black hole, sucking everything into itself including my left brain and my personality. Strangely enough I wasn't too bothered at the time. I was in another place entirely: Planet Coma. I coolly went through all the usual moves, poked the fire, laid out the envelopes, adjusted the typewriter. I just didn't *speak* until the scene was over and we'd left the audience baffled and the stage management in shreds. Afterwards, I lay on the floor in the wings, blubbing, until the late, lovely Deborah Kerr took me into her dressing room and gave me tea and sympathy.

Thank the Lord it's never happened since, but it took away for ever the blithe, confident 'swish of the curtains' joy I'd previously had on stage. Now I have a series of ever increasing rituals which I have to go through each night before stepping out from the wings. As the years go by I obsessively and compulsively add a new one with every new show, which dictates that I get to the theatre earlier and earlier to fit them all in.

Herein, The Naming of Parts, by M. Lipman.

First, there is the stretching and shaking out of limbs, jaw and tongue learned at LAMDA almost forty years ago. Then fifteen minutes of bizarre noises up and down the scales to get the voice coming from the right place. All this while making-up, dressing and, occasionally, steaming my whole head with Olbas oil. Quick pause for a Redoxin tablet, followed by the bit of over-annunciated Shakespeare – don't ask me which folio – uttered in the voice of the character I'm playing that night, beginning:

Thou art not thyself;
For thou exist'st on many thousand grains of sand
That issue out of dust . . .

Followed by a rumbustious rendering of:

Here's a to-do, to die today, at a minute or two to two.
A thing distinctly hard to say but a harder thing to do.

Then we'll add some siren sounds, some 'red leather, yellow leather' and a fast rendition of 'Six Scottish sock-cutters, cockily cutting socks', which, I should point out, is fun at a dinner party but not one to try in the karaoke bar or when the vicar comes to tea.

Now all that remains is the four yoga-breathing sniffs up each nostril, oh, and the new one – the one I sometimes forget so the curtain has to be held up until I've done it. Thirty-two rubs with a thumb knuckle under each foot, followed by three guttural chimp noises. *Voilà!* I'm ready. That's all it takes. Stanislavski didn't write about that little lot when he penned *An Actor Prepares*.

Needless to say, the shows and the discussion went well and I sort of slept, relieved by the knowledge that I would write about Prince Charles, whom I have a fair amount of time for. (Poor soul, he's just like me, he thinks his opinions matter. Might somebody, please, transfer the vitriol to the wretched members of staff who betrayed the Prince's trust?) It's now Thursday morning, and there's a dazzling page on the heir to the throne from Catherine Bennett in the *Guardian*. Eheu! I'll have to write about string theory again.

Over in Germany, the world has turned upside down. An actor has abused a critic. Apparently, German audiences are accustomed to seeing acts of bestiality, masturbation and naked fornication on stage – ooh, how that Ray Cooney does span the globe – but this time, at the Frankfurt Theatre House, during Ionesco's *The Great Massacre or the Triumph of Death*, when an actress playing a pregnant woman gave graphic birth to a swan, the critic, Herr Stadelmaier of the *Allgemeine Zeitung*, was heard to snigger in his front-row seat. Whereupon, one of the actors, Thomas Lawinky, marched into the auditorium, threw the swan at the critic, read out his scribbled notes and chased him out of the building.

'This was a physical attack on me, both on my body and on the freedom of the press,' said Stadelmaier, clearly not giggling now, nor indeed showing any humour whatsoever. The outcome? The mayor complained to the theatre, the actor was sacked, his fellow actors screamed that this was an attack on freedom of expression, the actor was offered a better job at the Berliner Ensemble and nobody went up before the beak. Max Clifford couldn't have arranged it better.

The Rangoon Show (1)

There was a programme in the *Dispatches* series called 'Burma's Secret War' which chilled me to the marrow. This is about as uncivil as a civil war can be. Reporter Evan Williams, a brave man and, at times, a worryingly puffed one, trekked for two weeks through the Burmese jungle, across enemy lines, with Burmese freedom fighters and medical workers. They were searching for the victims of ethnic cleansing, Kerin refugees, whose villages had been torched by soldiers of the military junta. Their stories of rape, torture and brutality were just what we have come to expect of this oppressive and increasingly paranoid regime.

'My little son left me only his palm,' said a worn, sweet-faced man, describing how he found his child's hand in the ashes of his home.

'We needed longer saw,' said a young doctor showing us the Swiss army knife he'd used to amputate the lower leg of a victim of one of the thousands of landmines planted around the village compound. 'Took too long.' Without anaesthetic – you bet it did.

'He was dragged from restaurant,' murmured a young wife. 'They would not give me his body.' Her arms softly shielded her small daughter. 'Army offer me sixty-five pounds for husband.' When asked where her daddy had gone the child stared and said, 'He's gone to buy eels.' An autopsy had shown twenty-four external wounds and severe bruising to his heart. Some eel.

Aside from displacing 18,000 refugees to live under plastic sheeting on the Thai border, and crushing and torturing any opposition (seven years in prison is standard for writing a pro-democracy pamphlet) the generals' chief source of fear comes from fifty million people's love and respect for Aung San Suu Kyi, their democratically elected leader. The Burmese have a way of smiling while telling of their terror, which pierces your heart, but when they look at the Lady, the Nobel Peace Laureate – speaking to them during a brief period of freedom from sixteen years' imprisonment – the smiles are all in their eyes. House arrest, her containment is called. It's a house surrounded by barriers and guards, a house which is crumbling around her in despair and disrepair. They won't kill her and cause international outrage, no, they'll just bury her alive.

All Aung San asks, passionately, of us in the West is that we *don't* visit her once prosperous and beautiful country. Travel agents are pushing Burma as a new unspoiled jaunt: come to Myanmar, see the palaces, museum and hotels (built by forced labour and enslaved children and owned by the junta); see the brand new capital city high in the mountains with its magnificent squares (created on the instructions of the generals' astrologer, to ensure everlasting military power). See one of the biggest armies in Asia (and the poorest people, ranked 190 out of 191 countries by the World Health Organization). Don't come, she begs us, *please don't come.*

The Lady's Not For Burma

She is a fragile, luminous, dark-haired Burmese woman who likes Bach and Bob Marley. She is remembered by those who knew her as a beautiful young woman, intense but playful, with a steely centre that contrasts with the flower she wears in her hair. She is sixty-three now, my age, a widow, a mother of two sons she has not seen for twenty-one years, and the elected leader of the NLD (National League for Democracy), a political party that has never been allowed in office despite, in 1990, winning 82 per cent of the vote.

I imagine her devout Buddhist faith is keeping her alive as much as any political ambitions she might ever have had to govern her beleaguered country.

She has suffered more in the last twenty years than I could endure in a day. Her plight haunts my mind and I fail to understand why the appalling lack of human rights in Burma fails to ignite political outrage in those who are so quick to condemn aggression elsewhere. Since we need neither oil nor gas from Burma, sanctions are the only expression of disapproval, and they tend to exacerbate the pain of the people, not the perpetrators.

Aung San Suu Kyi has been under house arrest in a crumbling house in University Avenue, Rangoon for the past six years and, before that, intermittently for the last thirteen. She is allowed no visitors but her doctor, and two Burmese housekeepers, mother and daughter, are her only companions. Her phone is cut off, her letters intercepted and her piano, a barometer of her health to the people who used to gather outside to hear her play, has quietly rotted in the humidity. In 1999, when her husband, the Tibetan scholar Michael Aris, was dying of prostate cancer, the generals refused him permission to see his wife one last time.

Her crime is her very existence. The evil and corrupt military generals who control this landlocked, once prosperous, now cyclone-devastated country, simply don't know what to do with her. If they deport her, she becomes another Dalai Lama free to roam the world raising consciousness about an oppressed people the world ignores. If they jail her in the notorious Insein prison (no pun intended, but Freud might say no accident either) then international condemnation of Myanmar – as the generals obsessed by astrology and superstition chose to rename the country – would increase.

She urges her followers to adopt a position of non-violence. Courage is certainly in her genes . . . and hard knocks her first school. She was born on 19 June 1945 to Burmese independence hero Aung San and diplomat Khin Kyi. Her father was assassinated when Aung San was only two. Her beloved brother drowned aged eight in a swimming-pool accident. She travelled the diplomatic route with her mother to India and Nepal and graduated from an Indian university and thence to St Hugh's College, Oxford, where she studied politics, philosophy and economics and met and married Michael Aris. Their sons, Alexander and Kim, were born in 1973 and 1977. She was known in Oxford to be a great cook, who could whip up a meal from American gourmet magazines on an academic's salary.

In 1988 she returned to Burma to take care of her dying mother and was plunged into a nationwide political uprising. She was her father's daughter and must have regarded the timing of the event as a kind of calling. She spoke out at rallies against the despotic military rule which had held power since 1945, calling for freedom and democracy. Five thousand people died when the junta responded with brute force, but the regime was destabilized and a general election called. Although Aung San was now under house arrest, her party won a huge majority of the vote, unleashing on her supporters another round of incarceration and torture.

In 2003 during a rare relaxation of her imprisonment she was ambushed and arrested by militia for travelling in a convoy. Dozens of her supporters were beaten to death. During non-violent demonstrations by Buddhist monks in 2007, she stepped out of her house to pray with them. After a brutal put-down thousands of these monks remain imprisoned. There must be times when she is devoured by uncertainty that her path is the true one. I was naively shocked when a Burmese restaurateur in London told me brusquely that she was constitutionally unfit to lead a party in Burma as she had married a foreigner. Then again, the issue of her sons and the heritage of loss and sacrifice she has handed on to them must cleave her heart in the long dark nights. She is a reluctant heroine.

In March 2009, the United Nations ruled that her detention was illegal under international law and also under Burmese law and the UN Security Council told the dictatorship they must release her. On 27 May 2009, her term of imprisonment was due to end. The generals have called what they refer to as 'free elections' next year. She is the greatest threat to the junta's hold on power. The thorny rose in their flesh must be dead-headed, but how without alienating even the few countries like China and India who continue to trade with the regime?

I have participated in fundraising for both the Burma Campaign UK and Prospect Burma UK. Evenings of poetry and prose, play readings and appeals by the score and a smattering of regular supporters like Jo Brand, Alan Rickman and Harriet Walter turn out for the cause, but how much can one achieve in the face of global apathy? In London's West End, alongside actress Miriam Karlin and forty Burmese activists in orange robes, I have chanted, albeit rather sheepishly, 'De-moc-racy, De-moc-racy!' from the open top of a Routemaster as Sir Peter Hall glanced up on his way out of the Haymarket Theatre.

In 2000 at the Women of the Year lunch we initiated an Empty Chair Award for a woman of distinction who, for whatever reason, was unable to be with us. Aung San Suu Kyi was our chosen recipient and I wrote a citation to her inspirational courage and forbearance, asking the 250 women of the year to join me in a minute's silence so that 'although she can't be with us, in some collective way, we can be with her'.

Then at the 2007 WOY lunch, a former Oxford friend of Aung San told me about her broken, untuned piano, and it struck me what a powerful symbol of sisterly solidarity it would be if we could literally take her a new one. Five women, powerful in their own right, if over-optimistic, put our heads together, sourced a piano, managed to get it donated, arranged cargo, musical scores and a documentary team to go with it, including myself. We figured that was what WOY was all about.

In September 2007 the monks of Burma turned out in their thousands for the Saffron Revolution, peacefully demonstrating about increased fuel prices, 19 pence a year, per person, spend on health care, forced labour, systemic ethnic cleansing of the many different Burmese tribes and almost half the national budget going on arms and the military for a country with no outside enemies. At the end of it, thousands of monks had been executed, thousands more detained without charge and tortured, a Japanese woman journalist had been shot and the whole massacre shrouded in secrecy from the outside world. It was no time for an actress to be delivering a large musical instrument wrapped up in ribbons.

Lately, news of the Lady has been fractured. Rumour said she was ill; she was on hunger strike; she had refused to see the UN envoy; she had not spoken out for over a year. Then quite suddenly an extraordinary incident was reported in the world's press. An unknown American, John Yettaw, swam across a lake to invade her house and grounds, which are watched at all times by soldiers. He appears to have collapsed exhausted and been allowed to rest there for two days. After which, both he, Aung San Suu Kyi, her staff of two and her doctor were arrested and thrown into Insein jail, accused of violating the terms of her imprisonment by allowing a stranger to invade her guarded compound. All that is known about Yettaw is that he is a fifty-three-year-old Mormon from Missouri and a Vietnam veteran. He is possibly unstable and claims to be writing a book about religious heroes. His defence was that he needed to warn her of an imminent attack. As it happened, the invasion *was* the attack. You may question how he got in to her compound so easily when it is under constant surveillance.

Prior to Yettaw's untimely arrival, Aung San's latest appeal for freedom had been denied by the junta. They have now found a reason to detain or jail her for up to five years. At her trial for the crime of breaking the terms of her house arrest, she represented herself in the kangaroo court. Aside from the first day, no international observers were allowed in. The British ambassador reported that she seemed strong and in good spirits and that she denied any part in this bizarre episode.

As of writing, Yettaw has been deported back to the States. Aung San is back under house arrest in University Avenue and it would be hard to view her situation with anything but despair. The outcome is not going to be in her or her country's interest. The 2008 Cyclone Nargis caused 134,000 deaths, millions were made homeless and the generals refused all offers of international aid. The roof of Aung San's house was blown off and she lived without shelter or electricity for a month.

The generals have constructed a new remote capital, Naypyidaw, in the jungle with hotels and designer houses and schools and hospitals for the military elite and their families. It is a human rights catastrophe and it might just be reported on page 26 of the *Guardian*. The United Nations occasionally send an envoy or bleat disapprovingly as do foreign offices here and in the US. Their efforts are useless. Nothing changes.

Aung San has more international prizes than I can list and won the Nobel Peace prize in 1991. She used the million-pound prize to set up a foundation to fund scholarships for young Burmese students to study abroad. They are, she says, the future of Burma.

The Rangoon Show (2)

Last Friday I cooked a brisket and carrot tzimmes for Friday-night dinner and invited my kids, my chap and my friend Heidi. It's a traditional, cook-ahead recipe which some believe sits on the chest for a couple of months after consumption, but one which I find cosy and tasty as all get-out. (I'll chuck in the recipe just in case you have a gap in your chest yourself.) During the boiling and skimming bit, Sue Summers phoned me.

'You haven't forgotten tonight have you?' She knows me of old.

'No,' I lied, I figured I'd invited her and Phillip Norman, her writer husband and had forgotten. 'Dinner will be about seven thirty,' I added, hastily counting brisket slices.

'I thought you'd have forgotten.' She sighed. 'We're dining in Cuddington with Sherry and the Bishop of Rangoon. I'm driving. It's black tie.'

I called Heidi and apologized. She said, 'At least I know it's a genuine excuse. No one could make that up.'

Then I called my friend Guido. 'Erm . . . I'm – we're apparently . . . erm . . . dining in Berkshire with the er . . . Bishop of Rangoon,' I mumbled shiftily, 'and . . . it's, er . . . black tie.'

'Oh, right,' he said, 'I've got black tie. What time shall I come?'

He's a very exceptional sort of a bloke is Guido. More of him later.

It was a stately Elizabethan home, blazing fires and dinner for thirty cooked by Burmese chefs. Sherry is a dazzling blonde dame, impossible to age, though younger than I am, in a black, sparkly, strapless gown and fun, lobster-shaped jewellery, who, along with her partner, Phil, a former Merseybeat, does derring-do missions at great personal danger up the Irrawaddy river to bring aid to the old soldiers of Burma. Bravery comes in most unusual shapes.

There was an ex-Chindit soldier among the array of distinguished guests, with his pretty Burmese wife. He thought I was Tracy Ullman, so, as a diversionary tactic, and not wanting to disappoint him, I asked him where he had met his wife.

'It was when I was parachuted into the jungle for the third time,' he told me. 'I hacked my way through to a Japanese prisoner of war camp, where I saw a sixteen-year-old girl through the barbed wire, cooking maize for the other prisoners. I took one look at her and fell in love with her bum.'

I hadn't seen it coming. His pretty wife had. 'He always says that,' she beamed.

Guido, who's visited Burma along with every other country on the planet, was quite at home among both the Burmese and the military. I asked the assembled guests to donate anything they fancied to my hoard for the TV show *Cash in the Attic* since I was doing it for a Burma cause and thus it was that I arrived home, at midnight, full of rice and bonhomie, carrying an exquisite Burmese military sword, which could probably slice through my over-wrought-iron front gate.

It was an unusual Shabbos dinner but one which I wouldn't have missed for all the 'A's in Mandalay. The bishop was a poppet who looked about nineteen in cardigan and mufti. The *Cash in the Attic* thing is going to be a trial though. I don't really have any antiques and when I promised to give my Joyce Grenfell gown and my Barbra Streisand autograph, my Virgin Virtuoso paintings and my Power Plate . . . the organizers had not gone through the door before I changed my mind and wanted to keep everything. Selfish! I cry. I should give them the Cartier watch that *he*, my mistake, bought me . . . or the diamond thing? Oh, what the hell! Give 'em my CBE medal! My Bafta! My Variety Club awards? How about my car? My dog? My kids? The sword didn't make it into the package what with health and safety at the BBC and I must admit it was a strange day.

198 I Must Collect Myself

But we raised £1,100 for Burma UK. And a bit of raised consciousness about one of the world's darkest secrets.

Oh, recipe as promised:

Brisket and Carrot Tzimmes

2½ lb brisket of beef
1 or 2 onions, sliced
salt and pepper
2lb carrots, sliced thickly
2lb potatoes, sliced thickly
2oz chicken or other fat
2oz sugar
juice of a lemon or ½ tsp citric acid

Put the beef and onions in saucepan, cover with boiling water, season with salt and pepper and simmer gently for one and a half hours. Add the carrots and potatoes and cook till vegetables are just tender.

Place the meat and vegetables in large casserole. Make a roux of fat and flour and add a pint of the liquid the meat was cooked in. Add the sugar or pour Golden Syrup over the casserole. Bake, uncovered, in a moderate oven for thirty minutes. Eat. Wash up. Diet.

Posey

Then there are the women who opt out completely. By the end of their thirties, they are sated, disillusioned by the chase, tired of the game and in search of an enlightenment they failed to find through either love or work. This led me to Posey. Posey is the product of the debutante system. She spent her formative years in a cold English aristocratic family, looking after her wayward but beautiful younger sister, and realized that to survive she needed a life line which held nothing in it of her own background. In a different age and class system she might well have become a nun. Or even a lady writer using a male pseudonym. I wanted her to be practising yoga throughout the whole speech – not an easy thing to do on radio – seamlessly like a kind of mantra.

Posey

(*A reserved woman in her forties. Nervous and with a strange rhythm to her speech as though speaking a foreign tongue. She looks at the floor except for when her eyes dart behind her.*)

It's hard to speak . . . I mean it's all so . . . another life . . . and not one I . . . Do I really need to do this? Well, I'm going to continue my yoga throughout. That is the agreement. We are on a routine here, you see. Sorry, but are you recording on that thing? May I look? (*She fumbles with it.*) Sorry. Oh well . . . needs must. (*Pose of the child.*)

I only remember Giana (*Pronounced Jaina*) and I did it for a season . . . all the presentations and curtseying to Her Maj and the parties. Oh. My what? For level? Oh I see . . . er . . . 1 2 3 4 5 6 7 8 9 10 . . .

(*Speaking carefully, woodenly.*)

It was totally exhausting. We never stopped. I mean, we all knew where we were going – Mondays the Early Bird. Two hundred of us. All knew each other – from brunch to lunch to tea to cocktails . . . to dance and gorge ourselves and then stagger home at two . . . I don't know how we got to college but we did. Next night the same at . . . L'il Scallywag's! Anoushka's, and on to oh . . . the one on the corner of B . . . Beauchamps Place – yes! Monks!

Guys and gels – moving in a great wave – no one really with anyone – wafting around the bars and the clubs, dancing and drinking. Actually, I always kept the drinking to . . . a min – Pimms – but some of them – honestly . . . vomited daily for the whole three months. Damaged people – hours spent at the dressmakers – the expense! Two of us! (*Salute to the sun.*)

Sex? Gosh, yes . . . Huge empty piles – weekend parties . . . parents off in the Bahamas. Actually, one wanted so much just to stay home and watch *Juke Box Jury*, with one's feet in a bucket. *Couldn't* though, you were on a roll and . . . (*The pose of the tree.*)

Marriage market? Well, some of them did pair off or drop out, yes. I mean I was eighteen and worried sick about Giana . . . drinking . . .

Er . . . Oh, Martinis, bloody Marys, Absinthe . . . *anything liquid,* really.

Eating? Course not. Sardines with the oil washed off under the tap so I had one eye on her going and comings – well, her finals, her – involvements . . . so many men . . . Mummy seemed not to worry, so I let it drift and when Caspar was around she was so 'up' and then when he wasn't . . .

Well, everything! She needed me for everything. Get her up, get her home, get her to tutorials, get her dissertation finished, make sure she had her inhaler. Why? No. Her work was always completely brilliant – she didn't have to open a text book – memorized it cover to cover . . .

Me? No, I was the family dunderhead. (*The archer.*)

Dozy Posey. No-go. No ambition, no push. Might marry a smallholder in Pembrokeshire and rent marshland to camper vans.

No, she got the looks too. Me? The patrician one. Daddy's chin – dead ringer for the Iron Duke.

She was *sooo* beautiful, you see, people just wanted bits of her and she . . . Just drifted into it, I suppose. Giana on posters, Giana on LP sleeves. Then suddenly, Caspar *enormous* with 'Hot Hand, Cold Heart', on *Top of the Pops.* As much coke as one could spoon in . . . please excuse the tired old clichés.

After we . . . after she wrote the book she just slipped from being Cazz's *chick* into being everyone in the band's *chick* and then everyone at the festival's . . . then suddenly nobody's.

Was I surprised? Good Lord, no. It was a question of *when* not if. I had my home line cut off, for fear . . .

Guilty? Me? No . . . yes . . . Probably. In the end I had to leave her to it. She told me often enough to pis— to stop 'cramping her style'.

Look, I left. I went far away. (*Pose of the tree.*)

The shrink said if someone really wants out, there's nothing anyone can do to stop them.

Look. I deserved a bloody life too, didn't I? Gladys Cooper's sister. Gladys

Cooper's sister? Left the theatre world because the audience hissed when-ever she came on stage. No, of course she wasn't. They were just saying, 'She's Gladys Cooper's sister, she's Gladys Cooper's sister.' Just a family story . . . No, never mind, forget it.

Sorry, but will that do? I mean, if you have enough . . .?

It's . . . er . . . just that Mama Rupu usually blesses the whole ashram at four so . . . I need to be there for the hugging. Oh, around six or seven thousand. A day, yes.

Yes. She hugs them all. In batches of twelve and gives them a toffee . . .

Well, I serve her. I am her number seven novice. Sister Immaculata.

Well, we wash her, feed her, travel with her, run the subsidiary businesses and take care of the pilgrims . . . and of course, supervise the hug. (*She laughs for the first time.*) Our reward is in our proximity to Mama Rupu.

Happy? Yes, I am . . . on a level of what? Oh, let's say 1 2 3 4 5 6 7 8 9 10 shall we? Very happy. (*Tongue out and roar . . . the lion.*)

But then, what is happiness, Miss Turner-Price, but the natural outcome of certain rules carefully followed?

Oh, never mind . . . forget it . . . I hope that I have helped your research and good luck with the biography. My mother must be delighted. Her life ended too of course. I was, remember, the sister of an only child. (*Harder laugh.*)

No, not for many years. Personal contact with the outside world is not per-mitted.

Miss Turner-Price, I, too, was astonished, believe me, when Mama Rupu gave her permission for me to speak with you. No, you are correct. Not pleased. Quite the reverse.

By the by, she thanks you for the generous donation your tabloid news-paper has made to our retreat. The new Centre for Spiritual Awareness will benefit hugely.

I must leave you now. It is time for daily prostrations. I hope my words have . . . made sense . . . I have forgotten how to . . .

Five years of silence is very . . . hard to break . . . And now . . . I have said almost my last words for another five. Well, just ten or eleven more perhaps . . .

Miss Turner-Price, forgive me, but I removed the tape from your machine. Namaste.

On Aiming to Get Michelle Obama's Arms Before She Notices and Wants Them Back

Twelve exercises to do when you're in the back of a cab/on a bus/no one can see you and you feel fat and old.

1. Belly dance sitting in your vehicle . . . can be done sneakily behind copy of the *Morning Star*. Roll your stomach inwards and outwards. Then to left and right. Ten repeats.
2. Sitting. Hold stomach muscles and core and lift feet off floor. Stretch legs out, heels together, then toes together. Do same when lying in backwash position at hairdresser. Must hold stomach tight though or back will go. Can even do similar on loo, mid-stream holding back with core muscles.
3. Stretch back of tongue out as far out as possible till you feel chest muscles rise. Relax then pull down top lip over teeth as far as possible for same stretch. Alternate. These are good for tightening loosening breasts and cheaper than surgery . . .
4. Pull down top lip as far as possible and smile broadly with wide mouth. Cover bottom teeth with bottom lip and thrust jaw up and forward. Alternate.

5. Tuck tongue beneath bottom teeth. Push back of it out, still curled as far as possible.

6. Sitting. Pull down back muscles beneath shoulder blades, hold down and tuck chin down. At same time, pull knees up so you go up onto toes. Add bent up elbows, make fists and move elbows forwards.

7. Spread arms, retract fingers, press balls of the palms forwards. Repeat.

8. Hold up finger discreetly in front of you. Look as far away as possible and then at finger. Repeat.

9. Eyes far left, eyes far right as fast as you can. Then pull back face muscles at sides of eyes until you feel ears move up. Alternate.

10. Waiting in a queue, rise up and down slowly on toes. Then press heels into floor.

11. Yoga breathe, press thumb to close left nostril, hold for seven, close right nostril, breathe out through left nostril, hold for seven, breathe in through left nostril, hold for seven, change thumb to left, breathe out. Repeat.

12. Weird one. Imagine a DNA spiral filling your head with windscreen-wiper blade edges. Visualize it turning from top of head, round and round, down through brain, face, neck, organs, cleaning and sweeping and removing clogged up matter, wherever it goes. Visualize it, actually feel it touching your insides. Turn it on its side for shoulders and arms. Send it down and round your spine. Visualize a small version of it moving through the length of your intestines, bowel and womb, send two spiralling round buttocks. Move all way back up to top of head again.

That's about it. Drink lemon and hot water as your first drink of the day. Add a pinch cayenne pepper and some fresh ginger if you're man enough to take it. If you wake in the night, make warm milk and sprinkle fresh nutmeg in it. Go back to bed and concentrate on the *out* breath, pushing your back muscles out every time you breathe. Keep Rescue Remedy in every handbag and fizzy vitamin C for a pick-me-up. If energy is plummeting, push knuckle deep into sole of foot and massage thirty-two times on each foot, then grunt 'Ugh ugh ugh' like a gorilla. Perhaps you should wait to get out of the taxi before you do this one. A shaman once told me to summon my inner frog!

If you get into a real panic, shallow, fast breathe like a panting dog or a newly pregnant woman at an NCT meeting.

Before using voice for speech or voiceover make a 'ff' sound then retract diaphragm, making gruff 'hgh' sound – not aspirate, but with sound straight from diaphragm.

Should anyone diagnose you with Tourettes Syndrome having watched all this, I never wrote this down and you never read it.

NB: When I appeared on Sharon Osbourne's chat show, a kind lady, Caroline, made me a hula hoop after reading somewhere that, as a teenager, I used to go on errands with my hoop spinning round me and return in the same manner, only with a bag of sugar in each hand. With obesity on the front pages as a kind of bogey man for society's ills, I took it up again and found I still adored it. What's more, it does trim the fat. If I diet, I lose all the weight in my face and end up looking like the late Sacheverell Sitwell. With the hoop, I can still eat the entire, sinful box of liquorice fudge that Amy brought me from Denmark, and hula the hips away. Do NOT try to hula the opposite way. Stick to what your body can do. Or you too will have an osteopathy bill which resembles a small mortgage.

Sharon, I read in her (going home present) biography, had her stomach stapled for weight loss, and surgery to pick up the selvedge. A nineteen-year-old girl on *Love Island*, with just a trace of puppy fat, was thrown into a very public depression because a fellow contestant called her fat. Overweight women may be refused the wherewithal to conceive by IVF . . . rampant fat-ism. Clement Freud summed it up on *Just a Minute* last week.

'If anyone tells me I'm fat,' he breathed darkly, 'I say, that's because every time I make love to your wife, she gives me a biscuit.'

Spiegel in Spiegeltent

I was taken to the circus last week. It was a belated birthday present from my friend Eve and, as birthday presents go, it was up there with a balloon flight to the Venice Cipriani (I expect) and dinner at Nobu with Nelson (Mandela not Lord or Eddy or the one who died propping up the bar in the *Archers*). It made me feel like a five-year-old kid.

Funny thing is, I never liked circuses in the days when I *was* a five-year-old kid. I always found them worrying and sinister. The strange off-kilter music, the imminent danger from lions and trapeze artists, the absence of discernible language and, worst of all, the anarchic men in grotesque face paint and electrocuted wigs who made everyone laugh but me.

This one, though, La Clique, was a contemporary circus. No animals, save some deliciously muscled men and lots of wonderful words, spoken and sung, which made me laugh and cry and, once or twice, made my jaw hang open like Gordon Brown before a fiscal pronouncement.

The whole thing took place in a Spiegeltent, a mirror tent, in Brighton. (Odd to think that Sam Spiegel was really Sam Mirror – it makes him sound a bit of a pussycat, which, from all reports, he wasn't.) It's a cottage-loaf-shaped canvas tent with a carved wood and mirrored frieze running round the top and in the centre, the tiniest, maybe 12 feet in diameter, round podium. It's warm and intimate and on this night absolutely packed to the rafters – had there been any rafters. Eve had worked with one of the performers, Ursula Martinez in Edinburgh, so we were given ringside seats, all of 18 inches from the cabaret.

I didn't know what to expect, which was an advantage. It started with a singer, Camille O'Sullivan, a minx with Kate Bush looks and a voice to hypnotize a viper. As she spun herself and the audience into orbit with a feline version of Jacques Brel's song 'We're on a carousel', I thought, Hello? I'm going to quite like this.

Two pin-striped, pipe-smoking gentlemen in bowler hats, one eager, one deadpan, confirmed this, as the latter, silently and without a bead of sweat, lifted the other high above his head while lying on the floor reading a newspaper. At one point he lethargically got to his feet, still balancing his partner on one hand and, as if that wasn't enough, to the sound of rending Velcro, both men ripped off their suits to reveal rippling torsos in Union Jack boxer shorts. My dears, birthday presents come no classier at my time of life.

Then we had a nice Jewish girl from Hampstead Garden Suburb in a red rubber dress, who specialized in scissor swallowing and pointed-stick-through-the-tongue twirling. In my mind I hear the scenario:

'So what's your daughter doing these days, Beattie?' I asked.

'Oh, you know, a bit of this, a bit of that – typing, cooking, sewing – sword swallowing. Listen, Millie, as long as the *kinder* are happy . . .'

Then came some dazzlingly cute trapeze work and then it was time for Ursula's strip.

Ursula's strip. Now, I'd heard about it from Eve but I couldn't imagine that removing a jacket, skirt and underwear with the right bolshie attitude could be that *empowering*. She had a body you could write to a catalogue for and she was going to have the best possible fun with it. She threw in a little light magic with a scrap of scarlet silk which she produced from various body parts along the way, and finished with a coup de théâtre which brought howls of appreciation from every corner of the roundest of venues. Like Gypsy Rose before her, Ms Martinez had the last laugh on generations of exploitation of her sex. After that little slice of variety, the bar did fairly decent business.

The second act gave us a witty and original sing-song, with an ancient Edwardian biddy called Ida Barr who, to our surprise, specialized in rap and body-popping, followed by a dark a cappella German version of 'Falling in Love Again' by a girl called Camille. Then a Russian girl with a dreamy expression did stuff with sparkling hula hoops and a jiggling leg that I don't have space or vocabulary to describe. The pièce de no-résistance, though, came with the placing of a claw footbath full of water in the ring and the solemn handing out of plastic sheeting to the front row, after which a jeans-clad Adonis, naked to the waist, slid into the water, stuck his feet into pendulous ropes and rose, damply, to the roof to spin, somersault and do worrying aerial splits before submerging himself and spouting bath water at us all.

The whole show, holding a Spiegel up to life itself, was a far cry from the last show I saw, which was *Hay Fever* at the Haymarket Theatre, and if I hadn't have been taken to the Brighton Festival, I would have known nothing about it. The Spiegeltent is rolled up now and the company goes off to Montreal and New York. Isn't there an enterprising young producer who would bring this bunch of wise nutters into a permanent home in the city, like the Roundhouse in Camden Town, so that lovers of what is, after all, the Spice of Life, could fill up on skill, sexuality and satire on a regular basis?

N.B. Hard to look back at the review wot I wrote here and not feel a bit prescient, because some enterprising producer did just that – brought the Clique to the old Hippodrome in Leicester Square and cleaned up. For a year! Hooray. Wish I'd thought of that.

Elsa's Dad

I wrote in my last book about my dear friend Eve, actress, poet, well 'over-sixties dance-group' member and general lesson to us all. She survived a hard Aberdeen childhood, losing her mother at twelve, saying goodbye to her father at sixteen and watching a loved husband depart to the arms of another in mid-life. Since then she has survived colon cancer, chemotherapy and various broken odds and sods with an equanimity born of living on nothing and always expecting the best to be round the corner. We met when she took part in Amy's first play, Sitting Pretty, *and have remained firm friends ever since.*

I suppose I wrote this piece in response to the story she told me, when we were on tour, about her father's affair and what she had said to him in anger. When writing this monologue it occurred to me that the father was looking for a way out of his obligations as a father, and her remark set him free.

Elsa's Dad

I don't know if you can hear me. They said you're – techni— in a coma . . . er . . . vegetative. So I'll just say this anyway, in case you can.

I came as soon as they rang me . . . er . . . Dad. As soon as I c-could get the children looked after. They play up if it's just a sitter from the agency and Susan couldn't come till she'd finished her usheretting – that's Jock's daughter from his first marriage – she's been with us for weekends since she was thirteen. Doesn't get on with her mother at all . . . but she can't stay up after eleven – she's swotting for her GCSEs, so there was half an hour to fill till Jock got back.

Then the train was delayed . . . we never found out why. Moth on the tracks probably. I m–mean at every s-stop he said something but his accent was impenetrable. Not his fault of course . . . there'll be no voice training. They'll have just flung him on board two weeks after he arrived in England – but . . .

Anyway I g-got here and I'm glad I did because your s-son looked out of it – exhausted – he can't make the decision about life support without me. No one's had the decency to tell me anything . . . if it wasn't for the tabloids I wouldn't have known you were even ill.

He should have got in touch earlier, I mean, I would have come if he'd . . . he said he found my address in an old diary of yours. I'm astonished you had it.

I can't believe I'm s-seeing you. I don't know that I would have known you if I'd seen you in the street. I mean I know it's you, but your face isn't . . . your bones are more prominent – and without seeing your eyes . . . it's a look I've seen before when I was going round hospitals doing research for M-m-matron Sue. Anyway, there's a look that people get – they . . . God knows, I've played this scene already – more than once – over my mother and my son. Episodes sixty and ninety-two – no, ninety-four. Kidney failure and motor-bike accident. I should be good at it by now.

Christ, I'm not doing it at all well – re-take.

I'd like to fill you in on all the years but it doesn't seem the time somehow. I'd like to . . . take your hand, stroke your forehead . . . I can't – I don't know you.

I'd like to have made my peace with you.

I've thought about you. Before every recording. Does he watch me in this? Does he know it's his kid getting great notices and fan letters and a *TV Times* award? Does he mention me down the pub – 'That's our Elsa, you know. My kid from the first Mrs T. Lost touch with her after her mam passed but I always knew she'd got what it takes.'

Liar. You rotten liar. 'After her mam passed' my foot! Didn't you mention me finding you with Peroxide Jean? With the orange panstick and the fat pencil-slim skirt? Did you forget that bit, oh Father mine?

Well it serves you bloody right, lying here with no speech and no sight, you bastard. Because that's what you've been my whole life to me – no sight no bloody sound.

And you've missed it all, Dad. Missed me and Jock falling in love in Rochdale Rep in the middle of act one of *French Without Tears*, and missed me being given away in oyster satin by one of the finest comic actors of his generation, and missed your first grandchild taking his bow in *Joseph and His Technicolor Anorak* and his wee sister going to kindergarten in her roller skates and Archie, the baby, who looked so much like you when the midwife handed him to me that I nearly handed him back.

Missed it all, Dad. And for what? A bottle-blonde with a bottle problem who made you think you were a Pearly King for as long as it took to drain your Halifax deposit account.

'Have you met my kid, Jeannie?' you said, standin' there in your string vest when I caught you out. 'This is our Elsa . . . fancies herself an actress, b-but she's got a b-b-it of a s-s-stutter; might s-s-tand in her way in the W-W-est End, don't you reckon?'

Yeah. Well. Wrong again, Dad. C-c-cos the funny thing is, I never stuttered again after you left. Till tonight. Once I gave up expecting it, I never needed your attention any more.

(*She gets up and goes to part the curtain, then turns back and looks at him.*)

How could you take it seriously? What I said? That's what I never understood. How could you think I meant it? I was sixteen for God's sake. When I s-said, 'If you don't give her up I'll never speak to you again for the rest of my life.'

'Do you really mean that, Else?' you said, and you put your braces on your shoulders. And you looked at me with those slate-coloured eyes that used to freeze me to the marrow when I was going to stutter and you were going to say something sarcastic about me in front of everyone.

And *of course* I said I did! . . . I was sixteen, Dad!

How the hell did I know how long the rest of my life was going to be? Eh? Answer me that, Daddy. Daddy, darling.

Dad? Was that your hand? Did you just move your hand then? Have you heard what I've been saying? Dad? You have, haven't you?

Nurse! Nurse! Quick! Get a doctor. Quick! He moved. He moved his hand . . . I didn't! I didn't imagine it, don't be ridiculous . . . He tried to take my hand.

I insist. I'm telling you that my father just moved his—

OK. Forget it. Just tell Barry, my – his son – that there's no way I'm agreeing to turn off his life support. OK? No way.

And don't mention him moving his . . . never mind. I'll be back tomorrow, Nurse, and the next day and the day after that . . . and I want his doctor and a physio in here, OK? (*She goes to leave.*)

I heard that. (*Head down, she takes a deep breath.*) I'm being a bit overdramatic, am I? All my life . . . all my sodding life . . .

It's just a job, you know. I do *know* real life doesn't only happen in the ad breaks! I don't actually think I'm matron of some bloody great hospital in some mythical bloody Scottish town that still has bloody matrons!

(*Icily*) Yes, well, you may well have seen me say it on telly but – unlike you, Sister, I know the difference. We don't do real life on a soap because you'd never bloody believe it. Now, if you'll excuse me, I'm gonna buy some grapes.

That poor old bugger with the wires in his chest and the tubes in his throat and the catheter in his cock is my *father*. As in 'Congratulations, Mr Cregan, it's a baby girl' father. And tomorrow I'll decide the storyline for the rest of both our lives.

I'm sorry. Sleep well . . . I'll see you tomorrow. Dad.

Osbourne No Show

I get irritated by chat shows. By the guests, by the hosts, by the audience, but, most of all, by myself. The night before, I get sleepless and snappy and on the day itself I rush out of the house and spend hundreds of pounds on new clothes which I take home, hang up and hate. Then I scour my wardrobe for anything I haven't worn on a rival chat show, climb into it with the help of a shoe horn and a lycra all-in-one which gives me four breasts, and assume a rigid, taut-necked appearance which lasts through the journey, the show, and finally into the canteen, where I gorge myself on carbohydrates and saturated fats to feel better.

The point is that there is no one left for interviewers to interview. It was all very well when Parky could sit and chill out with Bing and Bob or Lauren and Bette. It was magical to view their ostensible normality in the face of a Hollywood childhood, five vituperative marriages and 150 movies. Stylized normality, no doubt, but in the hands, in his day, of the maestro, Niven and Ustinov gave one-man shows of such off-the-custom-tailored-cuff distinction, that their performances could have instantly gone platinum.

Audiences would rush back from the pub or cinema to get the set warmed up for Parky. Will we ever forget his near coyness faced with his all-time hero, Fred Astaire? I thought at one point he was actually going to ask the frail old trouper if there was any chance of fox-trotting him round the studio. Terry Wogan out-twinkled him for some years, but, in contrast to Parky, his iconoclastic wit was at its most dazzling on radio.

It was an honour to be a starter when a big celebrity was the main course. I would tremble in the *hostility* room a bit, but as soon as I was in the other armchair, I would throw in a joke, a couple of stories about my mother and retire to watch the star sweep in. The lighting was kind, the set was bland, a nice silver car picked you up and took you home where you could watch it without wincing.

The trouble was, once the Yanks had taken their dollars out of the British film industry, i.e. Burton and Taylor were no longer ensconced at the Dorchester throwing rocks at one another, and films were made in tax havens or anonymous deserts, there were very few legends passing through town. So the focus changed to pop stars and politicians who were either adolescent, pompous or monosyllabic. DJ Simon Dee dropped – or was pushed – out of the race, Parky departed, huffed, for radio. Parky was always a televisual man. You had to see the suits, count the crinkles and assess the extent of the crush.

Mavis Nicholson and Gloria Hunniford were both excellent interviewers, well briefed, good listeners, and Russell Harty had a Richard Whitely-like appeal. You were agog wondering where the next size-twelve loafer was going to land. The two Clives, Anderson and James, were too egg-headed, both literally and metaphorically, to survive for long in a climate where asking Jordan if she'd ever *read* a book, let alone written one, were de rigueur. How could any of those gentle, amused souls survive once the plants had taken over the garden centre?

The three-headed dog at the mouth of Channel Hades was Barry Humphries' brilliant Dame Edna, where suddenly the interviewer was more important than the interviewee; Mrs Merton, who took the joke even further, Julian Clary and his wonder dog, Fanny. Since comedians tend to be mercurial creatures, happier with dogs than humans, and the British public more enamoured of their dogs than their other dependants, the floodgates opened for the canine as accessory. After all, it gave the host time to think. When the auto-cue rolled backwards, the creature could always be relied upon to pee or fart or do its business, giving the comedian time for improvised business of his own and endless Jack Benny takes on the studio audience. The viewers at home thought the host was both a natural and a man of the people because, 'That's exactly what your dad did when our Buster peed on the vicar's brogues at our Lilly's pre-nuptials.'

Enter, with alarums, the holy triumvirate: Graham Norton, Paul O'Grady and now, Sharon Osbourne, each with the lap-top-dog of their choice. Plus, since guests are in short supply and the public are weary of the same old celebs pushing the same old ghost-written prose, will you welcome, please, fusion-fodder of chat show/ *Generation Game/Surprise Surprise*. The host has to listen, speak, read the auto-cue and follow instructions through an earpiece while adding up winnings, giving out email details and being bitten. The guest has to be a bloody good sport too, willing to act as an innumerate version of Carol Vorderman while the host asks the studio audience general-knowledge questions of serious erudition, like 'For ten thousand pounds, did Matt Lucas and David Walliams star in a) Little Germany b) Little Britain or c) Little Venice?!' Magnus Magnusson must be spinning in his mausoleum.

For my appearance on Sharon's show, to talk, nominally, about my book *The Gibbon's in Decline but the Horse is Stable*, I was asked if I'd like to bring my Basenji, an offer to which any sensible actress of forty years' experience would say, 'Absolutely not. I'm talking about the International Myeloma Foundation UK where all the proceeds from the book will go – the dog will just distract . . .' Needless to say, as I said it I was packing her treats and her best Sunday lead.

The dog behaved impeccably. I burbled on like a candidate for *Love Island*, racing through the comic verses trying to get too many in at once, talking too much and saying nothing. To cap it all, I realized in the car on the way home that I'd had my skirt on inside out. Played like a pro, Mo.

Diva made further appearances on Paul O'Grady and Graham Norton's shows and was impeccable if dismissive. She behaved so well on the cover shoot for this book, posing and staring moodily into the lens, that I reckon Naomi Campbell should be tied to a breezeblock and forced to view her working style for a couple of hours. Watch and learn, Naomi, watch and learn. And she gets out of bed for less than a chicken morsel too.

Competitions

Does your life seem to be a competition? Did you win a place at the school of your parents' choice, compete in the inter-school balloon debating competition, buy a scratch card, scratch it and sob, send off two toothpaste caps and a photo of your feet to win an afternoon in Brent Cross with a depressive TV gardener of your choice? Do you vote interactively for Simon Cowell to be voted off the panel or some twerp to be thrown out of Celebrity Twerp house? Do you *care* who wins *Mastermind* or *Millionaire*, or race down to get the best seats in your local pub quiz or watch *The Weakest Link* to see if anyone is a bigger winker than Anne Robinson?

If you have answered any of these questions with a yes, then you are in the majority. I, who can scarcely contemplate *starting* let alone finishing a card game or a round of golf, salute you, for I am the founder member of the minority who couldn't really give a flying falafel who dares or who wins. League tables are out of my league, although I became a Manchester United fan by marriage and actually enjoyed, for a while, watching games from a totally prejudiced point of view.

Left outside was my position in the school hockey and netball games. My brother copped every nano-centimetre of the competitive spirit in our house. He captained everything from rugby to cricket and all the way to industry, and could hammer me at Monopoly, Beggar My Neighbour and, by means of a sponge bat and *spin*, table tennis, the only sport at which I *thought* I could excel.

The same gender bias went on in my children, in that for years, the boy had a gnarled sponge ball attached permanently to his foot and could attempt, even before his head had grown up to the pockets, a fairly mean snooker on his granddad. (Amy's just reminded me of a fearful row he and I once had during the game Cheat. I accused him of cheating – which he clearly was – and I went completely purple with rage when he pointed out that that was the whole point of the game.)

My daughter's sporting activities were entirely to do with who was in or out of the school gang and required hours of telephone time and plotting, all of which involved sitting for long stretches on her bum, hissing, and doodling all over the message pad.

Competition looms large in my world. There are more award ceremonies now than there are people to award twisted pieces of metal to. I've actually given an award this very week to the Best Chauffeur Limousine Firm at the World Travel Show. It was an odd event and many familiar faces were crammed into a small room in the basement of the Royal Opera House asking each other what we thought we were doing there.

Ruby Wax was scribbling her jokes down onto her clipboard as I arrived.

'How do you want to be announced?' she asked me.

I glanced over at a table beside her and saw Billy Murray of *EastEnders*. In 1969 he'd played my boyfriend in the film *Up the Junction*.

'Just say, "Maureen Lipman starred in the film *Up the Junction* in 1969, and hasn't done much since."'

Ruby laughed at that a lot, which was more than the audience did. All the presenters, munching on curled-up finger food, looked sheepish. We all knew we were there because, only a couple of days ago, exotic holidays had been offered to us. Peter Bowles, carrying his dinner jacket in polythene, looked ruffled, and Peter Davison blinked in puzzlement and shook out his DJ from a case on wheels. The stunning Jane Krakowski (*Ally McBeal* and *Guys and Dolls*) realized with despair that she was giving the *last* of forty-five awards and was doing it, like me, on her only night off from eight shows a week.

The organizer told us on no account must we speak other than to announce the winner's names on the envelopes. This worked like a red rag to a Taurean.

'Hello,' I said to the assembled bow ties and breasts. 'We've been told not to say anything at all – so would you like to hear a joke?'

'Yesss!' screamed back the crowd. It went down well and I was home by nine thirty having beans on toast in my evening frock. Nice. By the following day, the holidays had downsized radically from business class for two to the Indian Ocean to Dubai on an unnamed airline for one, so watch this space. I may be writing my next by-line from Bridlington.

My own experience of being on a judging panel is that half the judges vote for A and the other half vote for B, with such virulent dislike of each other's choice that C becomes *everyone's* second choice. After a period of discussion, muzzle to muzzle, with no one budging an inch, anyone with a life, desperate to stop eating hummus and crudités and drinking warm Chardonnay, votes for C. Therefore C – no one's first choice – wins the award. Alternatively, one persistent judge might well bore the cashmere off the others to such an extent that, to a Man Booker, they lose the will to Turner round and give in. Thus the money goes to *The Life of Pi*, elephant excreta and Ant and Dec.

Brittney's Got Talent

Shirrin from Model Habits and Brittney both belong in the same School of Performing Arts. Brittney, though, has a keen intelligence, although she won't necessarily have any art. She is in her early twenties and has dressed for the show in carefully thought out waif grunge. She has bags of confidence and belief in her own talent and a deal of chutzpah thrown in. She should be very convincing in her nervousness and her efforts not to cry. There is a caterwauling audience in front of her and a panel of judges who have got to know her and vice-versa over the past weeks. She will go far.

Brittney's Got Talent

(Girl who looks about sixteen, in sequined shorts and lurex bustier, addresses each judge in turn.)

Thank you . . . er . . . yes, I know I was dead nervous. But . . . aw, thank you.

Thank you, er, yeah, I need to work on that but . . . *(Laughs)* I didn't know it were that bad! *(Acknowledges audience reaction.)*

How do you mean? I picked it cos I liked it. It's one of Beyoncé's. I've loved her since I was born . . . Thanks, was I? Honest? . . . Thanks a lot.

(Tries to speak but chokes up.)

Sorry, it's just me nerves, I'm all right really. *(Cheer from crowd gets her smiling and waving.)*

It's me sisters . . . they're all here. Four, Clancy, Harley, Keeley and Charleez. *(Clearly she's been instructed to say next bit.)* They've all been a tremendous support for me since our mam d . . . our Clancy's worked shifts to get me this outfit and she's been stone deaf since birth . . .

No, it's not me mobile. No, that'll just be me ankle chain it's just ringing cos me knees are knocking. Sound man tried to get me to take it off but I wouldn't – it's me lucky anklet.

Well, from me mam and me uncle Trevor.

Just singing in pubs and that. It was always my dream to win a competition like this and get me mam and me sisters a nice house and that.

No, she's dead, like, now.

Thirteen and a bit.

Car crash. Four by four. Ran over her wheelchair like.

No, we haven't got a dad. As such. Just uncles. Me and Keeley had the same dad but he went off with a Sikh girl that worked in Superdrug. They live in Slough though now. We had a postcard from him when I got through the first heat. He'd seen us on telly in a bar in Paxos.

Oh, 'eck, I don't know really. Take us all on holiday first somewhere hot. Ibiza or Las Palmas. Then what I'd really like is to save enough to get our Charleez into a proper school with special needs cos she gets bullied where she is; and to be able to buy our Harley a trumpet cos she's dead musical but you have to have your own instrument to get in school band . . . Me? Oh, nothing really, it would just be enough for me to be able to put up a headstone on me mam's . . .

Oh, thank you. THANK YOU . . . I can't believe it! Hooray . . . YES! I'll see yezall next week then. Thank you.

Oh, thank you all . . . this means the world to me.

(*Runs off waving to audience. Removes microphone and takes out mobile phone from underpants. Dials.*)

Hello? Yah. Mariella? Did it . . . Not a dry eye in the house, darling. Sniffles all over the soundtrack. I'll be back at college in another week. Make sure my name goes on the list for the Chekhov try-outs. Ya.

Effing brilliant wheeze darling, and if this doesn't get me a frigging agent I don't know what will. *Ciao*, sweets . . . got to get back to the hostility room and pretend to quiver. What larks. Laters.

Wimborne Every Minute

Tomasina-Tomasina, the sat nav, took me to Dorset last week. She was very well behaved aside from telling me, unaccountably, on a very busy stretch of road just before the M3, to turn round and start afresh. I ignored her, reckoning she was just testing my resolve, and we proceeded apace. Naturally, Nats (angel in attic) had programmed Dorset in, and friend David re-programmed it at the other end, to please take this woman, daughter and dog back from whence they came, which she duly did.

Another notch in my cummerbund. I left all motorway driving to Jack for the full thirty-five years of our courtship and marriage. He didn't much like it either, but there were exhilarating times when we suddenly threw everything in the boot and set off for Cornwall, munching apples and singing songs from *Calamity Jane*. Times when I felt like Mr Toad on his way over to see Ratty. 'Poop Poop!' we'd say. 'This is the life.'

Now, on a fine sparkling day, Amy beside me, with the prospect of seeing godchildren and friends, spending a day on Bournemouth beach, and introducing Diva the barkless, to another chum Linda's four dogs, I was hugely cheery. We stopped at a hideous service station after junction 13, and, since it was a canine-free zone, sat in the car eating cardboard salads – no utensil provided – and watching the world wobble past on its way to Burger-Monarch, or some other such mince outlet.

On the car radio came Massenet's 'Meditation from Thaïs', which was the curtain music of act one of Amy's play *Sitting Pretty* and was also played at Jack's funeral. We didn't say much, just set off, with big grins on our faces, feeling he was with us.

'I always glance up at the overhead bridges,' I told Amy, 'to make sure no one's up there throwing rocks at motorists.'

There was a long pause . . .

'Do people really do that?' she asked.

'Yeah,' I assured her, 'there was a spate of it not long since.'

She chewed on her Werther's Original for a while, then said, 'Chinese people?'

It took me a while but I got there in the end.

'Rocks, darling,' I told her. 'It's rocks they throw. Not woks. That would just be silly. Why would they throw woks?'

She thought about it for a while, then said, 'Why would they throw *rocks*?'

Dorset and my godchildren were about as good as it gets. Kate and David and Jack and I met in Morocco, about twelve years ago, and as sometimes happens when one meets friends in later life, the bond was strong. Their mill house is cool and beautiful and, because I'm a stranger to the ways of the country – give or take the *Archers* addiction – I felt as though I was shrugging off a flaky metropolitan skin.

On the evening of 8 September, we drove over to Linda's to 'celebrate' the mutual birthday of our late husbands. It was always a source of joy and curiosity to us, that not only did she and I practically share a birthday (I once had a T-shirt made for her saying 'I will always be a year younger than Maureen Lipman') but that the men we loved shared one too. Our lives have had many parallels and in our youths we were often mistaken for one another . . . same mass of dark hair, same overbite, the same 'funny girl' sharp tongue and the same adoring bloke at our elbow. Now, outside the windows of her exquisite house, the landscape was a mournful navy blue of dark, rolling hills, illuminated by the biggest, fullest, orange-est moon we'd ever seen, and we shared even more.

Her three West Highland terriers and one black Labrador seemed to take kindly to Diva for a while, then something inexplicably canine happened and the youngest, a three-footed puppy called Sammy, began barking at her. The others, loyally, joined in, though Bobby the black Lab did it in desultory manner since he quite fancied her. Since she has no equipment for barking back she looked petrified, and held up her two front legs to be picked up.

'Wimp!' they barked. 'Wuss!' they yelped. 'Can't stand on your own three feet!' they growled.

Amy said she totally empathized with the scene from the school playground of her youth and took Diva out of the fray into the drawing room. Unfortunately, already in the drawing room was a large white cat, surveying her territory, which did not include the presence of a tiny tan twerp with a Danish pastry for a tail. The cat swelled up to twice her size, retracted her head inwards, arched her body high above it and issued a snake-like hiss.

In the end, I just carried her around all night like an accessory, and ate my turbot with one hand. It was, nevertheless, a stunning and final evening, and one which I knew cost my friend dearly. And I don't mean the turbot.

Country folk are incessantly telling you how wonderful the country is and both of my days away proved it to be so. 'You'd love it here,' they say, 'the community feeling is amazing. People rally round and help each other.' Walking round the village with Joe, my godson, he pointed out the 'honesty box', a basket of vegetables left for folk to take what they want and pay whatever they think it's worth. The metro-mind boggles.

On the Sunday I read an article by the renowned toff Julian Fellowes about how to be a good weekend guest. I was coiled up in a ball, with glee.

'Take flowers,' it said, 'to your host if you are under thirty, but nothing if you are over.' I'm over – I took. 'Eat everything you are given or just push it around your plate.' It was sensational – what's not to eat? 'If you are offered a walk on the beach, it is obligatory, so it's no good your saying: "I don't, frightfully, feel like a walk."' *Frightfully!* In what year – no, in what century is the *spiffing* old *cove* living? Nowhere did he say, 'be yourself', which is, after all, the reason why you're invited.

Later, heading for the M3, I felt a sense of accomplishment in having just made the drive and marked the occasion so perfectly. Still, London called. There was a prom to see that night at the Albert Hall, the last one of the season, and Alan Titchmarsh beckoned a green finger . . . Driving through Hyde Park, crossing the Serpentine, Marble Arch, the silhouette of the Eye, the skyscrape mural of the City and later, with Prokofiev ringing in my ears, finding even the Archway Road had a certain *grungeur*.

'Earth has not anything to show more fair.' It hasn't, as far as I'm concerned. I've been a Londoner for more years than I was a northerner, and you can't just give that up, for the sake of a rolling hill, a chirpy g'morning and a free courgette.

You Can Take the Girl Out of Hull

In my last book, *Past-it Notes*, I wrote a chapter called 'The Year of Living Dangerously', in which I told the story of my first new relationship, three years after losing my husband. It was a farcical story of a highly charged meeting, a tempestuous relationship and unattractive tears before bedtime. Looking back from the distance of another three years and in the calmer waters of a steady relationship with a grown-up man, I can only think that I was certifiably unbalanced or, to use the technical term, *somewhat off my squiff*.

Friends tell me they couldn't understand why I had fallen for someone so unlikely, people who knew him warned me off him, friends worried that I was not myself and appeared to be almost possessed. Of course they were right. I'd forgotten how heady it can be to be admired and, like a teenager, I could think of little else. It was vanity and it ended, like most vain projects, in disaster. Afterwards, I was laid low by a sort of battle fatigue that I'd never before experienced.

I resolved to learn from my mistake. I was better alone. I was coping so well before I met him and I would again. Then, on my penultimate date with Mr Wrong, at an event called Lunch With a Legend (or, as I misread it Lunch With a Leg End) I was introduced to the man with whom, three years later, I am still 'walking out'.

Two friends, Karen and Antoinette, had come to the lunch to hear me and had got into conversation with a tall, olive-skinned man with silver hair and a pearl-grey suit. He told them he'd come to hear me after seeing me in a programme about amateur painters (he was a good one himself). I came over to see my chums, he was introduced as Guido and he kissed my hand. That was it.

The ordure hit the fan with the Wrong'un about a week later. I went off, bleary-brained, to the Amazon – a sentence I never thought I'd write in my life.

The trip was organized by the *Oldie* magazine and although Mavis Nicholson, Rosie Boycott, sundry others and I enjoyed some sun, it was not all it was cracked up to be. The plan was that the ship would sail up – or was it down? – various tributaries to unexplored towns. The reality was that the unexplored towns didn't appear to know we were coming and refused us tender. We saw no animals, few birds and generally would have learned more about the Amazon in a pair of 3D glasses at the Imax.

Back home with a peeling nose, I set about pulling myself up by the bootstraps but found that just made my coccyx hurt. Out of the blue – and I was, very – Karen phoned to suggest I might like to meet up with Guido. I was adamant that I wanted nothing more to do with post-menopausal dating, ever again, particularly with men I'd met while public speaking in a hat. Untypically, she took my *no* to mean *yes*, found out his details from the organizers of the lunch, wrote him a letter and suggested he call me, which he duly did.

On the phone we talked a little about the Amazon, which he'd visited – I later found there were few places in the world he hadn't visited – but when he suggested meeting, I shrank back, only finally agreeing to see him for lunch on Saturday. I had a memorial prayer to say for my mother and he was, it transpired, a member of the same synagogue.

Before the service, over coffee in the lobby, people came up to chat. 'You look well,' was said more than once. 'I've been on an Amazonian trip,' I told them. When a tall, bearded man, in an astrakhan hat, limping slightly (reminiscent of Jack's pre-hip replacement gait) approached me, and asked me how I was, I told him the same thing.

'I know,' he said, 'you told me on the phone.'

He went to take off his hat, revealing a nobly bald head and leaving me thinking, who the hell was that and why does he think he spoke to me on the phone?

After the service therefore, I found myself lunching with a man I'd never seen before in my life. It was fine. I'm used to strangers and besides, he was reserved, cultured and had a self-deprecating humour. That was nice, I thought, no trouble, interesting company and I'll probably never see him again for the *next* sixty-three years.

Still, I couldn't wait to phone Karen.

'That man you set me up with . . . who was he? Yes, I know he's Guido, but there must have been another man with the same name, well, because – there . . . Didn't the one we met have silver hair? Yes, I thought so.

'Did he have a beard? No, I thought not. There must have been two . . . Yes, I know it's an unusual name but . . .

'Well, yes, but did you have the conversation about being an amateur artist with any other lone men? You only spoke to one single man.

'I don't know what happened to the dazzling Eurocrat in the grey suit who kissed my hand, either. He did kiss my hand, didn't he? Yes, I thought so.'

We laughed and forgot about it.

A week later he rang again with a suggestion for another restaurant. I figured I owed him lunch now, so I'd just do one more and I'd ask him about the sudden hair loss and chin addition.

We met up in Kensington. He was as beautifully mannered and charming as before. We laughed a lot and the conversation never flagged. At some point I took a large swig of the very good wine he'd ordered and said, 'You know when we met at the er . . . lunch thing . . . er . . . did you have hai— I mean, did you have, er . . . a beard . . . like you have now . . . at that time?'

He had – *has* – wonderful eccentric eyebrows which make him look stern. He looked stern.

'I've had a beard for fifteen years.'

'Oh, right. And . . . erm, did you have . . . er . . . hair? Did you have . . . er . . . more . . . then . . . than . . .'

'No. I lost my hair when I was in my thirties. As did my father.'

'Right.' There was a pause loaded with question marks. 'So . . . when you met me – I looked the same?'

'Well, you had darker hair . . . I think.'

'I had a big hat on.'

'No, you didn't.'

'I can show you the pictures.'

'Really?'

'And gloves. You kissed my hand.'

'Who did?'

'You did.'

'Me?' The eyebrows elevated and the beard retreated. 'I'm not in the habit of kissing ladies' hands.'

'You did. I thought it was sweet . . . and you wore a lovely light grey suit.'

'I don't have a grey suit, and if I did I wouldn't wear it for a luncheon.'

I couldn't wait for the end of the last course so that I could get to my land-line. 'Karen, ring Antoinette and ask her—'

'She's in Chicago with Ralph, he's playing—'

'I don't care if she's in Shark Bay twinned with Tatler's End. Ring her up and say – just answer *yes* or *no* . . . silver hair/beard/kissed hand/grey suit? Now.'

The call came back within the hour. Staggeringly enough, Antoinette said, *yes* he had silver hair, *no* he had no beard, and *yes* to the hand kiss and the grey suit. As they say in *Friends, Seinfeld* and anything with Ruby Wax in it – *Go figure*.

I'm afraid there is no end to this story. Just some run-of-the-mill magical realism and a conundrum or two. What Shakespearian plot led three intelligent and at the time sober women – this was a Jewish function remember – to see, quite clearly, and at the same time, a dashing Rossano Brazzi lookalike, who didn't exist, in place of the dear old version of Sean Connery, who did – *does*?

Obviously, someone – Puck, Gabriel Garcia Marquez, Angela Carter, Homer, Zelma . . . *Jack* . . . sprinkled fairy dust into the duck and ginger canapés ingested by three sane women, because they knew we had to be temporarily bewildered.

So, perhaps there is an end to our story, and it's a happy one because when he and I really looked, we saw each other very clearly, whereupon, as in all the best stories, friendship and companionship turned into love.

Still, having said all that, and in spite of my writing what you've just read, I was, *am*, determined not to let him be dragged into the three-ringed circus of the first relationship. No media interest, no appearances at premieres, no 'Can we snap you together, Mr Lipman?' That kind of attention by proxy is hard for any man to take, even if, like Jack and Guido, they are not in competition, but take pride in the good things I do. For my part, once again I have someone in my life whose decency I can look up to and respect.

It wasn't until after a year or so, that we, as a couple, encountered any interest from the press. Leaving a club restaurant one night, we asked for a cab, the doorman returned in the said cab and as we got in, the paparazzi appeared on either side. Instinctively, I flung myself against the right-hand windows, hands spread and then, when the snappers raced around the cab, across the left window. We drew off, turned a corner and went straight into a traffic jam, where, once more, bless their unsaturated hearts, they leaped, frog-like, onto the cab again. I was livid; he was sanguine.

Afterwards, he was phoned by the *Daily Mail* at home. He just put the phone down. I told him that's what everyone does when the *Daily Mail* phones. Two years later, the same paper *outed* us. The fact that I haven't spoken a syllable to the *Daily Mail* in twelve years didn't stop them, for a minute, from quoting me. In their book, why should it? With some satisfaction, we noted that every fact they printed was erroneous, save that I was sixty-three and he was a man.

Moreover, he is a mensch. Moreover even than that, he accepts that I live in a meandering basement flat with an over-indulged Basenji bitch, Diva, a morose male rabbit, Warren, and my spiky-haired PA Natalie and that I am a workaholic with a diary that accommodates three score and twenty people a day who want a piece of me, and the organizational skills of a broad bean. He is a traveller who wants to take me to Papua New Guinea and Khartoum . . . for a holiday! I feel faint at the sight of euros, am a pin-up to every mosquito in the twin hemispheres and, if pressed, admit to a fondness for Majorca.

A few weeks ago I took Guido to Hull. I always visit my parents' graves once a year and he volunteered to come with me. I told him the place got a worse press than it merited and I really built up its good points. It's quite complicated to get in to the locked cemetery so I arranged to meet an old acquaintance from way back, Stuart, at Brough Station, who would take us in to Ella Street Cemetery with a key.

It was dark and drizzly as Nats drove us to King's Cross but I felt my usual buzz as the train pulled out on time at 9.48 a.m. I love the country rattling past and Guido and I both buried ourselves in our papers, his *Times* and my *Guardian*, eating flapjacks and slurping coffee. Unfortunately, that was the last sane moment of the day.

There was a body on the line at Stevenage. It is impossible not to feel irritated by the dead man or woman – may they rest in peace, obviously – for not choosing a more selfless place to do it. It took five hours to get to Selby and then the train, for reasons not disclosed to its passengers, terminated there.

Oh, goody. Selby on a wet Wednesday, waiting for a relief train. We finally reached Brough around 3.30. What did we do before mobile phones? I must have rung Stuart seven times on the journey. Thank the Lord he's retired. Imagine if he'd been meeting us in his lunch hour. He was just as I remembered him, wiry of build, large of ears, with Hull's wicked sense of the absurd and dry-as-dust humour.

'Now then,' he greeted me. It's the northern now-then. It means hello, how are you, what's new . . . and then some.

The Yiddish language does it in one: 'Nu?'

Stuart had lost his wife, Joan, about the same time as I'd lost Jack. She was a pretty vital woman who had done amazing community work in Hull, but to me she would always be Joan Haas, pristine prefect at Newland High School in a navy blazer and striped orange and yellow tie. Stuart had owned menswear shops for the taller, bigger gent and once again Guido sat through the myths and fables of our Hullovian reminiscences, with beatific patience. He needed it. Stuart told me that Rita Charnah, a local pillar of the community, was now ninety years old, so I sent her flowers. It seemed opportune and my mother, Zelma, would have approved, although she hated being sent them herself . . . 'Too dear . . . and I hate arranging them. I never have the right vase.'

We approached the gates of Ella Street Cemetery and stood, stoically, in the pouring rain, as Stuart inserted wet key into wetter lock. He followed this up by removing a large hammer from his overcoat pocket and banging the other end of the lock.

'Er . . . why are you doing that?' I enquired, glancing over my shoulder.

He looked surprised by the question and replied, 'To get in.'

'But how will the next person get in then?'

'They'll hit it back the other way.'

'Oh. Right then.'

He bashed the lock into submission and we went in.

It wasn't all gloom. As we passed the headstone of a fairly prurient and curmudgeonly friend of my mother, Stuart remarked on how she'd had a reputation in her youth for being 'a bit of a goer'.

This got us tittering. I told them how, on one occasion in London, in the famous Elena's Etoile restaurant in Charlotte Street, Jack had, in secret, primed Elena, the Mâitre d', to know about all sorts of Hull women of Zelma's community. When Elena brought Zelma's coat she started talking about these people as though they were old friends of hers.

Mum was astounded. 'You know Miriam Bennett?' she breathed, 'and Jean Abrahams? You didn't . . . I can't believe it. How did you meet her?'

Elena carried it off like a pro. She mentioned another friend of my mother's. 'And Dora Green [let's call her], how is she? Still on the game?'

Zelma had to sit down.

'Dora . . . you don't mean . . . you're not saying . . . I mean she was known to be a bit of a goer but . . . go on . . . you're kidding me. Aren't you?'

It was a priceless moment and it was only when she saw Jack's twitching face that Zelma realized she'd been had. Still, ever since then Dora, this poor maligned woman, long since transported to her next life, has been the source of endless one-liners in our familial conversations. So much so that now even Guido is prone to talk with fond nostalgia of his breathless days with her when she was in the WAFs.

After the light relief came the visit to my dad's erstwhile Gentleman's Outfitters. Of course it wasn't at its best in the constant drizzle. Well, to be fair, it wasn't there. It's a DVD and games shop now. Dad's shop was next to the docks, which in Hull came right up into the main street, rather like a harbour. His advert in the local paper read: 'Maurice Lipman's shop is next to the docks. Drop in and see him.'

You can see where I get my wit from, can't you?

Next, we went to the nearby Ferens Art Gallery where they once commissioned a portrait of me from the artist Humphrey Ocean. The last time I saw it it was sitting rather queasily, I thought, in the café with one end of the canvas slightly rolled from the steam. This time it was, I was told, in the vaults. So, shaken but not too stirred, we descended to the barrels of the earth and canvases were rolled back like rugs in Harrods and suddenly, there I was, track-suited and soulful on a striped settee in my old house in Muswell Hill.

'Is that you?' said Guido.

'Yes,' I said proudly, 'good isn't it?' I always loved the painting.

'Doesn't look a bit like you,' he said.

'Does,' I countered.

'Doesn't,' he said. Fair do's. He's said it about photographs of my youth too. 'Who is it?' he'll say when I show him my glamorous image.

'It's me. I was twenty-one.'

'Doesn't look a bit like you. Completely different face.'

'Yes, well. That's what I looked like. Some people think I've hardly changed . . .'

'Harumph.' He can actually say it.

Next we had fish and chips standing up in a chippy in the main street. It wasn't quite as I'd remembered it but it was better than the down-south, whoopsie stuff that passes for F and C in London. Then I took him to the street where I was born, but couldn't remember the number of the house, so we passed on. Then I took him to the Humber Bridge, which is gorgeous, and he said 'harumph' to that too, and then we said goodbye and thank you to Stuart, got back on the train and went home.

In vain, I talked about the new marina – it was too wet to see that day – the fabulous aquarium The Deep, the Premier League football team, the round the world yacht race about to set sail from Hull Bunting . . .

'If I never see Hull again, it'll be too soon,' he said. He lives near Denham . . . twinned with Shark Bay, Australia. Don't make me laugh, sport.

Micheline

Micheline is based on a real-life encounter I had on a North London lawn, which left me breathless. The speaker is a faded blonde of South African derivation, once a bit of a dazzler but now looking slightly out of fashion. She's wearing a good silk blouse and skirt and high-heeled shoes which keep sinking into the lawn, which annoys her. She juggles a glass, a shawl and a handbag with not much grace and seems to have a kind of obsessive compulsive disorder as far as her favourite topic is concerned. Like Dinah with her pop star, she veers every conversation around to her favourite theme. She is poised, long-suffering and very certain.

Micheline

She's amazing isn't she, the way she brings everyone together? I really don't know how she does it. I wouldn't have the patience. And so easily . . . without fuss . . . I'd have to make it into such an *event* . . . every detail would have to be perfect and . . . and there she is with her big white doorstep sandwiches and supermarket wine and honestly, no one thinks any the worse of her. It's a lesson.

Oh, aeons. We were at college together . . . LSE . . . went our different ways but always kept up . . . I was globe trotting while she was running round the news circuit.

You? I suppose you media folks all move in the same circles, don't you?

Would you mind holding my glass while I . . .? It's these *heels*. I should never have worn them at one of Lottie's parties, three inches of North London loam. I'm going on from here – not sure I'm going to find a shoe-shine in Queen's Square . . . Thanks . . . er . . . I'll take that drink back now.

What's that? . . . To absent friends? OK. Why not?

Oh, you know about my . . . er . . . colleague? Well, since you ask, I am, yes. I mean as in touch as I can be considering that his mail is all vetoed. He's bearing up pretty well actually.

Interested in his work, are you? Well, I'm quite surprised to hear that from you. Well, from your writing – admittedly – bits in the crummy British press . . . well . . . well because your stuff is so partisan and, with respect, parochial . . . it's pretty in yer face Jew, isn't it?

Actually, he *is* quite a decent person when you know him – all this vilification at his age is appalling . . . You agree? You're kidding? You amaze me. I'm surprised . . . of course I am . . . Well, because I've yet to meet one of you lot – *your lot* . . . the lobbyists – who can get away from the personal for long enough to understand what he's really saying.

No – give me strength – he does *not* say the Holocaust didn't happen . . . if you read his last book, as millions of intelligent thinking people did, what he says and what most sane people would agree with, is that there were camps, but they were *not* extermination camps and the actual numbers were far—

Well, *I* don't know where they all got to . . . Israel, I presume. I'm sure they landed on their feet if all the reparation claims are anything to go by.

No, but I did catch the piece in the *Standard* about your slip up on the late-night politics show. Wow! She was really gunning for you, wasn't she?

Did you intend to make such a dangerous observation? Well, about life being held cheap for Palestinians as opposed to the Israelis? . . . Which soldiers were you talking about? The ones Hamas captured? They're not *still* being held hostage? I haven't read anything for aeons . . . I presumed they were back safe and sound. Come on, if two are dead, I can't believe the Israeli PR machine hasn't whinged on about it.

Tell me, do you actually ever go there? I mean, with respect, you Jews are always saying 'next year in Jerusalem', but you never actually go, do you? Do you feel at home there? Really? Even in someone else's rightful country?

Oh, you mean, your grandfather was born in England . . . oh . . . not in Vilnius or somewhere then?

Woah! Don't get overheated. Nothing personal intended . . . I'm just an interested bystander . . .

Your books sell well do they?

That *is* good for a minority subject.

Not quite up there with *his*, but . . .

I must find somewhere to put these huge crusts . . . Oh, thank you.

But you must admit, your Old Testament scriptures, well, they're incredibly violent, aren't they?

Do you ever wonder if your alleged persecution doesn't erupt *because* of your scriptures? Your God is *such* a war-monger! So aggressive! Always pitting kith against kin, isn't he? No wonder you all . . .

Sorry? Ask *me* a question? Sure. Why not?

Well, it depends what you mean by personal. Fire ahead, why don't you.

Have I *what*? I . . . I . . . beg your pardon? I can't believe . . . I mean! I just can't believe what you just . . . I mean . . . Why would you ask me that?

It is *not* a nose job. Jesus! Why would I need a . . . If you're implying what I think you are – I had a deviated septum . . . I couldn't breathe for Christ's sake . . . It's not a . . . a cosmetic thing! I mean nobody has EVER asked me that, in the whole ten years since . . . I mean, I've *never* been asked that.

Yes, I *do* resent it . . . I should think *so*.

Come back here!

I can trace my entire family back to the Huguenots you know!

No, I did not say *huge nose*, I said – oh, I get it . . . very funny . . . well, go ahead have a laugh at my expense . . . I suppose that's what they call Jewish humour, is it?

Memorials Are Made of This

I tottered out of another memorial service at the newly renovated St Martin-in-the-Fields church in Trafalgar Square recently, face streaked with mascara, shoulders braced against the inevitable biting wind, uplifted by laughter and strung out by memories. My chief concern was whether anyone would give me and my flimsy coat a lift to the nearest place where the stiff drinks were housed.

I don't know exactly how many such services I've attended this year, but I can tell you that it's five times the number of knees-ups. Clearly, my age makes me susceptible to losing friends and of course our children don't get married that often, nor do our friends have bar mitzvah-aged kids. Still, the ratio is chillingly unbalanced.

Last month it was a celebration of the life of the great comedy producer Geoffrey Perkins, struck down in Marylebone High Street on his way to a meeting with Anne Reid and myself about our show *Ladies of Letters*. The average age was, like Geoffrey's, early fifties and the stage was filled with his children and their friends talking about why they loved him so much. The 'show' featured songs and hilarious parodies from Angus Deayton, Clive Anderson, Paul Whitehouse and others, and though we laughed a lot, the pain in the room was palpable. I always have a moment of sheer fear that my tears are going to exacerbate to the point that I dehydrate and start to look like Benjamin Button at birth . . . 'No one ever said a bad word about Geoffrey,' said host Clive Anderson, 'and we don't intend to change that today.'

The present occasion was in memory of Sir Bill Cotton, a lovely man, former managing director of the BBC and one of its staunchest supporters. It was packed to the spire with hundreds of his devotees and when a soprano sang P. G. Wodehouse and Cole Porter's 'Just my Bill' from *Showboat* you could hear the teardrops hitting the pews. There is a wonderful monochrome stained-glass window above the altar, crafted by an Iranian woman, which is breathtaking in its simplicity, managing to look like Munch's *Scream*, the crucifixion and the human soul all in one abstract sweep.

The Ukulele Band of the UK stole the show with their rendition of 'Leaning on the Lamp Post' as it would have sounded in Stalinist Russia and Michael Grade was his usual witty and warm self – 'Bill and I went for a Chinese meal, whenever he was facing any kind of trouble,' he said, 'he preferred crispy duck to therapy' – until he suddenly fell silent, as the rising emotion in his chest forced his voice into a helium version of its former self. I recognized it well, from eulogizing at such occasions myself and nothing, but nothing – though you force yourself to think of dead puppies and massacred elephants – will stop the flow ... it was moving and tender, as though he was weeping for all of us.

I liked the story of Bill interrupting the *Eurovision Song Contest* dress rehearsal by storming into the producer's office with three angry, robed and turbaned figures, claiming that the Albanian entry *demanded* their song be heard! Now, Albania was not a part of the competition then and the producer was in a pool of diplomatic sweat until he recognized all four of the contestants as personnel from Bill's own office.

I never did a memorial for Jack because there were so many small tributes to him as the kids and I and groups of groupie Jack-lovers went round performing excerpts from his last autobiography *By Jack Rosenthal*. Still, one relishes the stories corroborating his benign, wry nature, when they come, and I relish talking about him and my late mother Zelma in public. Not every bereaved person enjoys such a privilege. Mostly, if a widow talks about the man with whom she shared most of her life, the most she can hope for, after a requisite period of mourning, is a parade of rolling eyes. Thank the Lord bereavement lets you down slowly, drip, drip, drip. The only advice

I would give to the widowed is listen to nobody's advice. The best advice you can give is to the friends of the bereaved: keep in touch, close touch, and after the first six months, keep in even closer touch.

And That's Jazz

An aficionado I ain't, but I know what I like and I liked Johnny and Cleo Dankworth. I have a trumpet in my study because of him, although I gave up lessons – in spite of my teacher telling me I had a good lip – and I can do a passable impersonation of Cleo singing the first two lines of 'If We Lived on the Top of a Mountain'.

I set out for their eightieth birthday concert, though, filled with trepidation, but that was because it was at the Barbican and I've never mastered Barbicongestion. I was expecting heavy traffic, confusion and a latecomer's seat behind a pillar. Instead, the journey was a doddle, the parking likewise, and the concert? Well, sometimes, music is the only language where I can really trust the words.

The audience became one body and I was the snapping finger on its left hand. Johnny may have looked his years when he came on stage but when he lifted his baton to conduct the London Symphony Orchestra and a jazz combo which included his son Alex on double bass, he morphed into a springy adolescent.

I like to watch musicians. They seem to be at home in their skins as the French say, in French. Their concentration is total and their lack of self-consciousness pleases me, and naturally I don't have to battle that familiar 'I could've done that part only better' feeling. The dame herself, dressed in a vibrant turquoise, moved me deeply with a song called 'He Was the One'. Her velour vocals have improved like fine muscat.

The Dankworths have done so much to promote all kinds of music and their theatre and music school, built at their home in Wavendon, Milton Keynes, has become the beating heart of fusion music and music with words too, because they are both great exponents of all kinds of literature.

So this February, I was delighted to be asked to contribute to the celebrations for the fortieth anniversary of the Stables Theatre. I rustled up a couple of Joyce Grenfell sketches which have always stood me in good stead: a short song called 'Hymn', and a sketch about a white woman on her first flight to America to meet her black daughter-in-law. It's a poignant and funny piece and one of Joyce's favourites – as was Cleo. They often performed together on musical occasions and the two couples were fond of each other.

I arrived in Milton Keynes, courtesy of Timothy West and Prunella Scales, old colleagues, and met up with other actors and musicians, all in Sunday mufti and wondering how they'd manage with no rehearsal. We all knew that Johnny was in hospital but the rumour was that he was being allowed out for the concert. We went through our sound checks on stage, I sang through with Laurie Holloway at the piano and we all waited for Cleo and daughter Jacqui to arrive.

When they did, it was clear that something momentous had happened.

Leaning on a stick, looking drawn, Cleo told us that they had been called in to the hospital that morning because Johnny's health had deteriorated.

'We got there as soon as we could,' she said, looking at the carpet and tightening her lips, 'but, sadly . . . it was too late.' She paused, righted herself and said, 'We lost him.'

It was one of those moments which etches itself onto your soul like a birth. Jacqui was quietly weeping.

'I'm not going to cry,' Cleo continued, 'I'll let Jacqui do that for me.' Another giant pause, then, 'We're going to do the show because that's what Johnny would want. We won't tell the audience. There's no point. They need to enjoy the show. Thank you all for being here. Now let's get on with it.'

She limped off into the theatre itself to rehearse. We all stood there in shock, then slowly followed her in, to watch her rehearse.

With a tender guitar player beside her she launched into, 'In this world, of ordinary people, extraordinary people, I'm glad there was you'.

It was painfully sad. All the more so because of her *truly* out of the ordinary resilience. The rehearsal went sombrely on, we munched a sandwich and drank tea as the audience began to arrive. Then, we changed our clothes in dressing rooms and loos, and, in my case, panicked that I'd chosen the wrong pieces and would offend Cleo.

The show was terrific of course. It was musically full of surprises with poetry and jazz and classical pieces, romantic ballads and Cleo's jazz version of the Shakespearian sonnet, 'Shall I Compare Thee to a Summer's Day?' I don't know how she and Jacqui and Alex Dankworth managed it, but it was an evening of sheer joy for the audience and real admiration for the rest of us. At the end, all the performers joined Cleo on stage for 'I Got Rhythm'. Then, interrupting the tumultuous applause, she took a step forward and said, 'Johnny wanted so much to be here tonight, but sadly for all of us, he passed away this morning. He wouldn't have wanted it to spoil the music for you.' The audience was stunned into silence. She thanked all the contributors and wished everyone a safe trip home. It was too much for me. My sense of the occasion was overwhelming. I took the mike and said the words that we all knew needed to be said: 'It has been a privilege,' I stuttered, 'and I don't think any of us will ever see a greater act of courage than we have seen from this family tonight.' The audience then gave them a standing ovation that couldn't come near what they deserved.

I got home at 12.45 a.m. and sat down to write this. I knew that I would forget its significance otherwise. After 200 words I found myself weeping and went to bed. At ten the next morning I went back to the typewriter. The phone rang. It was Valerie Grove, *The Times* journalist, a good friend.

'Mo,' she said in her Northumberland lilt, 'were you there last night? It must have been incredible.'

I tried to tell her exactly what it had been like but it was all so fresh that I choked up.

'Mo, you've got to write it,' she said.

'I know,' I sighed, 'but I can't. I'm speaking at a shul in Croydon and I've got to leave in an hour – I don't really know where Croydon is.'

'I'm going to ring *The Times* desk,' she said, 'you can dictate it.'

'No . . . it'll be all misquoted and I'll sound like I'm getting off on it and . . .'

Too late, she was already dialling.

Well, a young woman rang, I did dictate it and she reproduced it perfectly the next day, exactly as I'd felt it. This is it:

The Times 8 February 2010

There could have been no better tribute to Johnny Dankworth.

'It is what he would have wanted.' That's the cliché people use. Well, the cliché was newly minted on Saturday night. We had arrived, ready to celebrate the 40th anniversary of the Stables, the entertainment venue founded by Cleo and John at their Buckinghamshire home. It became a celebration of so much more. As ever, John's timing was exemplary.

We – actors, musicians, poets and friends of the family – were backstage, preparing to perform when Cleo and Jacqui (their daughter) returned from hospital. Cleo looked like an ageless icon.

She told us she had sad news: John had passed. He would have wanted us to go on, she said. The decision had been made – the 400-strong audience were not to know until the end of the concert. 'We don't want a wake, we want a celebration.' She would 'do her crying' later.

And so the show went on. Victoria Wood sang, Paul O'Grady entertained. I performed two pieces.

Accompanied only by a single guitarist, Cleo sang a beautiful song. Jacqui performed a piece close to her father's heart, telling the audience: 'Dad always liked this,' before correcting herself, keeping him in the present tense a little longer. For the rest of us backstage there was this knowledge that made it so poignant. The family went on, and the audience didn't know a thing was wrong.

It was not until the finale that Cleo told them: 'Johnny was very sorry he couldn't make it.'

The man whose music we were celebrating, and whose photographs were all around, had died. The whole audience just gasped. It just broke the place apart. People were shocked. They were shocked, first, that he had died, then they were simply staggered as they realized the whole family had just performed in the knowledge that their soulmate had gone.

Never have I seen a more valiant act of love than the one I saw that night. If Johnny had been there in a wheelchair, there would have been a strange sense of morbidity. Instead, he had never been so present. His music, his photographs were everywhere. It was swamped in feeling.

When a tenor sax player played one of Johnny's compositions, it was just as if he were channelling, quite frankly.

Every single aspect of the business he loved was at that concert. There were quiet moments, rowdy songs, rock, poetry, music, song. There was sentiment but no sentimentality.

Everything was exactly as John would have liked it. It was a rare privilege to witness, and to have been part of. We come, we go, and with a bit of luck, we leave something behind.

Johnny was a wonderful man, and in the end, music was the winner. There could not have been a better tribute. There will be others, but there won't be one like that.

'It is what he would have wanted.'

I went back to Wavendon for the memorial concert in Johnny's name. Again, it moved me tremendously, especially Jacqui Dankworth singing a song she had written to her dad's music. There was a beautiful picture of Johnny on the back wall and his spirit and ours just soared.

That night, because Cleo and Joyce had been friends, I decided that Wavendon was where we should try out *Mrs Grenfell and Miss Ruth* (titled, My Name With Yours).

The Wavendon audience is used to prose and poetry and music together. The seating is on three sides and rises to embrace the performer. And jazz audiences are used to the odd improvised slip-up. I think that Joyce, a hundred years after her birth, would have been tickled a rosy hue to hear the belly laughs her and Ruth's exquisite

material received that balmy night in July. I was incredibly nervous,
fluffed a few lines and felt I'd let myself down, but they gave Jane
Bower (playing Ruth) and me a standing ovation, and there is a show
there waiting to be seen.

Ladies of Letters

I had heard the radio series *Ladies of Letters* over the years in my fixed position as a passionate lover of Radio 4 and, aside from the performances by Prunella Scales and Patricia Routledge, two comediennes at the height of their power and expertise, it had never penetrated my inner fan, the one which makes one actually stop typing, poking bristly things down the loo or pretending to use the Power Plate, and makes one sit down to listen, feet up, with a cup of Ethiopian and a big grin.

So when, in 2008, Geoffrey Perkins, the late, great head of comedy at the BBC, then at Tiger Aspect TV and the man who brought us *The Hitchhiker's Guide to the Galaxy*, *The Fast Show*, *The Paul Whitehouse Experience* and – well, almost everything you've ever laughed at in the last twenty years – suggested serializing the original books for television, I was in two minds. One mind said, 'A sitcom with a starring role? At my time of life? Yessss!' The other mind said, 'This is entirely *literary* material – two women *writing* snail-mail to each other, for pity's sake! What will viewers, used to interaction with a red button on TV, helicopters arriving on stage, blue bottoms whizzing through a 3D fourth dimension and talking *owls* on film possibly make of two solitary women putting stamps on letters, talking about their appalling children and their thread veins? What's more, with postal strikes in the offing!'

Geoffrey was adamant and Geoffrey, adamant, was entirely

infectious. He was of small stature and had a youthful, mischievous face, which belied his enormous intelligence. I would be twinned, he told me, with Anne Reid, glorious Annie, of *Dinnerladies*, *In Love With Barbara*, and the controversial Roger Michell film *The Mother*. She was to be Vera Small, the louche, fluffy, ditsy one and I would be Irene Spencer, the one with the permanent poker up her jacksy. No surprises there then.

Many years ago, Julia McKenzie and I had waged civilized but attritional war over which of us would play Mrs Sherlock Holmes and which Mrs Watson, in a series devised by my late husband. Sitting in my living room, thin-faced, long-nosed, beady-eyed, slightly psychic, occasional smoker, I didn't think there was much of a decision to be made, but on such delusions do red-light projects stand and fall and, because neither of us wanted to be Watson, this one fell. Thankfully, Jules and I remained good friends.

Actually, it was the second time we'd disagreed about roles, the first being the original 1982 stage play of *Outside Edge*, a comedy by Richard Harris about amateur cricket. Jules and I had both been sent the script, both loved it and both chosen to play the same part – Miriam, the wife of the captain – a fact we both revealed at the Women of the Year luncheon, over the wall of two adjacent lavatories. Awkward.

As it turned out, on that occasion Jules was right to stick to her guns and Maggie, the aggressive, possum coat-wearing bricklayer lover of tiny Kevin the wicketkeeper, turned out to be a seminal role for me, one which I later recreated on television with Prunella Scales in the role of Miriam. Now, of course, Jules is enjoying success as Miss Marple, Ms Lumley is a goddess, Sue Johnston cleans up in all major TV roles over forty-five and one might almost think that, newsreaders aside, the older woman is thread-veining her way back into fashion.

Annie Reid and I went back even further than Jules and I. In 1969 I joined the company which started at Granada Television as the Stables Theatre Company. The discarded stables in a tiny street behind Granada was the site of the first attempt to produce small-scale new plays for predigestion before they appeared on television. It was a bold experiment, which ultimately failed, but which attracted much local and national attention and spawned a truly good permanent group of actors. It also brought me face to face with the man I loved for the next thirty-five years.

Jack Rosenthal was a scriptwriter, writing and producing his own series *The Dustbinmen*. He'd come from advertising into Granada on the first day it opened, working in promotions for nine pounds a week and thriving on the buzz of a new and thrilling adventure in northern television. He cut his writer's teeth on episode thirteen of *Coronation Street* and went on to write 200 episodes and produce many others. For me, the jigsaw was complete from our first date. I had my other half, my friend, my lover and my soul mate. We were partners in silliness . . . who barely stopped laughing for five years short of four decades.

At that time, Annie was playing Valerie, the wife of William Roache, still giving his Ken Barlow forty-one years and a plethora of wives later in the *Street*. Very fine she was too. Her partner in life was Granada's head of drama Peter Eckersley, and Jack and Peter shared an office and a second-to-none sense of humour. Peter used to remark dryly that they were going to shoot an episode of *Disappearing World* – in his office. At lunchtime, Margaret, their joint secretary, would play 'Zorba's Dance' on the Dancette record player and teach two left-footed men Greek dancing.

Annie recalled first meeting me in the Stables bar, and, later, as I was new in town, taking me out for dinner. In her words: 'You were this hippy girl in tinted glasses and afro hair with floor-length flowing clothes and beads and scarves and bells, and I was this plump Mancunian actress in a long-running series. You said, "Oh, it's going to be sooo fab! I'm going to start poetry groups and improvisation evenings and street theatre . . ." and I just sat there thinking, Oh *God*, I feel old.'

There were few opportunities to reminisce, though, as we packed in fittings and make-up sessions and sitting in on script conferences and readings and re-readings. The nature of the series is that the women write letters but rarely meet face to face. When they do, which tends to be only once per series, it's a disaster. They get vilely drunk and abusive and have nothing in common but envy. As the scripts trickled in from Lou Wakefield and Carole Hayman, who write an episode each then confer, the actual learning time got shorter and shorter. As deadlines appeared on further changes, it slowly dawned on us that, for Annie and me, whole days would be spent in front of camera, *alone*.

I had done enough monologues and one-woman shows for this not to make me overly blanch, but I don't think either of us, or indeed anyone on the shoot, could envisage how hard it might be to be alone on camera for days at a stretch without the rehearsal time one would expect in a play. No rehearsal time in fact. One week to go through changes with director John Henderson then straight on the set at 7 a.m., in character and committing the performance to high-definition film. Ten 22-minute episodes to be shot in six weeks. We had to shoot at least ten minutes of film a day. Learning time? With a combined age of roughly – very roughly, I'd like to stay on speaking terms with my co-star – 135 years, who needs it?

Then just as the scripts were being finalized, a couple of weeks before shooting commenced, the unthinkable happened. Annie, John Henderson and I were in a script meeting at Tiger Aspect TV in Soho, waiting for Geoffrey Perkins to arrive, when someone poked a head round the door and asked if John could step out for a moment. Something in her tone alerted us that this was serious and when John failed to return for longer than seemed appropriate for a query, we became a bit uncomfortable.

When he did return it was with an ashen face. There had been an accident. No one knew the circumstances, nor the extent of the injury, but Geoffrey Perkins, on his way to the meeting, had been mown down by a lorry, in Marylebone High Street. Wobbly, we drank too much lukewarm tea, waiting for more news, then slowly put on our coats, picked up our scripts and numbly made our way to our homes. There are some things that simply cannot be absorbed in a sitting.

There was an outpouring of grief when the news came that he had actually collapsed in front of the lorry and died. Heart attack we think. A young man, at the peak of his powers, married with two young kids. Richard Beckinsale, Philip Sayer, Diane Bull, Susan Littler, Katrin Cartlidge . . . Stephen Gately . . . all the other senseless deaths come back to warn us that we should live every day as if it was our last. Hundreds of his friends and colleagues gathered, stunned, in the foyer of the Drury Lane Theatre the next day, just to have a drink and hang about with his mates and his memory.

He remains massively lamented and his unique perception is irreplaceable. Matthew Francis, former director and administrator of the Greenwich Theatre, also known to me as Francis Matthews (I still have him in my phone book under both F and M. Good job his first name didn't begin with S, now I come to think) was drafted in as our new producer, with a mere fortnight to understand the brief, absorb all the requests for cuts and changes from different sources, get to know the writers Lou and Carole, who are feisty and colourful feminists, supervise the locations on a budget of gumfpence from ITV3 (who them, then?) and find disparate and hellishly cheap locations. In winter. To his absolute credit he did the job calmly, jokily and well, with nary a whinge, and has just gone and done it all over again.

The day before I began my first full day I realized that my hair was too funky for Mrs Spencer. Don't ask me why it took so long for me to realize this. Suffice to say that Pedro, Julia Mc's hairdresser of twenty-five years, lives round the corner and was drafted in to colour mousse my tawny locks down into a brown block, we left the regrowth grey sideboards au naturelle and Irene Spencer was born.

Nats was out of London, in Norway, for almost my entire shoot, working as standby art director on a film with Lauren Bacall and Brian Cox, for which, incidentally, some two years later, she and the rest of the crew remain half paid. Diva would have to learn to be a show-biz gypsy like the rest of us. Unfortunately, she had developed a night-owl disposition, owing to my theatre timetable, so she seldom rose before 10.30 . . . and then only for a cup of tea and some fresh coconut if there was any around.

Now she would have to learn to be a Winnebago dweller. Worried by this prospect I called Julia, a zany actress who had played my daughter in a film and was temporarily working in antiques, and she agreed to hear lines and dog-sit for the duration. It proved a tougher task than she had envisaged. She enjoyed the line testing, and was particularly invaluable to Annie, who found glancing at the lines on a distant monitor an impossibility and likes to speak them out loud to someone. I learn my lines on tape and developed a swivel-eyed tic into my characterization, making me look like George Cole in an early St Trinian's film. My requirements, therefore, were much more canine-oriented and not nearly so interesting to a young actress wanting to learn all about film making from behind the camera.

Needless to say, my young actress friend, wanting to be on the set all day, found Diva unrewarding work and told me so as kindly as she could. Working a twelve-hour day, I responded in kind, saying that there was bugger-all I could do about it and she'd just have to get on with it. Diva responded precisely as her name suggests she might, whimpering when left, yodelling through several takes and chewing the scenery. On one occasion, when I had to work late, I asked Julia to drive the dog home, where my nephew was waiting to dog-sit. As they arrived at the terrace Diva leaped up and down with glee, and so distracted poor Julia that she pressed the accelerator rather than the brake and drove her gorgeous Figaro straight into the front wall of my house. I was mortified, so was she and the damage was immense, both to her car and our friendship.

By the second series, Nats had given up the uncertain world of props and set design and was working full time as my PA, spending her mornings apologizing for me when I said I would be there and wasn't, and her afternoons happily racing round the parks and heaths of London with a pocket full of poo-bags, bits of liver cake and her best four-footed friend. Sighs of relief all round. A dog is for life not just for charisma.

As for *Ladies of Letters* it went out on ITV3 in 2009 with good pre-publicity and played ten episodes without much fanfare but, somehow, it seemed to catch on. It was hard to pigeonhole. It was wry, anarchic and unexpected and proper people, who generally wander up and down 200 channels without finding a single thing to watch, found it and liked it. It didn't patronize them. Quietly, we built up a following.

Then ITV decided, in their dotage – I think I mean wisdom but when did I ever fail to bite the hand that feeds me? – to take only the first six of the ten episodic episodes and show them on ITV1. It was better than a kick in the eye with a soapy Ugg boot but the schedulers could have served the show and the viewers better if they had used their formidable intellect and at least kept the story running and complete until the end. Hey, times are hard, the recession and changing forms of viewing have narrowed the habits of the faithful, and ITV has suffered from advertising belt tightening and, hey, we were given a second series – though, optimistic to the point of insanity, on an even tighter budget.

The show was nominated for the Comedy Awards, for best new sitcom, and I spent one of the more discomfited nights of my life enduring that little piece of purgatory. The event was held at the LWT Studios on London's South Bank. I used to work there a lot in the olden days, before butter was bad for you, and am as baffled by its meandering corridors as ever I was in the days of my comedy series *Agony*. The studio was very cold and goose pimples and mottled legs were as de rigueur as one-shoulder dresses and Kabuki shoes.

We *comical* people were greeted on arrival by a Perspex picnic plate – square, as befits trendy dining plates these days – with self-sealing lid, beneath which lurked what can only be described as a budget-airline snack dinner. I took out my mobile phone and photographed it to show to any people whose ambition it is to be famous. Inside were two lumpen samosas, one stale sausage roll, six knobbly breadsticks and a toad in the hole. Cold.

Vaguely, I recalled the previous year's Comedy Awards where the entire event dwindled into a food-throwing bash. Now I knew why. It's a funny thing – well, no, actually it is *not* a funny thing – but if you put together a roomful of comedians, and hungry ones at that, you can pretty well guarantee there won't be titter all night long. Instead there'll be tangible malignancy. Such was my experience of the event, sandwiched as I was between two lady writers who alternated between saying, 'Fucking boys' club, this is!' and 'I've got to get out of here and pick up my wife'. Jonathan Ross did what he does, i.e. make the best of poor scriptwriting, resorting to, 'I told 'em you wouldn't get that one – hardly got it myself' throwaways.

Know your audience is a lesson I've learned the hard way. As a young actress in demand for Jewish functions, I quickly found out that telling fond stories of my dad's tailoring shop in Hull went down a treat at Mill Hill Synagogue but fared worse than a pig's trotter at a meeting of elegant intellectuals raising money for an institute for stem-cell research in the Negev desert. It's hard to make professionals laugh. We've heard it all before . . . so if the topical stuff is weedy then why not just forget it, be sincere and get on with the prizes. I always joke that I travel with an acceptance speech in my pocket, even if I haven't been nominated. I'm half serious. If you're down to a final shortlist, if the papers have printed your name, if the camera is going to loom large on your good-loser grin, then why not gild the lily with a few well-chosen words writ large on a stiff card? It truly will not blight your chances of winning. Of course, no one can anticipate how nerves will stun you into paralysis, but that's where the stiff card comes in handy – and that's also where the censorship button in your mind should spring into action.

On the night of the Comedy Awards *Ladies* didn't win Best New Comedy but honestly and truthfully it wouldn't have been much better if we had. I remember journeys home from Bafta ceremonies with Jack, where we drove in silence, clutching either an award or a grievance, and the feeling was pretty much the same. A sort of hole in the gut from excess of supreme of chicken, self-deprecation, rictus grins and boned underwear. I've looked at clouds from both sides now – but I've also been on the panels. I sort of know how it works. A portrayal of any kind of disability will win. A person who's suffered a public divorce or bereavement will win. A straight person playing a homosexual will win. Anything too populist will not win – see under J. K. Rowling and *Avatar*. Actually, this year's Bafta and Oscars too were a crossroads in the history of film. At the post were the two directions in which movies could or should go. In the red corner, there was *The Hurt Locker*, an intense nail biter about bomb-disposal soldiers in Iraq and Afghanistan. Beautifully directed, cost a minimal amount, was acted by unknowns with spare truthfulness and was thought-provoking and topical. In the blue corner there was 15 million pounds' worth of blue-screen technology, computer-generated creatures from an alien CGI world, a couple of well-known actors yes, but not big salaries to pay and no awkward agents complaining that their clients won't countenance blue boobs.

In the event, neither film bombed, but the bomb-disposal film, rightly in my opinion, took home the Oscar. The ladies and gentlemen of Letters got it right, and actors everywhere breathed a sigh of reprieval.

Shut Up

A shutter and blind company are flooding my mail box and infiltrating my magazines. I won't name them because further publicity will only buy them more louvres, but it's not unrelated to Mr Clinton, ex-president of the United States – the one they called Sex between the Bushes . . . and, as it happens I still need two sets of shutters for the front bedrooms of my flat. I love shutters. They please me. They are functional and stylish and they do the job. I love them on old French chateaux in dusty celadon and I love them in faded green on my kitchen French windows.

It's these people who make them and purport to sell them who worry me. Sweeping generalization, I know, but the lofty woman who came to examine my faulty living-room shutters looked so far down her nose at me that I began to retreat into *Wallace and Gromit* speak, in defence.

'I'm afraid these shutters aren't really designed to be opened,' she Sloaned, flicking a piece of freshly striped hair back from her cashmere gilet.

'B-b-but . . . they're shutters . . .' I mumbled. 'Shutters are meant to open as well as . . . shut, aren't they?'

'Slats . . . Yah.'

For a minute I thought she was referring to my limitations as a housewife.

'One simply opens the slats to let in the light, yah?'

In my simple mindedness, I mumbled, 'Yebut . . . I mean, I see that . . . of course . . . but I like to look out.'

She looked from me to the outside courtyard as though I'd suggested a viewing of the London sewers by night. The courtyard looked back, empty of foliage, deadheaded of flowers, empty plant pots stuffed with half-eaten hay, practically signposted with the words, 'This way to the rabbit.'

Warren lives in the courtyard. He's an apricot velvet rabbit and his pod and run cost more than my parents' first home in Hull. Sadly the pigeons who circle above are not into real estate so they use it as an aerial toilet. We could run a small car on the amount they produce. I sort of took her point, except her point was not my concern. Ugly and unkempt my courtyard might be, but a blind man would be glad to look at it.

Which brings me back to the blinds. Because of this other shutter company's attitude, I followed up the trail of brochures in my mail and arranged for a fitter to come and advise on whether shutters could be fitted in an irregular space or whether I should have blinds instead.

We make an appointment in three weeks, which is the first time they have a man in the area. We swap numbers and addresses and I do the cute business about the flat being surrounded by scaffolding and skips and, needless to say, the fitter gets lost and never makes it here. A week later, at the second attempt, we fare better. The fitter arrives and studies the windows of both rooms, then sheepishly informs me that he's only started working for the company that day and he isn't yet qualified to measure for shutters, only blinds. He's a nice man so I don't hit him round the head with a rolled-up copy of the blind brochure, but ask him to phone a man who does. Which he does and an appointment is made for Monday.

Which, believe it or not, is kept. On time. Nice man. Measures up, advises, shows samples . . . will go away and send me an estimate for both blinds and shutters in a day or two. Whehey! He has a cup of tea and a chat about stuff he's seen me in over the years and he leaves and I never hear from him again.

I'm thinking nostalgically of white net curtains. *Frilly* white lace curtains. What's more, the kind that twitch nervously whenever her over t'road has a gentleman caller in a beige Austin Princess at three in t'afternoon.

Disco Must Go On

It's a grand life in the British theatre if your knees don't weaken and your brain cells don't reduce. I have the good fortune, in these days of disproportionate response and crunchy credit, to be in a HIT MUSICAL, *A Little Night Music*, at the Menier Chocolate Factory in Southwark Street. It's not quite Broadway, let alone the West End – I share my dressing room with seven pert-breasted twenty-seven-year-olds and a mouse with attitude, but the show sizzles with success and, right now, you'd have to hold one of my children to ransom to get a ticket.

The audience and the actors are very close to each other to the extent that they occasionally mingle and swap small talk. The proximity can be quite magical when a gorgeous blonde is singing 'Send in the Clowns' but it can be disturbing when members of the audience think they are in their own living room, or worse . . . A friend asked me what glue they used on my face to make me look so old and 'puckered'. I had to tell her that I was using a Shu Uemura powder base and the 'puckering' she'd seen was merely my own puckers, in close-up.

In my role as the elderly courtesan, Madame Armfeldt, I was sitting in my wheelchair in the wings waiting for my entrance. I say *wings* advisedly, meaning the two feet of curtained-off space between the stage and the rucksacks and sprawled Ugg boots in front of the front row. One night, for reasons later revealed to be not unconnected with alcohol, a white-haired member of the audience staggered to his feet, crossed the stage to the strains of Sondheim's dark and edgy lyric 'Every Day a Little Death', parted the velvet curtains and, with a hint of bravado, peed slowly into the wings.

It was bad enough for the audience but picture it from *my* point of view. For a minute I wondered if, unbeknown to me, some sort of puppetry had been inserted into the show . . . with sound effects. At the interval, the stage management, having cleaned and disinfected the area, politely asked him to leave as he stood at the bar attempting to order a beer. He was affronted at their audacity and made a noisy fuss all the way out of the building.

If you're thinking it couldn't get worse, you should have been in the house on Tuesday, when the disco across the alleyway held a private party. They do try to keep the noise down generally when we are performing, aware of the fact that gangster rap and nineteenth-century Swedish comedy of manners go together like marzipan and anchovies, but on this occasion the tiny theatre was vibrating with heavy bass and the merrymakers were whooping it up outside the venue, with Eminem's dulcet tones turning our delicate Mozartian operetta into 'A Little Fight Music'.

At the interval, I stormed out of the building, in full black crinoline and white pompadour wig, and through their open doors.

'What in hell's name is going on here?' I shrieked imperiously, oblivious to the effect my white face and ghostly apparel might have on the strappy stroppy teenagers before me. 'We're trying to do a period piece in that theatre and we can't hear ourselves think!'

They stared at me indifferently as the music ground relentlessly on.

I continued, 'Whose party is it?'

With pitying looks they informed me that this was the launch party for the new series of *Skins* – the explicit, cult TV show for teenagers. The sound of wind dropping out of sails was suddenly louder than the throb of guitars.

'Oh, my God,' I breathed, '*I'm* in that.'

(I'd accepted the part without reading the script on the strength of the stage directions on the first page: 'Auntie enters abseiling down a twenty-foot tree carrying a massive chain saw.')

However, whatever street-cred I might have earned through my episode vanished, in the very street I was standing on, dressed as a dying courtesan.

The realization came that this party was one I'd been invited to, but of course refused, on the grounds that I would be playing in a musical that night. I walked the ten metres back to Sondheim's Sweden, firmly accompanied by a giant security guard in luminous day-glo, wondering whether the fun would be over by the time *Little Night Music* finished so that I could pop in for a stately bop.

An abseiling grandma, a lady of letters, a nineteenth-century courtesan and a coffee-morning chat at a care home with a beautiful woman in her 106th year, who couldn't stop to talk because she was on her way to a bridge game. How lucky am I?

P.S. I abseiled with elan down the 20 foot tree and seamlessly removed my dungarees, revealing a simple but fetching house dress, prattling on throughout. It was great. They cut it.

Awards

This year's Bafta awards came and went and, since *Ladies of Letters* was seen by few people on ITV3, it didn't make even the long list. Annie and I were not invited to the event by the host company, Tiger Aspect, or by ITV3. I had never before fully understood that the production company actually has to pay a fee to nominate a show or performer.

Of course, we could have bought tickets and cruised down there, in pleated silk and too much blusher, but we decided against it. John Henderson and his hand-crafted crew were not going nor our writers, Carole Hayman and Lou Wakefield, or producer Francis Matthews. I looked at the photos the next day of Julie Walters in her leggings, Lynda Bellingham, possibly in a rubber dress, and Jordan in in a dress made of black ice, and felt just fine.

Still, soooo much work to make the show look easy and come in under budget and be funny and daring and different, and then it was as if we'd never been. The powers that for-the-moment-be in scheduling took the decision to put out episodes one to five in April and six to ten in October, thus spanning two financial years but leaving my character, Irene, in Australia, strapped to a bed in a strait jacket, having been sectioned by her daughter. That was not so much a cliff-hanger as a blithe walk across the Grand Canyon.

Instead of having my toes bleached and my hands henna'd therefore, I spent the day opening the Sir Nigel Hawthorne wing at the Garden Hospice in Letchworth in the morning, and judging the Stephen Sondheim Young Performer competition at the Queen's Theatre, Shaftesbury Avenue, in the afternoon. Both events filled me with a sweet, sad joy.

I unveiled a portrait of Nigel, painted by his partner, Trevor Bentham, and talked to the audience about my memories of him. I recollected how he was beaten to an Oscar by Tom Hanks for – oh, can you bear it – *Forrest Gump*, and how he was cruelly outed by the fiendish press after quietly living with Trevor for twenty years and despised by critics for his King Lear. We are not allowed hubris. Even Moses had to pack it all in before he ever saw the Promised Land.

In spite of myself, I found myself choking up and the audience joined me. I met cancer sufferers who were held in the arms of the hospice movement's creed and who spoke with such humour and fervour about its contribution to their survival. Cicely Saunders, the founder of the hospice movement, was, for me, the greatest hero-ine of the twentieth century. I wish more people could see what goes on in these airy light-filled rooms to elevate people's quality of life. Sadly we only see inside these places when we are in no state to do more than thank them. They are places of creativity, art, therapeutic relief and concentration on the individual. They do everything that the NHS was founded to do and simply cannot afford to do. In a mystifyingly cruel world, good and altruism is all around you.

Then a hot car ride to the Queen's Theatre where twelve young singers under the compère-ship of my chum Hannah Waddingham sang a Sondheim song, then a newly written musical sung to a cheering and wholly partisan full house. The talent was raw but daz-zling and the judging was made easy by the very last performer who showed us all how to do it and literally walked away with the prize. I had a drink with Julia McKenzie afterwards, and stood waiting for a cab home in St James. Finally, a car drew up with an elderly, olive-skinned gentleman in it who said, 'We met at the fiftieth reunion of Guido's and my English school in Egypt. Would you like a lift?'

With nary a thought of strange men in cars or don't talk to strangers, I thanked him profusely and hauled my sandal-burned feet into his welcoming car. I went home and watched some really good acting by George Clooney, Tilda Swinton and Tom Wilkinson in that much undervalued film, *Michael Clayton*, nodded sagely and went, more contentedly, to my bed.

Daftas

I wrote the Daftas after reading a very good article by Valerie Grove in The Times *about the incoherent and often inarticulate speeches given by Bafta-winning recipients. I have a love–hate relationship with award ceremonies. I'm old enough to have been award-winning, award-giving, runner up and veteran loser. These four speeches represent four different kinds of actor and there are no prizes for the one who I think gets it most right.*

Daftas

(All the characters give their speeches slightly crouching into the mike.)

Emma

Your Royal Highness, Members of the Academy, ladies and gentlemen. *(Big sigh.)* Thank you to everyone who voted for me. Congratulations to my marvellous fellow nominees . . . I shall treasure this award for ever. I promise it won't be propping up my bathroom door . . . it is going on my bedside table so it's the first thing I see when I wake up in the morning . . . to remind me it's just the start of a lifetime of learning my craft. Thank you.

Josie

(Big sigh.) Err, ohhh, I can't believe it! I'm gobsmacked. I never expected . . . Oooh, hang on . . . If I'd known I wouldn't have had that second vodka – that's your fault Jules! *(Big laugh, reels about a bit hanging on to lectern.)* Er, anyway, erm, Shit . . . Sorry, erm. Righterm, well, thank you, erm thanks to er . . . Vivienne for this *amazing* frock you lent me – s'wicked and you're such a geezer and I'll be all right when I get these frigging shoes off . . . Christ. My mind's gone . . . er . . . Doug thanks for picking me . . . Oh yeah, producers Jean and Henny and my agent, Lynda, for believing in me . . . wharra part – I just loved playing it – and Doug for your patience and . . . let me get my head together . . . Er . . . Yeah, OK . . . Jonas for the clothes – we had a ball and thanks loads for letting me put my input in. And Jane – my mate Jane – for the amazing way you made me look once we'd agreed on the look. And Hot Goblin for the incredible catering, although them onion bahjees were probably not your best idea during the naked three in a bed scene . . . erm . . . Shit this is heavy; I'll have to put it down – Oops . . . Oh heck! Oh what am I like?

Where was I? Oh, yes, to Dominic my co-star. I know we didn't always see eye to eye, well, unless he were standing on a box that is. No, I'm joking. And to Greta who deserves this award as much as I do, and Abigail, and Sarah, and . . . er . . . Ricci and . . . er . . . the other Abigail and . . . Oh no! I've got to mention Chalky and the entire crew who were so brilliant . . . And that's it really. I hope I haven't missed anyone – I'm that stunned. So . . . er . . . well, thanks. Sinsherly . . . shinserely . . . shit . . . this is un bloody blievable.

(She starts to leave then reels round and grabs the mike again.)

Ooooh. Sorry, I forgot the most important person of all, m-m-my Baz. *(She starts to cry.)* I'm sorry. I'm really sorry. I couldn't have done this without you – you turned it all round for me – and my dog Lebowski who's a cross Staffie-collie rescue from Battersea and keeps me sane and sleeps in my trailer . . . And everyone at Tantric Sweat Yoga . . . This is for you!

(Turns and comes back again.)

Oh Christ! Did I mention whosit – the writer – Sir Thingy? . . . Whosit-doodah? S'tom Poddart . . . Pom Tossard . . . whatever . . . oh, bugger it . . . I'll get ICA to send him a tree. C'mon let's 'ave a Krug . . .

Samantha

Gosh. *(Big sigh.)* Thank you. Your Royal Highness, members of the committee . . . ladies and gentlemen, friends. This is an unexpected bonus at the end of a miraculous year and I'm so grateful to be rewarded in this way . . . by my peers. Thank you all.

(And about fucking time too.)

I feel incredibly grateful to the *extraordinary* team I had around me who really made this award possible. To be singled out from such a distinguished group of nominees is . . . un – be – lievable.

(Actually, I saw the Dame in the Coward, and she did what she always does, and Lord knows why big Brenda got nominated – she probably came across for Sir Christopher . . . eurgh!)

I want to thank Christopher, my brilliant director, for having the courage to cast me in the part of Fionola Fluke. I did my best to dissuade him from hiring me – I mentioned several actors more suited to an *extraordinary* role like this, but he was his usual intractable self and thank God for that. I owe you everything, Chris! *(Blows a kiss.)* And more.

(I pestered that clueless git for months to give me that part and he still made me audition three times.) Without his skilful direction and overall vision, none of us would have seen our way through the complexity – the – the – utter density – of Dermot's *extraordinary* text.

(It was such a crap script! We had to completely rewrite the second act. Dermot and Chris had a fist fight at the tech . . . and the actors cobbled it all together in the last week . . . Poor old Hester still hasn't the vaguest idea of her lines.)

And may I also thank the glorious Hester Dellapiano, who has supported me so magnificently and handed this performance to me like a shining baton. (*Blows another kiss.*) Your generosity to the next generation is . . . well . . . *extraordinary* . . . I hope, one day, that I will do the same with equal grace to some *much* younger actor.

(Look at the old bat . . . she's spitting tacks! She'll be throwing in lines from the *Tempest* tonight in the hedge-fund scene. Thank God for the Botox, you can't see how livid she is.)

May I take this opportunity to thank my wonderful husband, Danny, who keeps the home fires burning.

(And just lost half a million at Crockfords which I'll have to cough up or he'll slap me around and I'll have to tell the *Sun* we were having rough sex again.)

And, well, just everyone who believed in me, when I doubted that I could make this transition from a Manx shepherdess in *Emmerdale* to Fionola the bomb-disposal expert in a modern Irish classic.

And blessings to my fabulous agent Bunty Brown . . . for believing . . .

(Who I'm leaving on Monday for one of the biggies – so yah boo sucks Tight-arse! for advising me I should stay on in *Emmerdale* for another year.)

This is such a proud moment for me. Thank you. Thank you all.

(YESSSS!)

Sir Barry

This is totally unexpected. And terribly . . . moving. I thank you, honour you, praise you, worship you and love you. You know who you are. Not just my producers and co-workers but the little people – Jack, my dresser and Viv, box office, and Stan, marketing . . . and Yetta, my Serbian house cleaner . . . You who do the *real* work, so that we poor mummers can take wing and fly too near the sun. I honour you all.

I know you can see it coming . . . but I couldn't live with myself without mentioning that as we pop a piece of marinaded guinea fowl into our mouths or take that second sip of Louis Roederer Cristal, there are poor unfortunates cowering in the Balawaran Delta, millions of fly-infested, orphaned, abused . . . Balawarans with swollen stomachs, squatting in their own ordure in that other theatre – the theatre of war – who may never have heard of the Orange Pepsi Daftas. The only *award* in their miserable lives, would be a grain of maize or a piece of bubble wrap to act as a shelter for their nakedness.

In their stead therefore, and to that end . . . I would beg you to support our forthcoming, week-long, Chaucerthon – Yes, we will be reciting the complete *Canterbury Tales*, twenty-four seven, over the Bank Holiday weekend – in Middle English – in the underground car park of the Royal National, sponsored generously by Classic Caviar, the Mayfair Truffle Company, and Oysters Direct.

Just – be – there.

This is, for me, a *truly* . . . humbling moment in time. (*He puts his palms together and bows.*) Peace, love, Namaste. Bless you. Safe journey home and how fortunate we are to have one.

Happenstance in France

This August, after a punishing schedule of eight months in the musical, preceded by, indeed crossed over with, six weeks intensive filming for *Ladies of Letters*, Guido and I decided to head for Heathrow and a fortnight that was half Irish and half French. To that end we no-frilled it to Cork, and from there to friends in Skibbereen for a reunion. Because that proved unbeatable, we then took Eurostar from St Pancras, and headed off to stay with Bruce and Sarah Hyman in La Baule for a week, and then Guido said we'd need two days at least in Paris – he knows about these things – so we booked a small hotel on the net. Nats got us upgraded on Eurostar by dint of me promising to play the trumpet down the phone for the desk clerk. It seemed to work. I only played two scales and he agreed to give me anything I wanted.

Because my character, Mme Armfeldt, in *A Little Night Music* spent most of the play in a wheelchair, folk did tend to think the job was a bit of a pushover. Those of you who spend *real* time in a wheelchair will understand that it brings its own rain clouds. Occasionally, it would set off – mid song – towards the footlights, the brake having been left off, or it had disappeared entirely, removed for an emergency and Mme Armfeldt had to stage a miraculous recovery and hobble on clutching a servant.

Ireland is the most healing place I know. Rain or shine I get to Skibbereen and jump in the lough I've come to appreciate and shiver in whose name is Lough Hyne – pronounced Loch-ine, 'To Life' almost – and it really is the cup that clears. The hedgerows along the narrow roads are packed with fuchsia making overhead arches of flashing coral and around every bend in the road there is a view of verdant eternity, dotted with villages and towns whose houses seem to have been painted by tipsy fairies on a late-night bender. We spent three days with our friends, who are variously, Belgian, Italian, Filipino and Egyptian . . . I'm from Hull and – hey – you can't get more cosmopolitan than that!

The food was home grown and the chat round the table equally delicious. The taste of my first Guinness in an outdoor pub in Baltimore is exhilarating. I never drink beer in England, save the odd shandy up the curry house, so I have nothing to compare it with, but I still declare, hand on stomach, that Guinness *in* Ireland gets better every year.

For twelve years Jack and I always visited our friends the Beards in Skibbereen, so it is a tricky business introducing a new partner into the equation; but fortunately, Guido sits easy in his own skin and has a fund of traveller's tales and he was soon clasped hungrily to the family bosom. It's quite a relief when your old friends like your new ones. He was in recovery from a hip replacement so we didn't venture far, two steps forward one back but, like I say, you heal quicker under Irish skies.

The one day at home to smother, then apologize to my dog, and we headed off to St Pancras and Eurostar to see more friends in Brittany. We do sound like cheapskates, I know. What can I say? Denial is pointless. I wish I could return the compliment but, frankly, I find running one household a tribulation, let alone a second. It really is a relief for me to board a train, not a plane, even though from Paddington, where I now live, the trip to Heathrow is twenty minutes from door to terminal. St Pancras is astounding . . . a triumph of renovation – gleaming and helpful and the train ride still seems like magic to my non-engineering ears.

We changed trains at Gare du Nord with a lot of dragging of unnecessarily heavy cases down the Metro to Montparnasse and remorse was muttered out loud by limping and non-limping travellers. Still, clean linen and crisp food restored our bonhomie as we puttered along, dazzled by wheat fields and terracotta tiles towards St Nazaire, where my chum Bruce and a carload of kids picked us up and took us to their white beachside villa overlooking the very beach where Monsieur Hulot, with his stork-like walk, so achingly stalked out his territory.

Bruce and Sarah have four children under fourteen, three large golden retrievers, one called Umbrage – as in 'If I go into town, will you take umbrage?' – one black labradoodle who *thinks* he's a golden retriever, three cats of various hues, three hens ditto and three chicks, bronze and cream with gaucho pants of feathers down to their feet. The Atlantic was as chilling as had been Lough Hyne, maybe even more so because the Gulf Stream wanders in to the lough in patches. But boy, did it feel good when you came out!

This part of Brittany is like England must have been about seventy years ago. Coves of sand and rock, shallow water, nestling cliffs, hardly anyone on the beach but us and a few French families picnicking, of course, very well. Duck terrine, crusty French baguettes and cheese to die for, *vin ordinaire* and peaches and nectarines. No flashy monokinis or lycra thongs or Lulu Guinness beach bags, no casinos or designer deckchairs. Be still my heart.

Every day we walked along the coast road to St Marc's beach and had bowls of coffee and crisp croissants at the Hôtel du Plage and picked up *The Times* for the Sudoku . . . Guido, not me, I hate anything that makes me feel stupid. England felt very far away. At night we ate royally. Bruce made his steak Port Charlotte with basil sauce and his famed rice pudding ice cream and we waddled our way into our little guest house *D'Amis*, over the other side of the garden, where we watched *Colonel Blimp*, *Funny Face* and *Monsieur Hulot's Holiday* . . . and other such current cinema vérité, on their home-cinema screen.

Colonel Blimp! What an astounding piece of work that was . . . it has resounded in my mind ever since. The ultimate anti-war film and as fresh and poignant and eloquent as it was at the time. Roger Livesey, Anton Walbrook and the divine Deborah Kerr in three roles. As for *Hulot* – I'd never seen it! Imagine my joy from the first shot of people on a train platform hearing the impenetrable tannoy announce the train – then all scurrying down the stairs to reappear on another platform just as the train comes in on the original one. I started to bark with laughter and became incoherent and incontinent as it progressed. No, Mr Bean, they really don't make 'em like that any more.

Sadly, during our enchanted stay, one of the chicks, the male one, Jeremy, disappeared. There was no sign of a struggle, no feathers strewn, and it was tragic to see the other chicks and hens searching for him. Sarah was heartbroken. I suggested, like the good Jewish girl that I am, that we should all pray to St Anthony, the patron saint of lost things, and put some money in his box at the local church.

'Honestly, it always works for me,' I told them. 'When Adam lost his passport and was up all night searching the house I begged him to ask St Anthony and he just scoffed and continued turning his house upside down. Finally, the morning of his imminent departure, he gave in and dropped to his knees and sarcastically asked his help. About ten seconds later his phone rang and it was Jack, saying he'd found it in the household files.'

Meanwhile I painted Jeremy in watercolours, feathered trousers and all, and wrote, in my execrable franglais: 'Avez-vous vu ce poussin en pantaloons, qui s'appelle Jeremy?' We put it in Le Tabac and waited in vain for someone to respond, although in our heart of hearts we all knew he was probably happily shtupping chicklets on another mini-farm and singing '*Je ne regret rien*'.

After a truly hedonistic week we headed back for two final days in Paris, staying at a tiny hotel in Montparnasse. We had our first meal in Le Boeuf sur le Toit, where Cocteau and co. paid for foie gras with hastily dashed-off cartoons, then awoke early the next day to do Le Marais, the Jewish Quarter. The museum was fascinating – although I always hear the voice of my young son once saying in Israel, 'Do we *have* to see any more interesting things?'

On the way back, I stopped off in an artefact shop and, after much deliberation, bought myself a new menorah, in green glass, Deco style, because whenever Chanukkah comes around I forget that the one my late mother-in-law gave me has no middle holder and wobbles alarmingly. Guido disapproved of my choice on traditionalist grounds but I bought it anyway.

On the way back to the hotel, after a tasty Moroccan lunch, I suggested popping into Notre Dame, which was less crowded than it had been the previous day. After all, where better to have a word in St Anthony's ear about a missing chick? Surely he couldn't have bigger things on his mind than that? We settled, bags and baggage – watches made from coconuts, yoyos, baby clothes, menorah . . . you know, the usual tourist stuff – into chairs in the central aisle and I muttered a few prayers on the topic of desperate hens. Then we left.

Halfway across the mighty square I yelped, 'Menorah! I left the menorah! Hang on where you are!' and, feet zinging and throbbing from the long walk and the crumpled Elastoplast within the plim-solls, I hared it back into the cathedral and to my pew. The bag had vanished. I stopped the first small brown nun with a collecting tin I found.

'*Er . . . Je cherche . . . er . . . Je quittez l'eglise depuis cinq minute, mais le sac avec mon menorah est disparu . . . er . . . mon candelabra Juife? Je suis Juife mais . . . j'arrive parce que un petit poussin . . . oh . . . sod it – Pardonnez moi . . . je consult l'information.*'

Bidding a halting *merci* to the sister of . . . mercy, I did the whole rigmarole again for the main desk. They just stared . . . and stared . . . particularly when I got to the *poussin* bit which, needless to say I didn't need to say, but as I ground to a halting stop one of them handed me a form and I left my particulars, not forgetting to write down the wrong name of the hotel, and I rejoined Guido in the square. He was rather relieved the glass menorah was lost but was kind enough not to say so.

Before we left the magical city on Thursday, we had dinner halfway up Monsieur Eiffel's glorious tower and covered the Musée d'Orsay from top to triumphant tail. Then, exhausted but mellow, we tunnelled our way home. At Friday-night dinner with friends I regaled them with our Notre Dame story, to much laughter, and on Saturday morning, when Guido went off to shul, I told my daughter, Amy, all about it. She was laughing fit to bust when the phone rang. I picked it up to hear ecclesiastical music and a voice saying, ''Ello . . . 'ello? Madame Leepman? Here is Notre Dame calling. I sink we 'ave found your candle holder.'

'Sometimes,' as Tennessee Williams once memorably wrote, 'there is God so quickly.' I'll keep you posted on the Jeremy front. If he comes back we'll have a hen party.

I rang Bruce in considerable spirits. 'They found my menorah in the administration office, has your chicken come back?'

It hadn't, but St Anthony was obviously working on interfaith relations. Bruce agreed to pick up the menorah on his way over and bring it to Paddington. I waited with bated breath and cleaned one shelf of my display cabinet. The phone rang. It was Bruce. He'd gone to Notre Dame. They were mortified to admit that the menorah had vanished . . . nicked from Notre Dame! Again. Bizarre. What could anyone who visits Notre Dame *possibly* want from a menorah?

The good news is that Bruce and Sarah bought new chicks. Amy, Adam and Maureen. Apparently Maureen is *very* bossy.

There's No Such Thing As Happenstance

On Eurostar, coming back from Paris, a tall, dishevelled man in his late fifties sat in the adjacent seat and began, straightaway, plugging in his computer. There was something very familiar about him, although at first I couldn't place him. Then it came to me.

'Andrew?' I said quietly. 'Andrew Birkin?'

He turned and out of a slightly ravaged blur, emerged the face which had been so impossibly handsome when I'd last met him almost forty years ago.

'It *is* Maureen,' he said, 'I thought when I saw but – you didn't look old enough . . . I mean . . .'

I laughed. Andrew is a very successful screenwriter – *The Lost Boys* – and director – *The Cement Garden* – and of course we had observed each other's progress over the years, but hadn't met since 1969 when, after I'd appeared in the film *Up the Junction*, he had appeared at the door of my flat in Battersea to offer me a leading role in his script adaptation of Thomas Hardy's *Jude the Obscure*. He is the brother of actress Jane Birkin and the son of the actress Judy Campbell, for whom Noël Coward wrote 'A Nightingale Sang in Berkeley Square'.

He was impossibly glamorous and upper class and out of my league, but I seem to remember us getting on well. The film was never made and I don't think we met again. I did know the woman who later became his partner, Bea. She was a professional photographer, who once took a classic photo of me and my kids as a first-night present for Jack's adapted musical, *Bar Mitzvah Boy*. It showed the three of us dressed up as the characters. A tiny four-year-old Adam in a prayer shawl, a six-year-old Amy in a fur coat and hat and me in hat and suit, gloves, bag, clutching them both. I keep it in a frame in the hall, which is engraved in copper with the words, 'The only son'.

Bea was a good friend of my old drama school chum, Lesley Joseph . . . in fact Lesley and I had been sharing a flat when Andrew came to call, twenty-five years before he met Bea. Are you keeping up? Sorry, it's complex I know. Bea was at that time married. I knew she'd then lived with Andrew and was saddened to hear from friends of the death of their beautiful son, Anno, aged twenty, in a car crash some years ago.

It was good to see Andrew and we passed the journey convivially. He talked about Anno, of course, and showed me a book of his prodigiously gifted poems. They almost seemed to anticipate his early demise. Bea and Andrew are no longer together but it appeared they run a charity in Anno's name in Africa and I happily agreed to read one of the poems at a fund-raiser next month. We parted warmly; he promised to send me the book and that was that. The book duly arrived. Anno's verses were haunting. I resolved to read them as thoroughly as I could and put them by my bed. Poetry has to be chewed slowly like food.

A week later, I heard from Lesley Joseph. I was due to be on her weekly radio show and it was cancelled suddenly. She wasn't well. I got through to her and learned that she would be going to the London Clinic for surgery. I promised to visit and keep in touch every day. After the operation, all was well but she had developed the usual anaesthesia nightmare of a blocked system. I knew it only too well from Jack, we called it 'the morphine brick-up'. It's painful, and delays recovery.

I remembered what we used to do . . . Rhubarb! No pills, prunes, enema, laxatives. Just rhubarb – without the crumble, natch. The magic potion. I popped into Planet Organic and half an hour later it was all stewed up with honey and I was on my way to Devonshire Place with a small, warm, Tupperware box, nestling against – well what else would a girl need in hospital? – reading matter. In the hope that she hadn't read them, I grabbed the poems of Anno Birkin.

I parked near the hospital, went up in the lift, found Lesley's room and knocked on the door. She had a visitor. It was Bea, Anno's mother, just back from Africa. You couldn't have written it. We fell on each other and the coincidence – ignoring the patient entirely, who sat shovelling warm rhubarb into her mouth. I gave Bea a lift to my place and she saw again, for the first time in twenty-nine years, her evocative photo hung in my new apartment. The best part was the text that came through en route: 'Thanks, love. Two minutes after you left, the earth moved. Hooray! Lesley.'

Caviar Caveat

After *A Little Night Music* was nothing more than a lingering melody, my plan was to take off for Brittany and Monsieur Hulot's beach again for the New Year. Guido got flu and couldn't come so the children and I spent a delicious week being blown about, playing parlour games and eating as if food was a banned substance. I wanted to take my hosts some caviar and sought out a little Iranian shop in West Kensington, which, I remembered from Chichester badinage, Diana Rigg had mentioned was reasonable. The day was pitch black, the rain threw itself suicidally at my windscreen wipers and the dog was unhappy in her showerproof coat and would only stand rigidly to attention. 'I do not exist,' signalled her body language. I couldn't see the names of the shops through streaming windows and, as they all looked Middle Eastern, I went up and down more times than was strictly legal before parking in a side street. Then, holding flimsy brolly in one hand and seemingly stuffed dog in the other, I splashed my way towards the parade of shops.

The spectacles are trifocal these days, so in order to read the words on the awnings I had to tip my head back. Umbrella water, held in a bent spoke, hurtled down my spine, but the words 'Iranian caviar here' rendered the wet bra almost an asset. Bearing in mind the shopkeepers would be Muslims, I held the dog well outside with my toe, and called out my request for a small tin of caviar. The head-scarved woman looked petrified by my demand and said so in rapid

Persian to her male counterpart. He replied in kind and she took out a mobile and muttered into it at length. I thought of ringing Dame Diana and asking if she'd got me into this because she wanted me thrown into the back of a van and deported, but her number wasn't in any address book phone search. I was questioned in a low voice about size and a price was agreed. It was like asking for paid sex. It was indeed cheaper than Fortnum's, while still managing to be half a week's wages on the London Fringe.

Time passed. I bought some chervil while it did, as the dog pulled and shook, indignant about the rain and the coat and the sheer ignominy. Finally a man arrived and produced a small tin from inside his clothing. I wrote a cheque – this being in the days when you could still write a cheque! (I bloody love cheques. How I'm ever going to pay my PA and my cleaning lady and my alternative-health practitioners, eh? I shall be permanently at the cash machine and that's a waste of time because I'll have forgotten my pin number for the nineteenth time and be too embarrassed to ask the bank for it again.) Then I splattered my way back to the car. As I was separating the dog from the tin and the coat from the dog, I heard the patter of wet flip-flops and there was the young burka'd woman, wet and even more petrified.

'Please . . . I make mistake . . . my fault. I tell you wrong price.'

I love this one. It's called *celebrity inflation,* a condition which arises from being recognized 'off telly'. I protested that she had given me a price and that was agreed, and I'd paid her, but her eyes filled up with rain water and she repeatedly told me she would get 'terrible big trouble for big mistake'. I, stubborn and resolute as you know me to be, wrote out a cheque instantly, for the second half of the week in a London Fringe. Then I drove home.

Caviar caveat. I have to tell you that the treat turned out to be an enormous and rather magical triumph in Brittany. Like Queen Esther's oil lamps and Christ's fishes and loaves, this tin refused to empty. Twelve people had it with blinis, sour cream, chopped egg and onion on New Year's Eve. A few had it the next day for lunch and after our return home, Sarah phoned to say they'd just finished off the dregs with their croissants.

Endgame

Finally, we did it. We began filming series two of *Ladies of Letters*, with Irene's sudden exodus to Australia, hotly pursued by a thug Vera had hired to take out a contract on her friend's life. Australia was represented by a dampish house on a bend in the Thames in the Shepperton area. The family – poor souls, foolhardy enough to rent us their house, left to live with relatives for a couple of weeks, leaving a film crew, fifty strong, in inclement weather, to write off their home.

I'm not sure how desperate I would have to be to rent out my home to gaffers and sparks and actors and caterers, dogs, kids and honey wagons. There is a tale of one famous writer who let the forces of showbiz have her fabulous Mayfair penthouse with William Morris skylight and came home to find a fabulous Mayfair penthouse *without* a William Morris skylight. Oh yes. Some waggish propman had seen fit to give the bottles of champagne just *one* extra shake before the popping-cork sequence. Draughty night, big insurance claim and the end of a moderately successful marriage.

After Shepperton, the rest is a blur. Wake at 5.30 a.m. Tracksuit, boots. Car arrives, old-fashioned tape recorder drones over and over the scenes I learned last night, and takes me to a small cubicle, somewhere cold, three to a Winnebago, porridge, tea, shivering climb into whatever Aideen the costume designer leaves out for me. We begin filming with Irene roaring drunk in her daughter's house, alone with child, so – nighty, slippers, bedraggled robe – then over to make-up. Wild hair, blotchy skin, last night's mascara. Props give me an empty bottle, line up and rehearse alone in corridor with John Henderson and run through the words and actions.

Episode five, Irene, drunk and friendless in Oz, I reel back from the front door into the hallway and get picked up on camera one, crying and meandering from bathroom to bedroom to room, where there will be another camera so I can lurch into his lens and fall out again. John is meticulous in his direction, both encouraging me to be bold and stopping me from boldly going where no self-respecting *over* actor would dare to go. When we're both satisfied that the scene is real and funny and tragic, he calls in the crew to watch from their specialized points of view, which they solemnly do. If I get a laugh, ta, it's better than a Bafta.

'Shooting this time,' yells the first assistant, and off we go. We film it once. Good for camera, bad for sound – a plane went over. Second attempt – good for sound, good for me, bad for shot of grip in hall mirror. One more time not so good for me, I reverse two lines and stumble. Four times lucky works for all of us – print. I rush off, change into twinset and brooch for a scene on first arrival in Oz, neat, expectant, full of promise, writing bragging letter re male admirer to Vera as I unpack my case. Then, satisfied with the take, I'm sent to change my make-up. A few Carmen rollers are bobbed in, a car drives me back to the set and we run through the twenty-odd lines and actions which make up the scene. My stand-in does what her name implies she does as the lights are adjusted and I mumble my lines to myself while the Carmens are taken out. Someone brings me a hot drink . . . we have sensational caterers called Hot Goblin and the thought of their exquisitely stacked lunch table is never far from my mind.

'How far is it from lunch?' I ask, plaintively.

It's 9.20 a.m. and I feel as though I've done a full day's work. We rehearse the scene as before, first alone, then, when satisfied, with the assembled crew, then we shoot it in two or three takes and I rush off to change for an outdoor scene in combat trousers and a Drizabone. In this scene, I'm sleeping rough in the outback, and having hallucinations. It's cold and damp but there's a thin sliver of sunlight on the crisp November earth as I lay down in a hole and the prop men cover me with wet leaves. I play the scene a couple of times through for John, wardrobe brush the leaves off me and we do it for the crew, then we do it again, picking foliage off between takes. 'Good. Onwards,' says John and I'm driven back to base camp for the next scene which, mercifully, is with my daughter, so I actually get the luxury of someone to talk to who talks back. After *twenty-two* changes of costume, we have *nine and a half* minutes of film – as opposed to the two minutes you would expect on a normal film of filming. I fold downwards into a car, reading tomorrow's lines in the gloom of a roof light, and am driven back down the packed A3 at rush hour to my flat, where I make a piece of toast and sit down to learn the next twenty-four scenes. With luck, on screen, it will look easy.

After four days, Annie comes on to do a day and I do the weekend again. It's feral. I have the bulk of the scenes at the start and Annie will have to work more days at the end. This is because they hire a location for a certain amount of time and all scenes that involve that house must be shot out of sequence. It sounds impossible and it is, but throughout, we laugh and eat and play practical jokes and complain and laugh some more . . . and it sure beats working for a living.

Six weeks later I'm finished, but on the last day of the shoot I drive in, not wanting to miss the last shot, the hugs and the champagne. I arrive bringing Vera/Irene/*Ladies of Letters* labelled wine bottles from Annie and me. It is precisely the same present the producer has brought for everyone, except for the different headshot on the label, so we all go home with two bottles of wine we'll never actually want to open. As before, we give silver postcards to John and Francis, stating 'Once again you put your perfect stamp on our letters.'

When it was over it was as if it had never been. The following March, ITV started repeating the series and once again, unaccountably, stopped after episode six. Yet they insist we make ten, ten are shown on ITV3 . . . and the series is episodic. Am I alone in my bewilderment? Yes, of course I am. This week there will be a screening of some of the new episodes for cast, crew and press. It's a stultifying thought that in the months since the shooting ended, just before Christmas, those poor boys, Hendo, Francis and the editor, have been staring at our jowls, overbites and wandering retinas for three months. Now that, in itself, to me, is worthy of a Queen's Award for Industry.

On 2 June the show went out . . . well, five episodes went out. It was received with extravagant praise by the reviewers and the public response was terrific. Most newspapers don't do ITV3 in their listings but we made respectable figures. The last episode finished with Irene strapped to a table in a home, having been sectioned by her daughter in Australia. It was very bleak for a sitcom and there was no announcement afterwards to say that the series would be continued in October. This lady may just have to write to the man at the top. I did. I'm not holding my breath, but a friend of a friend of the girl who cuts the hair of one of the writing team said she's heard it will be on ITV1 this summer. I don't know when, so just stay in for a couple of months, will you?

As of July 2010, it is going out on Sundays at 6 o'clock on ITV1 and so far I've missed every episode, but the word on the street seems good. Figures are okay too and the number of times punters say, 'Don't see you much on the telly these days, Doreen,' is dwindling.

Darius

Darius is different. He's a ghost. I started from the words, 'Don't scream! Oh, please don't scream', then suddenly found it all started to rhyme so just went with it. Aside from the last speech in 'Daftas', Darius is my only male . . . and you can see right through him.

Darius

Don't scream! Dear lady, please no screams! I hate it when a maid
blasphemes.

No! – Madam cease – pray you be calm; I am deceased and
mean no harm.

Lawks a'mercy – 'Tis enough! See, I tremble thru' my ruff –

I do beseech on bended hose: don't do another one of those!

You heard my voice? Forgive my stare – across dimensions this is
rare.

I realise chills run down your spine, but I am merry, not malign.

Though goose pimples may stand on you; I will not lay a hand on
you.

Although, I am distrait and dour, and odorous as an open sewer,

I am, despite decomposition, a well-adjusted apparition.

There now – all your teeth are chattering . . . I have no teeth,
which is not flattering.

But why recoil from one who's spectral? There's hundreds on the
roll electoral.

Was that a smile? Almost oblique . . . a dash of colour to your
cheek!

'They' hate that I'm still funny, dead. I'm always being punishèd.

Oh what the hell – I think I'll risk it – Thank you, I will have a biscuit.

That cupboard yonder might be handy . . . perhaps a noggin of
the brandy?

I fain would pour it, in your stead, were I not carrying my head.

You peer at scars I cannot hide, and trails of fetid blood that's
dried.

Crepuscular deterioration? 'Tis standard with decapitation.

'Twas done in but a single stroke. It stained my doublet . 'Twas
bespoke.

The other world? A kind of Hell? I'm not at liberty to tell:

Spirits may not shake a teacup, 'til we've signed a legal pre-nup;

My crime was murder with intent and, no, I was not penitent

He was a lowly theatre critic who said my Lear was 'paralytic'.

I merely stalked him through the greenery and brained him
with some heavy scenery.

The axe-man put a bag on me. Now I'm a soul in agony.

Condemned to moan in marble halls and, ev'ry night, to walk
through walls.

Eternal torment can be humdrum, forced to ponder one
conundrum –

Help me, maid, 'ere I implode: Why did that chicken cross the
road?

'O ghostly guest,' the maid replied, 'It crossed to see, on t'other
side,

The Duchess, straining from her throne, to *lay* a large foundation
stone.'

Met My Metamorphosis

'As Gregor Samsa awoke one morning from uneasy dreams he found himself transformed in his bed into a giant beetle.' This is the famous first line from, as the advert used to almost say, 'probably one of the most famous . . . sagas in the world'. It's the first sentence of Franz Kafka's novella *Metamorphosis*, one of the great classics of the nineteenth century. When the email came asking me to play the mother of the giant woodlouse, I hadn't read the book. When I sent away for it, it came in comic-book form, which was very readable but probably cheating. The film was to be produced and directed by Chris Swanton, a former editor, who has been obsessed by the book for much of his life. There was a tiny budget, a tiny cast, tiny salaries, a six-week shoot in a tiny studio and, with a tiny, scarcely imperceptible shudder, I agreed to do it.

I'm quite glad I did. The company of actors was jokey: Robert Pugh, a sprawling, craggy Welshman, with a marvellous self-deprecating humour; Laura Rees, a young, straight-backed and clear-eyed actress with an uncompromising style; and Chris New, a young man of a thousand voices as the voice of the creature. His woodlouse impersonation was as good as his Ian McKellen and he had me doubled up in the between-take pauses.

It was boned corsets from 7 a.m. to 7 p.m. There was little to learn – mostly mother just screamed, fainted and had asthma attacks. There was some trouble with the six different beetle models. They refused to do what they had been commissioned to do, namely, respond to magnets under the floor and look like anything other than beetle models, so CGI, computer-generated images, had to be called in. They cost an arm and eight legs. Time was lost which couldn't be made up but everyone retained their patience and we finished only a few days later than contracted. It will be a one-off, if ever you saw one.

Stephen Berkoff had triumphed on stage in his own adaptation of the book and no lesser woodlouse than Roman Polanski played it on stage in Paris. He'd tried for years to make a film of *Metamorphosis* and if *he* couldn't get it off the ground, then who could? As we filmed the news came through of his arrest in Switzerland and the gossip was rife. There is some conjecture that the Swiss could even have done a deal with the CIA to extradite Polanski in exchange for backing off investigations of numbered accounts in their banks.

Polanski had been going in and out of Switzerland for thirteen years. He owned a residence there and paid taxes. On the night of his arrest he was due to be honoured at a Swiss film festival. The crime he committed thirty years ago was a very serious one. To say that he has paid for it by becoming an exile, looking over his shoulder for all these years is not enough to appease the media and the public, although it clearly *is* enough to appease the victim herself. She is a forty-four-year-old wife and mother who has publicly forgiven him and does not want him to be extradited.

Roman is a scarred human being, a victim of the murder of his mother and siblings under the Nazis, and the horrific murder of his wife and unborn child by a drug-crazed cult. The question of why the victim's mother took a thirteen-year-old girl to the hotel of a director with his reputation will never be answered.

Still, survival is in Polanski's genetic code and survive he will. He edited his last film in a Swiss prison, and later while electronically tagged in his apartment. He is in good spirits, I'm told, and at the height of his powers as a director.

I think the reason that *The Pianist*, in which I played the mother, was such a good film, and will be a classic film, is that there are no heroes. Just survivors and the hand of fate.

Meanwhile, if *Metamorphoses* gets a distributor it will be an art film. We still have one shot to pick up at this juncture, three months after the last day of shooting, and it has to be on a Manchester tram. I really hope for everyone's sake that the insect can be made to work. Animation is so sophisticated these days and viewers are schooled to expect so much. Once the model insects had been fired we, the actors, were all acting horror and revulsion at a small, yellow tennis ball on the end of a boom pole held aloft by our first director. It's quite a test of something or other and we all did it with real relish. Coming soon to a flea-pit near you.

Spiked

I don't know if it's synchronicity or coincidence or even some mighty 'upstairs' storyboard but something is pointing me towards the work of the greater spotted Goon, Spike Milligan.

After a busy day fundraising at a school in Swiss Cottage with Kathy Lette, we had dinner at Lizzie and Barry Humphries' bibliotheque of a flat where she told us how she had been a Spike Milligan groupie and, at the age of fifteen, followed him all over Australia.

Strangely enough, Spike's widow Shelagh was at a birthday bash I'd been to the night before and we'd talked about the odd coincidence that Nats, my PA, had lodged with her a year or so before coming to me. Synchronistically, some weeks before, I'd had a marvellous lunch in East Finchley to talk about raising funds for a statue of the dear fellow. It was held in the house of two of the most fervent collectors of tchatchkes (collectable odds and sods) I've ever seen. As I said at the event, that I somehow, over dessert, managed to volunteer for:

'The idea for tonight's fund-raiser came from the Milligan Society, who kindly invited me for a home-cooked lunch in Finchley to explain their idea to raise a statue to Spike in Finchley. Well, since I now live in Paddington, I accepted. You know actors. We'd go anywhere for practical food. As Max Bialystock said in *The Producers*: "I hate actors. They're animals – ever eat with one?"

'The writer Bernard Slade, when he was a child, told his father that when he was a grown-up he wanted to be an actor. His father replied, "Er, no son, you can't be both."

'When Spike was given a CBE for services to comedy, he wrote: "I can't see the point of it really . . . a Commander of the British Empire. They might as well have made me a commander of Milton Keynes – at least that exists."'

Oh, incidentally, I heard a wonderful exchange at the *Oldie* lunch between Spike and Richard Ingrams:

Spike: Why are you serving bread and butter pudding?
Ingrams: Because it's Lent.
Spike: When do we have to give it back?

Anyway, back at the Finchley lunch, I heard a voice say, 'Well, surely, it wouldn't be too difficult to mount an evening to raise a few bob for a statue, would it?' With a small internal whimper I looked round the table and realized it was my voice that had said it. Everyone but me was nodding and smiling.

Six months, 263 emails, eighty-five text messages, the loss of Joanna Lumley, Barry Cryer and sundry others later, three hundred people packed into the lecture theatre of Middlesex University in a room with as much atmosphere as the moon. Then Joanna was recently seen cruising down to Luxor, charming the muslin off old Muslims. Yep, she gets the engagements on the Nile and I get the marriages made in Hendon. Still, are we downhearted? Well, yes, a bit, actually.

As for Barry Cryer, well he sent a joke, which was cheaper than coming on a bus from Hatch End:

Three men in the desert. The English Protestant said, 'Crikey, I'm thirsty, sooo thirsty . . . I must have some water.'

The Protestant Irishman says, 'Aye, but I'm thirsty! I'm that thirsty . . . I must have a whiskey.'

Bringing up the rear, the North London Jew says, 'Oy, I'm sooo thirsty, I'm sooooooo thirsty . . . I must have diabetes.'

Just for good measure, I'll throw in the one about the matchmaker, who tells a young man he's found him the perfect bride. 'She's beautiful,' he tells him, 'really gorgeous. She cooks like a dream, she keeps the house spotless, she knits, she sews, she loves children . . . she's perfect.' Glumly the young man asks, 'Is she any good in bed?' 'Eh . . .' replies the matchmaker, 'some say yes, some say no.'

The proposed bronze statue of Spike on a park bench by artist John Sommerville will cost £50,000. Aaargh – it's a wonderful evocation of the man, sitting in the corner, cap on head, elves and fairies carved into the wood, but I got to wondering what sort of statue would Spike have commissioned of himself?

I asked his publisher, the poet Jeremy Robson, who published many of Spike's books, beginning with the *Goon Show Scripts*, which sold 160,000 copies and was a publishing innovation at a time when scripts were never published. After racking his brains for some time, he said, 'You do know that Spike started every poetry reading by saying: "I thought I'd begin by reading one of Shakespeare's Sonnets. But then I thought, why should I? He never reads one of mine."'

It occurred to me that a statue of William Shakespeare with the caption 'Spike Milligan?' beneath, would have most amused him no end. After all, it was he who wrote:

Said Hamlet to Ophelia, I'll do a sketch of thee.
What kind of pencil shall I choose? 2B or not 2B?

I asked a few luminaries for an opinion. Tom Conti said, 'A statue of Cary Grant.' Great minds . . . Comic actor Robert Longden, who worked with him on *Treasure Island*, got right into Spike's fertile mind, suggesting, 'A Statue of Ben Gunn, reading a book which is upside down, sitting on an unexploded bomb, with a constant loop of Spike's theme tune played on an out of tune piano.' Composer Denis King's suggestion was a life-sized pigeon with a tiny statue of Spike on its head. (Pigeonholed again.) And journalist Valerie Grove suggested – a yellow spike. Perhaps it should just be a bronze of Spike on the telephone with the caption: 'Hello. Stat-ue?'

I never knew Spike personally, but I do subscribe to the general belief that he was a bit of a wayward genius. One of those rare renaissance men, like Noël Coward, who can do it all, someone who this often quite narrow country doesn't quite know what to do with.

I was present on the night he received a Bafta award from HRH Prince Charles and responded to the Prince's eulogy by saying, 'You grovelling bastard'. It was an incredible moment, at once excruciatingly funny – and – excruciating. Essentially the kind of spontaneous, hair-raising, dangerous moment that recalls the Fool in *Lear*, Max Miller and Lenny Bruce and anticipates *Monty Python*, Sacha Baron Cohen and Chris Morris. He was the Salvador Dalí of the world of comedy: iconoclast, wit, surrealist, cartoonist, warrior, worrier, musician, poet and player prince.

Like Denis the Menace, he had madcap mischief poring out of every pore. One night in one of his stage shows he sat on the edge of the stage and said, 'Sorry I'm late folks, I've had a three-day cancer,' after a pause, he added, 'And now for the world's most embarrassed silence championships.'

Have you ever wondered who writes the jokes we all email to each other? Spike wrote some, but he didn't make crafted jokes, they were too premeditated. I wasn't a Goon aficionado but I barked out loud while researching the address at some of the wit which leaped unescorted by propriety from his shapely lips.

One day he came into the office he and various other comedy writers shared, which was over a betting shop in Shepherd's Bush, and was aghast to find tea leaves poured down the lavatory. He marched into the secretaries' office and yelled,

'Who's flushed tea leaves down the lavatory?'

There was an embarrassed silence broken by the voice of the newest girl, who had only started work the day before.

'I'm awfully sorry, but I'm afraid it was me.'

Spike looked long and hard at her and said, 'I see that you will meet a tall dark stranger.'

Spike once phoned a friend who answered, 'Who is speaking please?'

'You are,' said Spike.

One night a neighbour knocked on his door, after ten at night, and said, 'Saw you on the telly last night. Brilliant.'

'Right,' said Spike and shut the door in his face. A week later he rapped on the same neighbour's door at midnight. When he answered it, Spike said, 'Saw you mowing the lawn yesterday. Brilliant.'

I especially enjoyed his absurd one-liners and his reflections on the Almighty.

'Is anything worn under the kilt?'

'No, it's all in perfect order.'

'And God said, Let there be light, and lo, there was light around the Electricity Board and a voice said He would have to wait until Thursday to be connected.'

'And God said, Let the earth bring forth grass, and lo, the earth brought forth grass and the Rastafarians smoked it.'

Once, at a birthday party, he mused, 'Anyone can be fifty-two but it takes a bus to be 52A.'

His frequent depression took the form of a deep melancholy. He was in a glazed state at the *Oldie* lunch I referred to earlier. To cheer him up, Barry Cryer leaned across the table and said, 'You realize there are a lot of paedophiles here, Spike.'

Spike regarded him mournfully and said, 'Why do you hate us?'

I wonder what Spike would have made of current events like the March TV debate between the three putative leaders?

A teacher in a Hackney comprehensive says to his class, 'Hands up everyone who's a Gordon Brown fan.'

All the kids raise their hands except Johnny. The teacher asks why not, and he says because I'm not a Gordon Brown fan. The teacher asks why and Johnny replies, 'Because I'm a Conservative.'

Teacher asks him on what grounds he is a Conservative, and he replies, 'My mum's a Conservative, my dad's a Conservative, so I'm a Conservative.'

His teacher says jeeringly, 'If your mum was an idiot and your dad was a moron, what would *that* make you then?'

Puzzled, Johnny says, 'A Gordon Brown fan.'

Barry Cryer once said, 'I've never known anyone who could be so consistently inconsistent.' Spike's take on Barry was, when he saw him, to shout, 'Cryer's here . . . take my jokes! Don't hurt me.'

Q. Why does Finchley, former constituency of the Cross Iron Lady, need a statue of a Puckoonish comic with a genius for mayhem who took all our minds off everyday, parochial small-mindedness and did what comedy is supposed to do: examine a skewed civilization and, by mocking it, restore proportion.

A. It doesn't. But then did Kensington Gardens need Spike to paint blue trousers on all the fairies and elves carved into the rotten old stump of a tree?

I'm sure of it. If just one child regards Spike's work with wonder . . . and if one solitary soul sits down on the bench beside Spike, unplugs his iPhone, removes his iPod and looks into the twin faces of comedy and tragedy and smiles in remembrance, then, yes, that statue is worth it.

Finally, I leave you with Spike's assessment of his own career: 'When I look back, the fondest memory I have is not really of the Goons. It's of a girl called Julia with enormous breasts.'

The unrehearsed concert on Sunday 18 March 2010 was a triumphant success. We had jazz and poetry from Spike's daughter Jane Milligan. Victoria Wood, who stepped in to save the day having thought we were unveiling a statue, not cavorting around in order to get one, donned a pink woolly hat and gave us topical comedy and a sketch set in a coffee shop which had the house braying with laughter.

Young Jessie Buckley from *The Search for Nancy* and *A Little Night Music* sang jazz classics with the sweetness and finesse of Cleo Laine and Judy Garland rolled into one, and I did what I do. Oh, and ran the book auction with the Mayor of Barnet. It was an old-fashioned variety bill, played in full fluorescent light with a sound system based on British Rail's best, and it couldn't have been bettered. Tickets were cheap and we only made £3,500 but we had a ball. So far, we have half the donations we need. If you like the model and the idea then send a donation to The Spike Milligan Statue Society, 17 Abbots Gardens, East Finchley, London N2 0JG.

And that, folks . . . is chutzpah. Leo Rosten's definition of which is a small boy peeing through someone's letterbox, then ringing the doorbell to see how far it went.

A Day in Reality

I'm supposed to be writing this book. Therefore, with my customary gift for prioritizing, I accept two dodgy jobs, both of which interest me for all of the two minutes it takes to say, 'Oh, go on then, it'll only take a couple of days.'

The first is *Celebrity Cash in the Attic*, which I have never seen but which promises to take away some of the stuff which clogs up my flat and auction it for the charity of my choice. Gloria Hunniford's name is mentioned. (I really like Gloria. She's a proper TV journalist, always professional, well informed, interested and relaxed. In short an interviewer in her prime, whom television has relegated to daytime in order to accommodate camp comics.) They come to my flat. Lots of them. Men, women, boys, girls, cameras, tripods . . . the dog loves it – endless opportunities to show off her beauty and her tricks.

I've been asked to do this by Anna Roberts of the charity Burma UK. It aids the Burmese people who lack food, health, human rights and education. Every cause is a good one, but this one just ain't populist. Britain neither wants nor needs anything from Burma – oil, rubber, tourism or allegiance, so it's hard to raise money for them.

Jonty Hearnden is tall, mild and kind. He knows his onions. Worth his value as a valuer. I show him mine – valuables that is – dragged out of the back of cupboards very late the night before. Should I give him the Chopard and the Cartier, bought for me by Mr Wrong a few years back? Yes, I should. Will I? No, I won't. We discuss my bronze chiffon fifties dress, with bolero, worn in *Doctor Who*, my strongest contender for big-time dosh for Burma UK. *Doctor Who* memorabilia goes for a fortune, doesn't it? I throw in the John Myatt painting of John Constable's *Haywain*, painted alongside my own at the scene of the original one for a Sky Arts programme called *Virgin Virtuosos*. His looked Constable-ish and mine looked chocolate-box but the *frames* were fabulous and his fame as a painter is growing, years after he was jailed for forgery. Then we add a charming mahogany dressing table, painted with turquoise flowers, an autographed *Re: Joyce!* programme – no, not by me, but by the elusive Barbra Streisand, and a host of fabulous stage costumes, including the trompe l'oeil ex-libris jacket which I was photographed in for the cover of my fifth book, *You Can Read Me Like a Book*. The filming at my flat is pretty endless, as we do everything at least three times, but another day is still required.

I was driven to Derby, yes Derby! Why in heaven's name Derby? Arriving at 8 a.m. at an auction room on an industrial estate, alongside the usual car showrooms and oriental food warehouses. I've done my own make-up and hair as one now has to in TV, and there's nowhere to change but the staff toilet. Gloria arrives, flushed from a nightmare journey from Sevenoaks, in a lovely sage-green velvet coat, and we sit around for two hours as the auctioneer goes through three hundred lots before ours. The crowd there was as eccentric as befits an auction room and considerably smaller than I'd envisaged and I worried vaguely that nothing would sell. A *Doctor Who* fan found me in the café and said he'd looked up my fan club on the net and found I didn't have one. I told him it was early days, I'd only been at it for forty-three years.

The mahogany dressing table was first up. The auctioneer made no mention that it was mine and to my disappointment it went for forty quid. In fairness that is exactly what Jonty said it would go for, but I was as gutted as a Hull midfielder and said so. It was so *pretty* and I remember the day Jack and I found it. In those days, I had a Victorian bathroom, and had the whole bath hand-painted in floral blue and white, to match a Victorian chamber pot by the same brilliant scene painter, Chris Clark, who later painted the trompe l'oeil, ex-libris jacket. It was a perfect match. I'm not being over sentimental here . . . I don't need it, this flat requires modern stuff . . . it's just that . . . well, ahem, say it Maureen . . . it felt unfair to the table, after thirty years of good looks and good service.

Still, onwards, my friend Richard Price's antique map of Burma fetched another forty, the paintings were withdrawn as no one was interested ('Don't give up the day job,' being Jonty's more than fair assessment), and the Streisand autograph a couple of hundred. In between lots, the director, who'd clearly had enough of this particular gig, snapped instructions at us to walk in, out, tell stories, look animated as a listener, etc. Finally, I asked her if she was happy in her work and if so perhaps she might treat us to a little of that happiness. It didn't go down terribly well.

I got into the trompe l'oeil jacket and flogged it myself for a couple of hundred pounds and a thin, bespectacled woman took on the embroidered silk, fur-lined Chinese coat from my hippy years. Later she told me she kept a market stall and would wear it to keep warm. Aaaargh! Possessions, Maureen, just possessions. Let it go!

Finally the *Doctor Who* dress came up and the phones started going. It sold for £400, bringing my donations to Burma UK up to £1,100 and removing my sense of failure. I'd left too early for breakfast, there had been no lunch hour and, since it was Passover and I could eat no bread or cake, dark, Satanic sounds were coming from my innards as they bundled me, the remaining costumes and the two hulking great paintings, unwrapped and unprotected, into the back of the eponymously named People Carrier. I threw a muted wobbly, hauled the pictures back out, told them to send them wrapped as they'd received them, and swept off.

That was yesterday. Today I'm thrilled and delighted to be back at the computer. The whole house upstairs has gone away for Easter and there's only me, Warren sitting in his plant pot and the floor of Ti's flat above filled with workmen doing an Irish jig. I am happy. That's twice. It's almost becoming a habit.

The other job was called *My Story* and since the world tells me stories whenever I go through a strange door, I thought I might as well do it as an employee. This one, again, is cheap TV, no hair or make-up, a skeleton crew and one day for each story. But my, they were interesting stories, culled from thousands sent in by members of the public, in response to a request for real-life experiences.

The first story concerned Julie Wassner, a woman in her late forties who at seventeen, living in poverty in the East End, with strict and undemonstrative parents, had given up a child for adoption. Afterwards, she found forming a relationship difficult and the thought of having children appalled her. What if her daughter came back and asked her, 'How come you could look after them but you couldn't look after me?' She began writing scripts and, needing a literary agent, went to see Michelle Kass. They had a good meeting, during which a secretary brought in tea and they agreed to meet again and discuss representation when Michelle had read her stuff. Later that night she called Julie at home and said, 'Something very odd has happened, and you'd better sit down.' She told her that the secretary who had brought in the tea was a temp, filling in for a couple of days, and that when she saw Julie's name on the script cover she had almost fainted. She believed Julie was her birth mother.

They met in Kew Gardens by the pagoda, which is where we filmed them. They were cut from the same roll of linen. Peas in a pod. 'You've got my face,' her daughter said when they met. Both of them met their life partners shortly after meeting each other, as though the missing piece of themselves had been found, freeing them for someone else. To me, they appeared as easy and familiar as though they'd known each other all their lives. Which, I suppose, they have.

Julie is a larger than life blonde, bubbly broad, who has written *EastEnders* for eighteen years and other series, including *London's Burning*, where she met its originator, Mr Jack Rosenthal. She remembered him coming in to complain that the series had moved too far away from its origins and that sex had replaced drama and comedy. That's my boy. We had the most fascinating and easy two days together. I didn't know if her story would be picked by the celebrity panel, but it certainly did it for me.

The following day, I went to Ramsgate to meet the woman of the second selected story. She was the survivor of a perfect marriage. I use the word advisedly. Three well-balanced children, a husband with whom she never had a cross word, a grand Edwardian double-fronted house in a garden square, most of which was their garden, friends, dinner parties, gardening and a translation business which they ran together. One day her husband said he had a surprise for her. She went across the road to the garden where he was trimming the hedges. The only surprising sight was a pair of brightly coloured gardening gloves, which she didn't comment on. Still promising her a surprise, he tied a narrow necktie round her eyes. She giggled helplessly, because she could still see. Then he hit her over the head with an axe and left her for dead.

When she came to, he was sitting on some stone steps watching her and she was lying face down in the gravel about twenty yards from where it happened. She says she felt no pain and has no memory of how she travelled that distance. She remembers him saying, 'It's not supposed to take this long' then he held down her head and hit her with a rock. She remembers nothing more except crawling inch by inch, the hundred or so yards to the entrance to the square, where a Catholic priest found her and summoned an ambulance. Her son appeared, seeing an accident from his bedroom window, but with no clue that the bloodied wretch before him, ears torn off her head, swollen and blood-soaked, was his mother.

During the time it took for her to crawl the distance to safety, her husband changed his clothes, put the old ones in the washing machine, sent some emails, went to the shops for some cigarettes and came home. As the ambulance was leaving the last thing she remembered saying to her son was, 'Don't let your father come in the ambulance.'

Ten days in intensive care and weeks of rehabilitation followed, at the end of which she and the children wrote impassioned pleas to the courts begging them not to sentence their father, her husband. He served a six-month remand and a two-year suspended sentence, during which the family took him back into their home and their lives. I found this the most surprising part of the story.

They are no longer married, you'll not be too astonished to hear. He never explained his psychotic episode either to his family or to a psychologist. Nobody seems to have recommended that he might have needed help so that he didn't fracture the skull of someone else in three places and rip off their ears. It was all not quite kosher and I couldn't put my finger on why. But I reckoned, in terms of a knock-out competition, it would be the story which gets published and appears in every bookshop in the land the following day. I was wrong.

The third one involves a child being kidnapped from the family home and taken to Thailand by his father, and the desperate attempt by his mother and her brother to steal him back. I flew to Belfast for this one. The mother was courageous. The son, now a student at university, gave a moving speech of gratitude to her. They cut it.

The rest of the show was given over to a panel of experts, one of the stories was selected and by the following morning appeared in Waterstones for public consumption. The programme ran at peak time on a major network. As a lady of letters, I'm jealous of myself.

Julie Wassner, who'd given up her daughter, won the judges' decision and her book was published as soon as the TV company decided where to schedule the programme. Waterstones, having invested deeply in this project, waited with bated breath.

I, meanwhile, recorded all the presentation pieces to camera. Three times. Each with a different haircut, in varying degrees of Force-10 winds. Once in Richmond, once in the East End and last week in St Katherine's Dock where the tourists came in groups of forty with a multilingual guide, the parties of schoolchildren ran amok around the yacht base, the bridge rang with bells every time a boat went through, and people who'd known me, my father and my relatives, and whose daughter's wedding I'd forgotten I'd attended, all stopped for a chat. Why did I have to do it three times? I asked that question myself, but I think, like the transmission dates, it's just to cover their arses from every side. Wish I'd covered mine. It all looked, as they say, a bit pear shaped.

I did the voiceover a few days later, which meant seeing myself in wind, hail, rain and with no make-up department and a blocked tear duct. I looked like I needed to be steam pressed.

Grumpy? Old? Woman? Well. Ye-es. Television politics always brings out the best in writers. We love to bite the hand that feeds us canapés.

Niamh the Naive

On the theme of women alone, I wanted to write about an abandoned wife who suddenly found herself back in contact with all the things she was before she became a wife – the things that turned her on, like cooking and making love and being needed and admired. Niamh (pronounced Neeve) the Naive came from my experience of being admired after three years of widowhood and thirty-seven years of loving one man. It is quite dizzying and, in retrospect, one becomes a bit of an embarrassment to one's friends and relatives. In my case it was a mistake but even given that error of judgement it wasn't a waste. It led me out of purdah and into something infinitely kinder, quieter and more rewarding. Similarly in Niamh's case, I feel that, whatever the outcome of her September–May relationship, it will restore her self-confidence and give her back what her marriage seamlessly removed. Namely, herself. I made her lover a Polish builder because all the cafés I frequent are staffed by Polish girls and my street seems to be populated by Polish builders, to the extent that I sometimes wonder if Poland isn't empty and falling down. Of course, the fact that Niamh is baking a cake all the way through her conversation is hard to show on radio, but it should be indicated by sound effects because it is indicative of the pleasure she is taking in the sensual activities of life.

Niamh the Naive

(She is an Irish woman, attractive and lively, in her late fifties. She is making a cake throughout and has popped it in the oven by the end.)

Do I? Really? Do you really think so? Everyone says that. It's ridiculous. I keep thinking what did I look like *before*? Coffee? I'm doing a coffee cake, so will you hang on? I mean, thank you, but . . . for heaven's sake some people say the most personal things . . . No, of course they are happy for me . . . well, some of them are . . . one or two have been surprisingly beady . . . Oh, well, you know . . . 'Way to a man's heart *really is* through his stomach then?' One, who shall be nameless, said on the phone, 'Just make sure he's not after your money.' Well, yes, it *was* Renee since you ask, how on earth did you know?

Renee? . . . Really? Why frustrated? She and Simon? Oh, I see . . .

What is a *white* marriage exactly, I've never really known. No. Is he? Simon is? No. Surely not . . . he's a magistrate, isn't he? Oh, I see . . . *underneath* his robes . . . fancy. *(She is beating the mixture vigorously.)* Beats me . . . No wonder the children call me Niamh the naive.

The thing is . . . I thought all that was over. Well, you can always tell the re-marriers, don't you think? The *juicy* women. They're not going to let the grass grow for long, are they? Birds and the b's I call it. Boxing, bridge, ball-room, boob lift, Botox.

(She squints into measuring jug, sieving in flour, then rubs it off her cardigan.)

I've got to concentrate with the whites so – sorry . . . light whisking's the trick . . .

Of course, the men *always* find someone, of course, even the pikestaffs. Look at Emlyn Wishart, well, I mean, you couldn't fancy him with *parsley* round and a pesto crust, could you? I know, he *does* look *exactly* like a monkfish. And he reeks of Corsidol and talks in clichés from *Reader's Digest*, you know:

'How are you, Emlyn?'

'Oh, over-worked and underpaid.'

'Nice jacket, Emlyn . . . '

'Hong Kong. Twenty-four hours. Free suit with every tie.'

Such a poppet, Louise was, as well, and he gave her a dog's life. Sagittarius, though – born to suffer . . . did you ever go there for dinner? He would ridicule her from hors d'oeuvre to Ferrero Rocher and compare her Mediterranean vegetables to mine and rhapsodize about my brulée when hers didn't caramelize and both of us wanted to stab him with a cake fork. It made it so *awkward* to have them back . . . I used to curdle my hollandaise on purpose.

(*Adds vanilla and other spices.*)

Make your own vanilla sugar . . . much cheaper . . . it's a Jamie Oliver. There we are. Sorry about the noise. All done.

Then five weeks after the cremation, when we're all leaving casseroles on his step and texting every day, he hooks up with Justine . . . Yes, there has been talk – well she's served him whisky sours for long enough, she must know what she's taking on. Now we know why he spent so much time in the clubroom . . . of course it's quite a catch for her . . .

No, I didn't mean that to be funny . . . No, honestly, I'd forgotten about the monkfish . . .

Anyway. Me. I was just bobbing along merrily, friends, contract whist, gourmet club, Alison and the boys on weekends. And of course if I did have to go to a function there was always Miles – he'd come with me at the drop of a hat. He can talk for hours about stuffing a poussin and dries his own fenugreek and everyone loves him. Humphrey's marvellous about lending him out . . . but romance? Well it never entered my head. I'd put all that behind me . . .

I just use a pastry brush and a fish knife dipped in cold water . . . see? Just falls away . . .

Gideon and me? Coming up to thirty . . . well, we were so used to each other. Like a pair of old pouffes, no, not that sort . . . Oh, you are the worst. No, we never rowed . . . that would have involved passion – only about my one a day habit . . . couldn't sleep in the same room as me after I'd had a

Consulate. Well, of course all that side of life had been gone for a long time – well, since his tennis elbow and the ruptured disc of course – but it wasn't a priority. Cuddles are best, anyway . . . *I* thought so . . . but clearly, he didn't . . .

I never really found out how they met . . . The kids say she booked him for stopping in a residential parking zone and he charmed her into an eggplant parmigiani – seems she thought spaghetti came in hoop form – and she tore up his ticket and escorted him back to the pound.

(*She uncorks Cointreau bottle.*) Oh certainly . . . and another on the way. Imagine, a three-year-old at his age. Poppy. He's besotted. Brings her round while Lovely Rita's at hot-stone therapy – which she seems to be a lot. I wonder if it's not a euphemism.

Poppy? Strawberry blonde with folds of fat . . . Just like him. But, ooh, 'Just taking Poppy to baby juggling'. . . 'got to pick up Poppy from violoncello grade two . . .' Never had a moment to take *Alison* to the swings of course. (*Throws in a shot of liqueur.*) Too busy building up a portfolio to die for, which the wife's blown already on Anya Hindmarsh handbags. (*Takes a generous swig herself.*)

Hanging on by a thread – hedge funding his bets . . . apparently. Forty-six redundancies so far and more to come.

Does what goes round *come* round though! (*Laughs and pours another.*) Don't some folk just 'flop upwards'?

Stefan? Oh, I was buying the studio flat . . . he was distressing the shared lobby . . . I just thought, 'What an attractive man' but no more. I asked him for an estimate to paper over the magnolia Lincrusta throughout. I had a salmon and asparagus pie in the oven and some passion-fruit brûlée . . . Well, I made a rule after Gideon that I was not going to live on M and S lean cuisine, and I don't. His nostrils were flaring like a Bisto kid's and I heard myself say . . . 'I'm just going to have something very simple and a glass of Montrachet' – not sure he understood a word I was saying, my Polish being as strong as . . . as my resistance . . . and by the end of the evening, honestly . . . I *know*!

He seems to – yes. *Staggering*, isn't it? I'm quite *ga-ga*. Haven't read a *book* or watched *TV* for eight months. If he's *there* I'm cooking for him and he's *gazing* at me adoringly or . . . if we're out it's just through the door and up the stairs flinging each other's clothes off . . . *I know* . . .

Don't you love this consistency . . . mmm – childhood. When Mum gave us the bowl and a rubber spoon?

No stop it . . . it's awful really . . . silly adolescent. (*Licks fingers slowly one by one . . .*)

Alison just rolls her eyes and does sick acting. Thomas thinks it's cool. He's doing D. H. Lawrence . . .

Quite. Well he's so affable, you couldn't not . . . but Ali's rather hoping he'll go back to Sopot when the flat's painted. But there's always the very backs of the cupboards and the underneaths of shelves, by which time the Farrow and Ball Dutch pink will have faded to magnolia and Stefan will just have to start all over again . . .

(*She sighs and pops cakes in the oven.*)

No, Ali hasn't said a word to Gideon . . . how would she put it?

'Mum's fine – if you count being wrapped round a thirty-year-old Polish builder most of the time, fine.'

Have *you* seen him? Gideon, I mean. Oh, well, when you do . . . would you mind mentioning that – you know – that I looked well.

(*She lights a candle and uses the match to inhale a cigarette.*)

Oh and Viv, just tell him I've finally found someone who shares my love of cabbage pie with whole garlic cloves . . . and iced Glenmorangie in bed and . . . a cigarette . . . after.

Maintaining Your Election

Every protagonist in every joke ever written, has to have someone to look down on. Fact. Political correctness has robbed comics of the whole nine yards of protagonists and victims. I can tell a Jewish joke but a Gentile shouldn't. I can't do an Irish, black or Asian joke and only very brave Muslims or Chris Morris can do Muslims.

Anybody can do politician jokes though, and animals and kids and the aged. They can't fight back or put a fatwa on you. And *blondes* for some reason have taken the place formerly held by the Irish in England, the Kerryman in Ireland, the Poles in America, the Newfoundlanders in Canada or the inhabitants of Chelm in the Yiddish-speaking diaspora.

Just before the election I heard a gates of heaven joke. It concerned a prominent politician who suddenly died and found himself at the gates in the presence of St Peter who asked him whether he'd like to spend an hour in heaven and hell to decide which one he'd prefer to spend eternity in. Confident that he was going to prefer heaven, the politician took the elevator down to hell, where an affable Devil was pouring champagne, while canapés of delicious caviar and truffles were going round the exquisitely dressed guests, some of whom the politician had known well during his life. Music was played by former stars of the firmament and the conversation was sparkling; he could see no reason why this place should be regarded as hellish.

St Peter suggested he take a look at heaven and they travelled back up in the celestial elevator to a landscape of soft clouds and winged angels playing harps to attentive men and women of spiritual bent.

When asked, the following dawn, to choose between the two eternities, the politician sheepishly admitted he preferred hell and was duly taken back there.

To his shock and dismay, hell was a different kettle of *poisson* entirely. It was boiling, damp, stinking and everyone worked in ordure and constant pain, loading sewage for a terrifying Devil.

'But this is so different!' he exclaimed. 'Yesterday, this place was divine and now it's evil and disgusting. Why did you trick me like this and change it?'

'Oh, it hasn't changed, sir,' said St Peter, smiling. 'I thought you of all people would have realized it. Yesterday we were canvassing. Today you voted.'

I had that in mind when an invitation came to join Paxman, Dimbleby and Andrew Neil on *Election Night 2010*. I was more than keen to accept. It is as rare for me to be in the eye of the storm as it is for Barbara Windsor to win *Mastermind*, specialist subject, photosynthesis in bi-annual deadly nightshades. The London marathon runs past my door in Paddington when I'm in Cockfosters buying gravy powder. The changing of the Guards takes place fifteen minutes down the road, but I've only ever seen it on a telly in Curry's shop window. I slept through the London hurricane and couldn't understand why, as I drove through Regent's Park on my way to film a BT commercial – wouldn't you know – all the trees were on the ground . . . you get the picture?

I remember where I was when Princess Diana died. I was having Shreddies in the kitchen . . . and, no, I didn't even nearly choke. Kennedy? It flashed on the screen at the cinema . . . er . . . Lennon? . . . er . . . don't remember. 9/11? Yes, I was about to open a new play in Southampton . . . a comedy.

So I thought I'd go along to the BBC boat, see a few old friends, impress the cognoscenti with my grasp of proportional representation . . . pour a cup of hot coffee on A. A. Gill, you know the sort of thing. What larks, I thought. What sharks, as it happened . . . what debacles . . . may I remark, as we fought to disembark.

My peripatetic brother accompanied me. Geoff's a world maven on tourism and he and I can argue politics for Harry, England and the Home Counties. Guido and I had been outed by the *Daily Hobnail* that week, with every fact only ever so slightly right, so lying low was a given. My brother was flying to India the following day, Icelandic ash permitting, to chair his own meeting, but unlike me, he enjoys living dangerously. Fifty years of jet-lag ensures that we never actually finish a conversation, but we've perfected the skill of arguing in his sleep.

We arrived early, me in shivering lack of clothes, and started sipping wine at nine thirty. The food was, of course, canapés of no protein or carbohydrate content, as in thinly sliced courgette wrapped round some sort of slidey stuff like cream cheese, so by nine forty-five, I was awfully jolly. Friends were meeted and greeted and opinions sparkled and fizzed, Cap'n Andrew Neil of the crinkled bob greeted us from the poop deck and told us we were in for the most exciting night of our lives and it went steadily downhill from there. Jane Asher, Clive Anderson, Helena Kennedy, Alan Yentob, David Liddiment, Stephen Morrison . . . all the network head-rollers, sportsmen, odd politicians – well, they are on the whole. Yes, all the great and the near great were there, swapping polling-station stories and badinage and agents, glued to the minute-by-minute drama on the large screen monitors.

At which point, they all went dead. The monitors I mean, not the guests, which would at least have been worth having a recount. We neither heard nor saw a thing for the next hour and a half. Well, until a burly bloke in a yellow jacket nudged his way port through stars-aboard, narrowly missing eminent and legless guests with his horizontal ladder, and endeavoured to fix the fuses.

By now, we were all trying to desert the sinking shit because we knew Petty Officer Neil would shortly be asking for our opinions on how well hung a hung parliament should be . . . and there we were, gathered around someone with a news app on their iPhone, drunk, hungry and in total ignorance of the results.

You had to laugh. By now a famous star had arrived and a make-up girl was filling my brother in on how she had gathered up the flesh of someone who shall be nameless into a sort of bunch and clipped it under her wig with a bulldog clip. Darling, I couldn't have liked it more. Geoff and I headed for the gangplank to find a gate-crashing Kathy Lette arriving so she and Geoff went in for more serious flirtation and we learned that hundreds of the voting public had been disenfranchised in several of our democratic boroughs and that Robert Mugabe was on his way over to show us how a fair election should be run.

As I stepped into the salty air and goosebumps sprang to my attention, a waif in an electronic earphone and a clipboard hauled me back aboard saying Andrew was ready for me aft and I was ushered, in some hysteria, into a middle seat between Toby Young of *New Yorker* fame and Alistair McGowan of 'if you close yer eyes he could be Rory Bremner' fame. Toby burbled, I became earnest, i.e. boring, and Alistair did an Eddie Izzard impersonation. The whole thing took thirty seconds, after which Guido texted me that he was going to bed cos it was the worst election-night programme he'd ever seen.

Geoff and I came home. He put the TV on, although I begged him to go to bed as he had to be at Heathrow for 6.30 a.m., but he refused. Twelve seconds later he was fast asleep with his computer on his lap and there he remained. I crept in at 6 a.m. to wake him and he was dressed, showered and Skyping a colleague in a voice which could have shattered concrete. That's my bro'.

Gordon cut a tragic figure the next day and I remain one of his supporters, though perhaps he is not the man to fight an entirely televisual campaign. The British public said gorbals to Mr Rupert Murdoch's opinions of whom they should elect and remained impervious to the pretty face which the media insisted they had fallen for. Tories and Labour stalwarts are wooing young Cleggover, like tutors at a freshers' week meet-and-greet and frankly, my dears, we couldn't be more hungover. This space is not even watchable. The BNP was thoroughly trounced and humiliated. The sensible citizens of our deceptive, sceptred isles had the last word.

Artie: Play To The Gallery

This observer of the species came about because I was, and remain, fascinated by jobs which require an inner life, possibly with an internal dialogue going on. I always stared at the librarian and wondered if in some way she was judging my choice of books. Similarly, with the security guard, the bouncer, the guardsman in the Busby on duty I always wanted to know what game they played to stave off the hours of boredom.

In my day, every moment is different, every hour contains so many possibilities I do wonder what inner resources I would have, given a job requiring me to sit on a stool for eight hours and watch the public in all its crazed mundanity. When Michael Parkinson asked me, on Desert Island Discs many years ago, how long I would last on the island, I replied 'About twelve minutes.'

Artie: Play To The Gallery

'It starts here on your left, yes, madam. Early draughtsmanship in evidence . . . An' you follow the exhibits round inside the rope, keeping left, into gallery two and so on and so forth. My pleasure. Yes, miss, head-sets are over by the information d . . . Yes, sir, it starts here, the early draughtsmanship in evi— Er . . . no, my dear, cloaks on the next floor . . . Well, son, you follow it round to the left, within the rope and into gallery two and so on and so forth . . . Yes, the guide book will be as good as the headset but . . . by the information, my friend . . . you're very welcome . . .'

(Here's a big one. Look at him. Stand close up and his features are gross, heavy but from back here, he looks distinguished almost. I bet that suit's seen better days . . . I reckon he's a retired businessman. Something in the City . . . taken hisself off to adult education classes cos of she don't want him around for lunch. He's doing fine art, that's what he's doing. Couldn't get in to the Reubens' nude models – booked up well in advance even for members. Shame. Come in on the train from . . . Windsor! That's it. The clue is in the newspaper . . . too thin to be a tabloid . . . and he's had a flutter between the station and here. I'll *wager* . . . an' he'll drink the winnings on the way home.

Schoolteacher that one. Chose those colours with no respect for herself. Look at her shoes. Heels chewed. All her pockets full up. Treats and poo bags, I reckon . . . took her dog – no, dogs – out before she started out for school . . . You can see the tiny grey hairs on her cuffs . . . schnauzers maybe? Might've been pretty once, but disappointed. Notice her dealings with the kiddies . . . no patience. Driving her potty but she can't afford to give up . . . needs the full pension . . .)

'Excuse me! No mobile phones, please, and no cameras, er . . . madam, would you please communicate that to the class? Madam . . .?' She's plugged in to the headset. Lawd spare me! 'No flashing, madam!' Ooops, that's got her attention!

(The one with her's got more about her. Eyes in the back of her head, that one, and they seem to follow you all over the room. I like her cagoule though . . . that's foreign, that is, and it's seen a bit of travelling. Bought that in . . . somewhere Nordic – Finland? Siberia? That's what she wants to be doing, travellin' far flung, can't afford it though . . . Geography's her thing, I reckon, not art but she's 'ere for the extra pay. Yes. That's it. Look how she's lingerin' over *Coupling Couple*, and she ought to be hurryin' past it – kids are 'aving a laugh but she's lost in it, poor cow. Oh, that says broken home . . . hubby left, back to training college, pronto, finish what he stopped and here she is. Mauve, paisley skirt fits where it touches, nice thighs through the tight skirt though, might be a bit of a goer, nice creamy skin . . . redheads are different they say . . . more up for it. Even different smell I've 'eard . . . What colour's Molly's hair these days? Dunno that I know . . .

Now then, now then, who's this comin' in and movin' round like a flippin' fish on a beach? What's little one's game, eh? Not what you'd call a classicist, tartan shorts, little black pork-pie hat, holes in her stockin's and studs – everywhere . . . White hair with bits of orange. Somebody's daughter that . . .)

'Oh yes, miss, you'll find that one in the third room, the exhibition builds up slowly and the early work shows his early draughtsmanship then . . .'

(Oh, yuck! She's got one in her tongue, bleh, makes your stomach turn a corner. Whassit for? Agony. Must be something to do with rumpy pumpy. Nothin' in my Molly's portfolio, I'll wager. Sod it . . .)

'The headsets are over by the inform—'

(Oh. She's gone then. Thanks very much for your time, Mr G. My pleasure, Ms Glasgow South . . . Straight into gallery three to clock the Rape of the whassits . . . typical. She's probably going to talk about the whole exhibition on some art critics forum on channel 112. She got the looks for it. I can see the light would bounce nicely off the planes of her cheeks. Good angles. If you don't mind Goths.

I need to stretch my legs. Been on this stool for too long. Cuppa tea and a gasper. Where's my young relief when you need him?

People though, eh? Know what I mean? He gives us two eyes, one nose, one mouth and – wallop, not one of us looks like the other. Amazing really, innit?

Uplifting work, though, watching people. Gives you a lift. Not boring. No, no. Nobody's boring. I mean if someone is that boring, well . . . that's interesting, innit?)

'Sorry Sir – I'm on my break now . . .'

(And the same to you with a frame round. Human race in all its whatsits – manifestations. It's an art form in itself.)

If You Want to Put Something Back, Make it the Seat of the Lavatory

My friend Paula Swift is training me to say 'No' to things. She recites various scenarios, like 'Hello, Miss Lipman, I'm from the Leeds home for retired bombardiers with carpal tunnel syndrome and we were wondering if we could count on you to cut the ribbon on our new aromatherapy and wheat grass pressing centre, on 24 September 2014? There's no money, I'm afraid, but we know a bloke with a van, who'd drop you off nearby and we might be able to get you a pie for the journey back. Please answer by tomorrow at the latest as we need time to get a leaflet altered.'

Then she makes me say in a zombie-voiced way, 'I'm sorry. I – am – unexpectedly busy for the whole of that decade. Here is the mobile number of Dame Helen Mirren.'

So far, Paula doesn't think it's going that well. Charities and memorials, memorials and charities . . . raising a statue in Finchley, painting a deckchair for a Suffolk hospice, doodling for neurofybro-matosis, robbing my own attic for Burma, chatting to the old folks for Mill Hill JACS, drawing the raffle at a shul tea party in Croydon. I'm not complaining . . . well, I am a bit . . . I mean it's not Sir Bob Geldof but it *is* time consuming and time is going at a frantic rate.

I was sixty-four in May and I can't be! Not sixty-four! Not me! I'm thirty-four . . . aren't I? In my head, I am. In this business, we have to do our thing. We have to use our good fortune to help. If only to thank the patron saint of showbusiness, St Palladium, for the occasional moment of bliss, which comes as a by-product of having a vocation.

Some people last year, at a fund-raising gala for the Hampstead Theatre Club, bid several thousand to have me host a fund-raiser for their Cystic Fibrosis Evening at Sketch. Almost a year later we'd agreed on a time and several thousand more emails later it was the Sunday in question. I phoned to ask exactly whom or what I would be hosting, i.e. introducing, later that night. The organizers called me back.

We'll start with a talk by the physician from the hospital in Israel, who'll talk about cystic fibrosis.

Do I introduce him?

No, our chairman will do that.

Right, so then I do the auction?

Er . . . no, we have two professional auctioneers from Christies to do that.

OK. So what do I do?

Oh, just the after dinner speech.

It was four o'clock. The event was at seven and there *was* no after dinner speech. True, I had a case full of printed postcards, with acronyms and synonyms and abbreviated punch lines, fit to make a dry eye run rheumy, but no, I had no After Dinner Speech.

(The Roman gladiators are fighting the lions for their lives. The lions are winning. The most junior gladiator goes in the ring. The crowd roars. He circles the lion then goes up close and personal to whisper in its ear. The lion skulks shamefacedly away. The slave is given his freedom, but the emperor asks him what he said to make the lion skulk away. The now freeman reports, 'Nothing much, Excellency. I just asked if he'd be willing to say a few words after he'd eaten.')

I flailed about for an hour, putting material together, but then I reckoned it was more important to put *myself* together, as navy tracksuit bottoms, white face and red eyes could make me look overly patriotic. My friend and I were picked up in a small two-seater containing another passenger and transported to Sketch in Conduit

Street, a Dalí-esque nightclub of great beauty and elegance where 150 of the great and the near-great monged and thringled safe in the knowledge that they looked chicer than Anna Wintour's sunglass bureau and would shortly be parting with volumes of pocket money to win a holiday they didn't need, all in an exceedingly good cause.

Well, the physician covered cystic fibrosis movingly and at some length and the auction went on at least five lots too many and the audience all got going-going-going overload and then, without pausing for dessert or drinks, I was thrown on and readers, I died. This lot was not a lot I'd bargained for, with my stories of Zelma's tooth and Hugh Jackman's day off and what an old lady said to me outside Tesco's. All the jokes were politely received with an air of – that was maybe funny the seventh time I saw it on my iPhone, but now . . .? After a while, my tongue dried up and clamped itself to the roof of my mouth and my voice started breaking like Will's in the *Archers*.

I made it through for about twenty minutes and then I fled for home, slightly teary, saying, 'Never, ever again.' A few days later they rang to say £90,000 had been raised but, even then, my spirits failed to rise with it. I hate being bad at anything. Still, I did meet Paulette there and Paulette does vintage clothes and offered to find me something to wear for the forthcoming Olivier Awards, for which I had a nomination for Best Supporting Actor in a Musical. I'd planned to wear a very simple Jaeger crêpe and satin cut on the cross number with the black wrap I'd brought back from the Maldives, made from banana fibres. Well, someone had to buy it – er, three of them! Then days before I'd dropped in on Ray Harris in Westbourne Park Road and bought a little black silk, pleated dress with a weird, pointy skirt and now here was Paulette with tales of a shawl of Egyptian agate and the promise of a Knightsbridge boutique of other little silk cocktail dresses. I raced there through the rain sporting a strange plum-coloured head recently acquired at a local salon.

Suffice to say that on the Sunday of the awards, I required a panel of experts and three different kinds of underpinning. I felt vaguely sick as I sat down to write a few words of artfully ad-libbed material. My speech began with a reference to this, and the thought that nominees didn't write speeches out of superstition that if they did, they wouldn't win.

'I would thank Trevor Nunn for casting me, against type, as Madame Armfeldt in *A Little Night Music* . . . and for bringing out my inner courtesan.'

It would be an in-joke. When the notices had come out last year at the Menier Chocolate Factory, the *Telegraph* critic Charles Spencer, complaining that I was miscast, wrote that to him I would always be Beattie in the BT commercials. We all knew exactly what he meant by that. As far as I was concerned that was his problem. I had cracked wheelchair-bound Madame Armfeldt and I knew it. She was haughty, despotic and far-seeing. There was bitterness beneath her crust and her wit sprang from her weariness. Hugh Wheeler had written the dazzling book, as he had written *Sweeney Todd* and *Sweet Charity*, as a play with songs and I discovered something new to play around with every night of the five-month run. The cast were young and ridiculously talented, particularly Alexander Hanson and Hannah Waddingham, who played the ex-lovers, Frederick and Desiree, whose plight is described so poignantly in her song, 'Send in the Clowns'. Most of my scenes were with a thirteen-year-old Grace Link who had the gravity of Alice and the mischief of Pippi Longstocking.

Because of *Ladies of Letters*, I had joined the cast a week late. My joke was that because of this I only caught the very *end* of Trevor's introductory speech.

In fact, some weeks before, when Trevor had popped round to the flat to talk to me about Madame Armfeldt, I had confessed to him my own misgivings about being the object of desire for acres of high-born toffs. I was never overly secure as a woman loved and lusted over. In my mind, I'd end up paying *them*. He had no such misgivings.

'She's witty and intelligent,' he told me. 'Therefore . . .' (His all time favourite word. I've never heard anyone else use it as he does) 'that's all that powerful men require. The rest they can get anywhere.' This spoke to my heart and my art and I never looked back.

When, therefore, Spencer (the man who'd basked in his own appraisal of a nude Nicole Kidman as 'Theatrical Viagra') flipped off his shabby analysis of my performance, I flipped off a note to Chris Hastings at the same paper, enclosing photographs of a few other well-known famous courtesans, namely Wallis Simpson, a woman for whom a kingdom was lost, who looked like a Boston terrier, Camilla Parker Bowles, at best as cosy as a pair of Uggs and Dorothy Jordan . . . well, it was hard to tell with all those ringlets, and threw in the original Mme Armfeldt, Hermione Gingold, a sort of fifteen carat sparkling Harpo, for good measure, and, finally, a snap of me in *Ladies of Letters* wearing a green bathing suit and matching wig and wellies. It did the trick and was published in the *Telegraph* over a half-page spread. Radio 4's *Front Row* followed up on the story and, inevitably, I received a good-natured postcard from C. Spencer saying, 'I gather lunch is in order. It shall be at my expense.'

Dame Judi was very cross indeed with him, at the time, for the last review he gave her for Madame de Sade. I thought of inviting her along, but I think she may have smacked him one with one of her awards. When we met, as arranged, at Café Anglais in Bayswater, he was looking suitably sheepish and I was sitting behind a cardboard cut-out of a naked Nicole Kidman. We had a very jolly lunch and I bet he tears the shit out of me the next time he reviews me.

A Little Night-Night Music

Wednesday was matinee day and I was due at the Royal Albert Hall to address 2,500 members of the Women's Institute. I don't think I took it seriously enough. I read the literature on Tuesday night and saw that their agenda was: Care not Custody, Women and Violence and Women and Climate Change. Remembering how the WI took Tony Blair apart, I scribbled a few notes down during my break in act one of the show. Later, I took an age to get to sleep, because I was worried and, consequently, woke late at nine thirty. I threw on the cream and white Adolpho Dominguez suit that has seen me through so many similar occasions, and wrote a few snatches of prose until 11.30 a.m. when a car came to pick me up.

The Albert Hall is a spectacular architectural masterpiece at the best of times, and on this day, from the wings, as I crept in and peered round a corner, I saw tier after tier of women on every level of the magnificent edifice, and I mean thousands and thousands and thousands of them. My lower intestine lurched and I almost ran for it.

They did give me a tremendous ovation, though, and laughter broke the barriers after I asked them to test the microphone by saying, as one: 'Doesn't she look thinner in real life?'

There was more laughter through Joyce Grenfell's 'Useful and Acceptable Gifts', a sketch written by her in 1933, based on a meeting of her real Women's Institute in Berkshire. It was after performing this at a party that Herbert Farjeon asked Joyce to be in his new review. Her answer was, 'But, I can't possibly . . . I'm married.'

It went very well. I could have done another ten minutes – and probably should – but there was a matinee to do and an evening show and chums for dinner afterwards. Back home at midnight, impossibly tired, I felt the need to dress up in an inflatable-horse costume which Alex, the electrician, had lent me. It slowly deflated, leaving me standing in a limp pile of slightly smelly plastic horse. Guido regarded me wryly, wondering what he'd got himself into, no doubt. How surreal is my life? Fingers on the buzzer and no conferring or just phone a friend and ask.

Theatre life continues to be weird. We are closing before the proposed twelve-week extension because the bookings dip dreadfully in August. It's all beyond my comprehension. But I let it go. The countdown to the last few weeks is tender because by now we all love the way the show keeps getting better and better. I feel as though Mme Armfeldt is crystallizing. I do less and less as the nights go by with better results. Also I've stopped bothering about fellow actors losing laughs because they don't say them as I would – or listening out for someone who plays *against* the lines. This makes me very happy. There are pranks in the wings whenever Kelly the countess and Alastair the count are reconciled and walk off stage. One night I'm in the wheelchair – kneeling – with big shoes on my knees, Toulouse Lautrec style, another I'm lying drunk on the floor with a bottle, or have my entire dress over my head and glasses over the top of my hair.

I spoke to the Chocolate Factory's producer David Babani in the last week about *Smash*. *Smash* is Jack's only stage play, a satire on the adaptation of his Emmy award-winning play *Bar Mitzvah Boy* into a stage musical. It has a chequered past. I toured with it in 1981 with the stellar cast of Nigel Hawthorne, Stephen Moore and Peter Blake but, after great notices at Richmond, we never reached the West End. It could have been because of a personal calamity affecting the producer Michael Codron or the pressure of Jack's own agent Peggy Ramsay on Michael *not* to bring the show in.

I'm terribly protective of Jack's work. All writers' wives get like that over our mates seemingly being overlooked. When Jack first sent *Smash* to Peggy, she made no response for a month and, without telling him, I phoned her office and told her he was very nervous waiting for her comments. Foolish move. She called me 'Jack Rosenthal's impossibly ambitious wife' forever more. Ironically, I got to play Peggy Ramsay, whom I never actually met in person, in Alan Plater's play *Peggy For You* at Hampstead Theatre Club and the Comedy Theatre. If there is an after-life, she must have been spitting bulldog clips.

I had, after Jack had died, sent the play to Kevin Spacey at the Old Vic, but he never replied. I was prepared to berate David Babani for not replying but the wind went from my sails when he told me he would really like to stage it next year. I was choked and tearful. We talked about getting Stephen Mangan and maybe Jonathan Lynn and it was so exciting. Watch this space though. All producers are Max Bialystocks at heart.

Trevor Nunn couldn't make our last night – but gave us all a farewell drink in the theatre bar. Hugging Hannah and Alex to him, with their heads down, it was clear to foxy old me that he was telling them he desperately wanted them to do the Broadway version of *A Little Night Music*. I'm five yards away, and horribly jealous. He comes over and pours honey in my ear about how all those months back I said I couldn't play it and then I brought so much to it and I am faint from what I can't say. This is what happened when *Oklahoma!* went to Broadway. The show will go, completely recast apart from one actor.

In *Oklahoma!* it was Josefina Gabrielle, the triple threat, who sang, danced, acted – all brilliantly – and performed the dream-ballet sequence herself, a feat which had never been seen before. She was difficult to replace. My part was the old dry-as-dust settler, Aunt Eller, and America was teeming with actors who were ripe and right for the role. Still, to misquote Oscar, 'To lose one Broadway opening is unfortunate, but to lose two can only be regarded as callousness.'

This time would he take Hannah Waddingham, who was statuesque and stunning with a three-octave voice, in the role of Desiree? Or Alex Hanson, the consistently reliable and solidly excellent Frederick? To compound my agony someone sent me a review of our show from the *New York Times*. It says and I quote shamelessly:

As Madame Armfeldt, Ms Lipman becomes the unmoving, magnetic focus of a show as frantic with farcical activity as a Keystone Cops movie. She spends most of her time in a wheelchair, playing solitaire and exuding the kind of boredom that suggests she belongs to a higher order than anyone in her range of vision. Miss Lipman carefully husbands her effects; her vocal inflections, whether she's speaking or singing, are limited to perhaps half a dozen notes; her facial expressions are even fewer. Yet when she arches an eyebrow or lowers her eyelids, she holds the stage more unconditionally than a naked chorus of strippers turning cartwheels ever could.

I wrote to the critic, Ben Brantley, saying, 'My late husband always said, "They'll *never* understand what you do. You make it look too easy." For once someone has. Thank you.'

Last night we had our last two shows – and they were spectacular. No indulgence at all and we took a minute off the evening show. The audience reaction was tremendous. They threw flowers all over the stage. We took eight curtain calls and a few tears dropped onto the green.

The next few days were strange mixtures of relief and loss. The cast have all been my children. We've had bowling parties for Gabrielle Vick's birthday, spent New Year's Eve singing at my place, cheered Jessie Buckley and Kelly Price's impromptu torch songs at the Ivy Club, huddled in the dark and cold theatre as Trevor's notes ground to a halt, warmed up together every night at the half hour call, solved each other's inflection and disappearing laugh problems, passed around deodorants and throat pastilles, told each other off, chased tiny mice from beneath our costumes, blown out the candles on the cakes of our three interchanging stage children – all that aside from the pleasure of playing the wry wit of Wheeler and Sondheim to packed appreciation eight times a week.

The cast agreed to meet up at a Swedish restaurant in Marylebone as soon as we all got back on our feet. Only Alex Hanson, it transpired, went to Broadway and he had a pretty gloomy time for nine months. Hard to say why, but he had a dream rapport with Hannah and the rest of us, which couldn't be repeated with Catherine Zeta Jones, and the divine, eighty-four-year-old Angela Lansbury. The cast didn't have the magic gel that we'd had over dim lights, packets of crisps, thudding bass from the club next door, overhead trains during 'Send in the Clowns' and, of course, the joy of the odd member of the audience who chose to use our set as a toilet.

Alex Hanson was the quiet lynchpin of our production, so I can see why Trevor chose to take him to New York. I'm told he was even better at holding it together on Broadway. When the Tonys were announced Catherine Zeta Jones and Angela Lansbury were nominated, Alex was not. He'll now play the last three months with Bernadette Peters and Elaine Stritch. Different light, different night, different music – Miss Jones got her CBE but he was our very noble knight.

This year I was honoured to be a judge of the Stephen Sondheim Award for the best student performer. They were all so good. So very accomplished and talented, and there was a worthy and unanimous winner. But the overall winner is Steve Sondheim himself. A proper, living genius, whose complex work will ripen and improve and become more accessible to each coming generation. I hope his comment on seeing my Madame Armfeldt was accurately relayed to me, 'Mmm . . . When she first came on, I thought she was too young, but after a while I really believed she'd f***d all those guys.' I'm faint with damned praise.

Rosh Hashana Dinner

What pleases me is that I seem to be having adventures again. It's been a lean couple of years for both jokes and adventures. Amy and I were driving to Gerrards Cross to have a fish dinner with Guido and his daughters and sons-in-law. In my childhood we never made much of the night before New Year other than, after Dad got home from shul, having apple and honey for a sweet year. It was up early the next morning, and on with the grown-up hat to see and hear the shofar blown – always with difficulty. The shofar is a twisted ram's horn, blown during the service to shatter our complacency and make us face what we must change about ourselves in the new year. We then have one week to think about our sins, until Kol Nidra, the night before Yom Kippur when we spend the day fasting and praying. My mother, who was very Jewish in her heart and in her rituals, but almost entirely ignorant of the reasons why, broke the fast first thing in the morning, with a nice cup of tea . . .

'Weeell . . . What does it matter?' She then took light snacks only for the remains of the fast day and carried a packet of Polo mints in her bag with which to tempt my children during the long hours in shul.

Nowadays, probably because migraine has made me used to days of fasting, I find the twenty-four-hour fast very easy and rarely want to break it when confronted by the groaning table in the evening. I think Zelma's pact with her God was one of the best relationships of her life. She talked to Him very much as she talked to her lady friends, chatting of this and that and asking His help for the most prosaic of problems, from choosing a carpet to persuading a Mancunian scriptwriter to marry her daughter.

Certainly, she had a righteous death. With scarcely a day's illness in her life and looking as beautiful at eighty as she had at forty, she donned her new hat for shul, one Saturday in December, had a heart attack and was dead on arrival at the hospital. It was a blessed end, particularly because she would not have made old bones as they say, happily. Her appearance was everything to her: 'I love the way I look,' she said once without a trace of arrogance but merely as a statement of fact. 'The only thing I'd change is my varicose veins and the size of my feet.' I see her reflected in my performance as Irene in *Ladies of Letters* and would willingly suffer size eights and blue veins for just a shred of her bonniness and structure of bone.

So often, these days, I long to hear her inevitable reactions to anything a bit out of the ordinary. Last Friday Jonathan Ross interviewed Tim Burton and Johnny Depp about the forthcoming film *Alice in Wonderland*. They had both grunged up for the event, making Jonathan look like George Clooney. Tim was a bad-hair day mass of tics and twitches and Johnny wore a hat with some of his long hair plastered down by his horn-rimmed specs. I thought they were sweet and funny but the room was pregnant with the sound of Zelma not saying, 'Ugh! Can you believe what they look like? Is it fancy dress? 'ow can they come on television looking like that? Are they mad? Is he a film star? Ugh! Ronald Colman must be turning in his grave . . . don't they make spectacles of themselves really, though? Don't tell me you think they look nice, Maureen? You don't! Ugh – I'm going to make a cup of tea, I can't bear looking at him, does anyone else want one?' The truth is that nowadays I tend to agree with her in her absence.

'One day,' said Arthur Miller, the playwright, 'you will get up in the morning and find yourself shaving your father's face.'

So, it's New Year again and Amy and I prepare to drive to Gerrards Cross. She wears the pale pink tie-up twin set I've bought her for the new year and I wear a new linen trouser suit I've scoured Westbourne Terrace for the day before. Quite why, with a wardrobe heaving with barely worn clothes, I persist in believing that the new year must be seen in wearing a new suit is something only Zelma and Carl Jung can possibly tell me. We take a carrier bag of wine and chocolates, a change of clothes for overnight and, in a small box, a Brora pullover for Guido, to see in his new year in sartorial warmth.

I have driven to Gerrards Cross many, many times and know the route well, so I have no need to take sat nav along with me. However, I've never driven to GX with my daughter beside me and we do not draw breath as we speed along the A40, talking animatedly as the red-gold ball of the sun plummeted down towards the horizon and the upshot was that I miss the last turn-off to GX before the M25.

Unknown motorways I do not do. Jack did the motorway driving and I did Hyde Park Corner. It was a totally satisfactory division of talents. Since Jack's death, I've solved the dilemma by driving miles to avoid a motorway. Now, at 7.20 p.m. I find myself going the wrong way down – up? – the M25 in heavy traffic, with no idea how to get off it *and* the heavy knowledge that once I do get off it I'll never find GX as I've only ever approached it from one direction. Furthermore it is now twilight, my glasses are dirty and I've begun to babble incoherently.

'I'll never get off it – oh, Maureen, you idiot! Why did you . . .? He'll be upset if we're late . . . I can't believe I didn't turn off at the tur . . . I always turn off . . . all the times I've done it, and I've never . . . How could I miss . . . Ring Guido, darling, ask him – No, get a pen so's you can write it down . . . Oh Lord, they're coming in from all sides at me . . . Where the hell am I?'

Suddenly I see salvation parked on the hard shoulder. A police rescue jeep. I swerve viciously in beside him and almost get my buttocks sliced off getting out of the driver's seat, trying to stop the two officers from leaving.

'Yes, madam, try not to kill yourself, we're not worth it.'

'Sorry . . . but I've never driven on this motorway and I'm lost and it's the new year tonight' – they look askance as well they might – it's September, after all – 'I missed my turn-off and . . . and how do I get to Gerrards Cross by eight o'clock?'

'Right. Calm down . . . you are who we think you are, aren't you?'

'I am. Probably, but I'm not as sharp as I look and I'm getting myself in a state.'

'All you need to do, Maureen, is drive on to junction fourteen and—'

'Junction fourteen!' I yell in disbelief. 'But I haven't even passed junction one yet and dinner's at eight and—'

'No, junction fourteen is the next junction ahead.'

'But . . .'

'Don't worry about junction one, Maureen, this is an orbital road remember.'

'But . . .'

'That means it goes round.'

'But . . .'

'In other words, it didn't start when you got on it.'

'Oh right. Yes. Of course. So . . .'

'So drive on to junction fourteen, yes, and when the road becomes six lanes—'

'SIX LANES! How will I . . . where should I . . .?'

'Just remain on the left and go all the way round the roundabout and head back down this road until junction sixteen and—'

'Junction sixteen,' yells Amy from the car window, 'that's where Guido says to get off.' He was on the mobile giving directions.

'But you said junction fourteen!' I accused the officers.

'Yes, Maureen. Going up. But this is coming down. You go off at sixteen and turn left onto the Birmingham Road . . .'

At this point my knees gave way. 'Birmingham? Birmingham as in . . . Birmingham the city?'

'Well, you don't go all the way, you . . .' They looked at each other. 'Shall we? We've got to go back and it's not much of a detour?'

At this point I threw my arms round the nearest one and yelled, 'Yes! Oh yes! Thank you so much. I'm sooo . . . you are sooo wonderful. I'm soo grateful!'

Before they could change their minds I leaped back into the car saying 'Great. We've got a police escort!'

'I thought we might,' said Amy grimly, and we were off. I clung to them like grim death and when another car moved in between us I turned my hazards on him and effectively blinded him into another lane. We followed them, up, round, back, off, and safely to a roundabout I thought I recognized, whereupon I waved triumphantly and attempted to drive off in the wrong direction. They flagged me down to the even harder shoulder and then, mysteriously, a sign came up on their back window. I couldn't believe my eyes.

'Did you leave that Brora bag outside?' I asked Amy.

'What are you talking about?'

'The sweater for Guido?'

'It's on the back seat. Why?'

'Because what else can they mean? On the back of their car. Look at what it says.'

'What?' said Amy. 'What do you think it means?'

'Well, pullover,' I said. 'It says pullover. Did I drop it? How could they possibly know?'

Her face said it all but I'd got it already.

'No. Oh. I see. Pull over! Oh right, I geddit. It was just a momentary . . . Right OK.'

I got out of the car.

'Now. Are you quite sure you know where you are, Maureen?'

'I do. I'm so grateful, please come and . . .' No, I couldn't really invite them to dinner . . . I opened the boot and yanked out the carrier of wine.

'No. We can't. Not allowed. Thank you, but no.'

I stood there nonplussed. Minussed yet. 'Am I allowed to give you a kiss?'

They looked at other. 'Well . . .'

I kissed them and waved them off mistily, and proceeded to Guido's dinner table and apple and honey and a sweet, laughing start to the new year.

Later Amy confessed that her greatest fear was that the police jeep would be suddenly sent off by central control, on a dramatic chase at 90 miles an hour to some bullet-spraying heist and I would be tearing along behind them still expecting to end up in Gerrards Cross and arrive at Guido's with two cops, several robbers and a warrant for all our arrests.

Diary of a Woman Not in Total Control of Her Freedom Pass

Guido and I drove to Bournemouth for a speaking engagement at the Bournemouth synagogue – well, someone's got to do it and it's hardly likely to be Gerald Kaufman – via lunch in the New Forest with some old friends of Guido's whom he'd met on a trip to Siberia. Derek and Alison are hippo fanatics. They live in a glass and wooden house and if there was one replica hippo in the house and garden, there must have been 200. Even the dining table was a full-sized bronze hippo supporting the glass through which its head and flank protruded. There should have been a house sign outside saying 'Hippodrome'.

I've long been fascinated by our anthropomorphization (can that be right?) of our favoured animals. When I saw a Basenji for the first time, my immediate thought was, 'Gosh, that looks like me!' Jack always favoured rhinos and tortoises, because of their carapace, which made them look so ancient. Birthdays and Christmas time he got inundated with them – cards, artefacts, footstools, wall hangings, wooden ones, paper ones, biscuit tins – until he finally admitted that if he never saw another puckered old hide in his life it would be too soon . . . I had the feeling that included mine.

Lunch was all very jolly and the intrepid travellers, even now planning another expedition to the frozen north via Edinburgh,

Norway, and places with far too many consonants in their names for my liking and not enough deckchairs, welcomed me – the girl whose idea of an adventure holiday is Porchester Baths – with open arms and delicious nosh. I was pretty overexcited to see the ponies rambling free as we traversed the forest. Who needs abroad? I ventured to say this to the man who spent the first six weeks of his retirement ambling across India with a pack on his back.

'Look!' I yelled, townie in pointy-toed court shoes that I was. 'Look at all the stuff! That's bracken, that's gorse, that's heather, that's springy turf!' There were all the things I skip over when reading novels. We actually saw two hares as big as Diva. The trees were in full blossom. During the weekend I saw a bluebell wood for the first time. I'm not sure we had them in Hull. It took the breath from my body, with its beauty and a veteran actress's thoughts turned towards a country existence. It's OK. It didn't last. Two days of grandeur and rustic splendour and I'm yearning for a pothole and a snarling man in a white van.

It was a mere thirty minutes from Sandyballs – I know, but the house *is* actually built on a ball of sand – to Bournemouth and the Cumberland Hotel, where I'd last holidayed, with my parents and brother, some fifty-six years ago. The hotel was an art deco building of the type I love, looking like a white ship about to set sail, but the decorators have been in and redone it in the style of the left side of Satan's brain. It is so red and so black that it's hard to believe the Royal Mail hasn't sponsored the paint. Our room had a massive black and red floral wallpaper that punctuated my sleep like a Grimm nightmare. We dressed up posh and Jennifer, an old friend from my Hull childhood, came to pick us up and take us to the dinner.

The three weeks before the event had been fraught with calls and emails from Thelma, the organizer. Boy was she organized. Every detail of my arrival was covered like a minor Olympics. Times and dietary requirements were checked and rechecked until I almost had to prevent my PA snarling down the phone: 'We are good people . . . why are you persecuting us?'

Of course, when I saw her my heart melted in several places. It is because of women like Thelma that Judaism lasted 5,000 years and Rome survived the Punic Wars. Tiny in stature and as brown as only a woman who walks miles along a promenade every day going from one good deed to the next can be, she was slightly hyper. She had been up since dawn supervising the meal for 188 people, and also attended a somewhat unattended stone setting and supervised all the last-minute crises, of which there were many, inherent in a dinner for 188. She was dainty as a moth in her navy and white jacket and flowing skirt and she made the ideal dinner companion in spite of leaping up thirty or forty times during the meat course to improve whatever needed improvement.

After the coffee was served she mounted the podium and, clutching copious notes, proceeded to read out every job I'd ever done, including radio, lingering over the failures and peaking with a season at the Old Vic with Sir Oliver. At some point during the forty-three years I leapt out of my seat and begged her to stop and let me on the podium and the evening got riotous from that moment on. I'd asked her over dinner what they were hoping to raise funds for and she mentioned that they dearly needed two new ovens, a freezer, some crockery and a decorator.

My first words on reaching the hand mic, which had to be raised by at least two feet from Thelma's height, were that I knew my place. 'I stand here before you this evening, not as an entertainer,' I told them, 'not as an actress or a Jewish mother or a Lady of Letters, but as two ovens, a fridge freezer, a canteen of cups and saucers and a can of Dulux gloss – magnolia.' It went down very well and no one laughed louder than Thelma.

We staggered back to our scarlet box and slept the sleep of the overfed. The next morning, declining the tempting offer of a trip back to the shul to play Jennifer at table tennis, we walked the length of the promenade until Guido spied a helium balloon and decided we should go up in it, which we duly did, had a lovely panoramic view of Bournemouth bay and came straight back down again.

Then, stirred but unshaken, we headed for home and a quick change of clothes for a livery banquet that very night at the Mansion House in London . . . for actuaries. Guido explained what they were to me on the way there – like auditors but without the personality. It was awfully posh – the Egyptian room where we dined was quite beautiful. We passed around the loving cup. After you have drunk

from it, you turn your back to the person currently drinking, to protect him from being stabbed in the back as he imbibes. Manners!

But, my dears, have you ever helped anyone into white tie? It's
like keyhole surgery. What a preposterous invention and what discomfort it ensures for the wearer, and for why? Studs in a
hard-fronted shirt had me in three different pairs of glasses, sometimes all at once. I ask you again, for why? Cufflinks that link to
nothing but four flapping pieces of cuff ... Cummerbund!
Cummerbund! ... What in Escoffier's name is that all about? A
pleated belt around the waist, in the very place that stops you having
one, and the most complex set of fastenings outside Wormwood
Scrubs. Then the wing collar which has a loop on the back for the
white tie to be tied through, except you don't find that out until
you've fastened it without seeing it – through a series of adjustments
of the overhang on the string of the tie, which must be slotted into
a slot in a series of slots, to contain a T-shaped hook and fix the bow
beneath the wings of the collar. Then, crouching, pink faced, with
your glasses on your head, you do it all over again.

It's 2010 for pity's sake and my chap is going to sit all night with
a panel down his front that is stiffer than a new clutch. And, well –
for why? I remember how my dear Jack hated his 'monkey suit' and
how I used to watch, fondly, as his bow tie moved slowly round the
back of his head and his cummerbund grew narrower as the evening
wore on. In empathy, I bought him a maroon velvet jacket with frog-
ging, which hung lovelessly in the wardrobe till the moths got it,
while he stuck loyally to what he knew and loathed.

The thing is that when they stand before you, all formal and tentative for approval, flickering like a black and white film, they look so
damned appealing. Maybe it's the thought of the trussed-up evening
that lies ahead of them, but I've seldom wanted to take a bloke's
clothes off more than when I see him about to sally forth in strictly
formal attire like a frozen emperor penguin with an egg on its feet.

The following day I set out to see an alternative thyroid expert in
Crawley. It started when I treated myself to a lifeline check in a
church hall in Cricklewood. A friend of mine had casually gone along
for the five tests on blood, cardiac, bone density, cholesterol and
whatever the fifth was, and found herself, two days later, having

emergency brain surgery. No kidding. I'd booked myself into that church hall before you could say hypochondriac.

My tests showed up nothing but slightly high cholesterol. I took my test to my GP who advised me that it could be as a result of low thyroid and suggested thyroxin. My mother had taken it for years. If there was a way not to take it, I would find one. Which is why I was at Victoria Station, staring at the automated ticket machine like a Papua New Guinean tribesman stumbling upon Paris Hilton.

My train left in four minutes so I pulled a Zelma. 'I wonder if you could help me to do this?' I batted what's left of my lashes at a man who clearly knew the ropes. He looked at me and smiled.

'The last time I saw you, Maureen, was twenty-five years ago, when my wife and I were sitting at the next table to you, at an outdoor café by Sydney harbour.'

He got my ticket. I forgot to watch, thus ensuring I will have no idea how to use the machine the next time I need to. I said goodbye for another twenty-five years and started running. The train went from platform 16 and I was at platform 1. By the time I sat down in the compartment I was very, very short of breath and I could feel the hairs on my thorax vibrating. Still, I texted and phoned and read my free *Independent* through Clapham Junction, Redhill and Gants Hill until I heard the tannoy crackle and pop: 'The next stop will be Crawley, next stop Crawley.'

After promising the concerned disembodied voice that I'd leave none of my valuables behind on the train, I hopped off and walked round the block, following my Google map to where the road I wanted clearly wasn't. I headed back towards the station, only stopping to register the street sign which proudly boasted the cleanliness and floral cornucopia of the civic centre of Horley. I skidded to a halt, Scooby-Doo style. *Horley?* Not . . . Crawley then, where I was due in ten minutes. The ears were going as well as the thyroid. I headed back to the station and informed the ticket collector of my problem.

'A lot of people make that mistake,' he smirked. I waited for the next train. When I got on it smelled of very, very, smelly dog. An American bulldog lay across the compartment floor surrounded by assorted shreddings. His owner was a large friendly woman with a shaven head, micro shorts, studs and tattoos who was taking him to Brighton for the day. 'You are who I think you are?' she asked me.

'I expect so,' I replied, and we passed a cheerful couple of stops in doggy conversation, as you do, until I arrived at the right Crawley and had my hypothyroidism checked. I'm on something bovine and my levels have levelled.

I love casual banter with strangers. The cab driver on my last leg home told me he'd had a very, very camp man in his cab that morning. He was dressed in tight leather trousers, a ruffled shirt and sported white-blond hair in peaks and a spotted handbag.

'Take me to Bond Street, fast as you can,' said the man. 'I'm very late for an appointment.' Then he added, 'I'm a stylist.'

'You don't say,' said the driver, 'and there's me having you down as a spot welder.'

Sandi or 'No Probs'

Some women are unhappy with their lot and take it out on their patrons. Sandi is an Australian mammographist in a large London teaching hospital. She is assertive, brisk, a bit tight lipped and wishes she were somewhere hot. She's had her walking boots on for some months now and is frustrated in all senses. Although she longed for big city life, she finds the, let's say, cosmopolitan make up of the patients she deals with less than satisfactory.

Sandi or 'No Probs'

Have you filled in the form, madam? The form for screening? Do you understand? THE FORM FOR ... OK, has your wife filled in a form, sir? We send a form out – OK, can you fill it in for her ... Righto – I'll get you one, we keep running out of pens hang on ... and do you have a doctor's letter? Oh. (Spare me.) DOES YOUR WIFE – Oh, thank you.

Yes, I'll be with you in one minute, madam, we are quite busy today – there you are, sir, bit chewed I'm afraid.

Next, Mrs Ros ... er ... Rossenfa ... Ah, you're here ... righto ...

No, most people find the unit quite easily but we are in the middle of building works at present. Did you bring a form, Mrs Ros ... enballs. Oh, well, whatever ... Did you bring a form with your doctor's letter? Oh, you don't have either. Righto.

Any special reason for this scan – have you found a lump or any unusual puckering? So, it's a routine one because of your age. Sorry? I missed that ... SIXTY-ONE did you say?

Would you fill in the form now. Oh Lord (*Sotto voce*), another one. Can I take that pen back, sir? Here you are, madam ... when you've completed it, strip to the waist please and leave your clothes in there – and wait here in the reception area ...

(*Sing-song – she's said it before.*) I'm sorry, we don't have any hospital gowns in this department.

I don't really know the answer to that, Mrs ... er ... Ros ... er, madam, but I assume it's financial.

Well, I don't see how you lose dignity when you still have a vest on.

Er ... Breast unit? We tend not to get too many men in here.

Well, I don't know why they spend so much money on what you term stupid sculptures and can't afford gowns. You'll have to ask them in admin.

Yes, well, some people might think a cappuccino bar *is* more important than a hospital gown . . . look, this is really not my patch so if you could just . . . (*Sotto*) Perleeze!

OK. When you're ready Mrs Rosenf . . . just in here – sorry it *is* a bit nippy, but if you could just pop your left breast on the steel slab for me . . . hold this bar, would you? Sorry, yeah, my hands are cold – I have to spread it across the slab this way . . . We need four pictures that's all . . .

RELAX your shoulder please or this won't take – could you just hold that *other* breast out of the way, please? Cheers – and turn your head right round to the other corner.

I realize it's f***ing uncomfortable but hang on in there and (*Pause*)

Have you done anything nice this weekend? (*Clearly speaking over her answer.*) Terrific. Lovely. Sorry to haul you around. I hope that's not too sore. It's the really firm breasts that feel it the most so *you* should be OK.

Have you had this procedure before? How do you mean in the car park? Oh, I see. In a mobile breast unit? Quaint. All right, breathe out and relax again . . . hold the other breast away from the machine for me and look over your right shoulder . . . I'm just going to have to lift it further over – sorry, I know it's painful, soon be over.

RELAX! Please leave that arm where I placed it . . . I did it for a reason and – hold it now and (*Pause*)

Any plans for the Bank Holidays?

Oh nice.

Just two more with the machine on the tilt. Just place the original breast on the slab again and face this way. Sorry to manhandle you but it saves time and excuse me if I lift it a bit more and spread it over there and under here – thanks. Sorry, Mrs Ro . . . madam . . . but it won't take if you don't . . .

RELAX! Breathe out and . . . Jesus . . . Thank you (*Pause*)

Did you go away for Christmas this year?

Just asking . . . Well I'm sorry if it gets on your tits. (*Without irony.*) Oh, funneee.

One more to do. Yes, it can be a little . . . distorting . . . but frankly, breasts like yours are a nightmare for a radiologist.

Well, I don't know what they'd be for an accountant, Mrs Rosenf . . . what an odd question. Just turn the other way and spread that left one again and move your hips over here and look right, and this may feel a bit more pressure but – I beg your pardon?

Lift the machine off? I can't do that we're behind schedule already . . . Well, I'm *sorry* if your breast feels like a piece of ox tongue.

Most people don't complain QUITE this much but . . . one minute, one minute and it'll be over so – just hold absolutely still . . . one more second and (*Pause*)

Have you seen *Avatar* yet?

I see no need for that kind of language, I was only enquiring as to – I certainly will! And thank *you*. That's all I need, so if you'd like to dress now in the cubicle . . . and you'll be hearing from your doctor in four weeks with the results.

It takes that long because that's how long it takes.

There is a form to fill in if you are dissatisfied in any way with the service you have received.

I'll try to remember that . . . but I don't always feel like smiling forty times a day, unusual as that may sound. (*Sotto*) Miserable old hag.

I said 'Don't forget your bag!' (*Long sigh . . . examines nails . . .*)

Mrs Ilana Popadopoulous – thank you. Do you have a form from your doctor? . . . Thank you, that's brilliant and just slip off your clothes to the waist and – S'cuse me a mo –

Rosie . . . can you get me a hazelnut cappuccino on your way . . . Oh, no, forget it.

Crosspatch Sit by the Latch

On Friday 7th of May, I set off for Dorset to watch my godson Joe Payne sing a startlingly good version of 'Moon River' with a damn fine school jazz band. I got a lump in my throat. The next morning his mum took me to see a bluebell wood. The lump, which had taken all night to go down, came right back up again. The morning after, Guido and I went to the house of my good friend and birthday twin Linda Agran, who has moved to a new house in Wiltshire and wanted to christen – although that's not quite the right word – the New York-style bar she's had installed. No matter how far in opposite directions our lives diverge, we pick up the threads in about thirty seconds flat. There are as many fissures and ravines in our hearts as there are in our necks but they are nurtured by the crème de la mer of laughter.

We raced back on Sunday for another reunion of Guido's old school friends from a Cairo school that closed in 1956. There's loyalty to the old school ties. Back home, I must prepare an hour's chat for the Swindon Book Fair on Tuesday and a fund-raising address for Hammerson House old people's home on Wednesday. My old friends Annie and Astrid will be flying in from America on Monday, volcanic ash permitting, and so sofa beds must be erected and duvets sourced and lunch at least thought about.

There will be twelve of us seeing *Hair* on my birthday and nostalgia will mess up my remaining eyelashes as I recall how often, as drama students in the late sixties, we would climb up on stage and sing 'Let the Sun Shine In' wearing clothes from Granny Takes a Trip and smelling of patchouli. On this occasion, I pondered the distance between stage and dress circle and stayed put with an indulgent smile on my mush. 'I Met A Boy Called Frank Mills' was Jack's favourite song. It sings in the same way as he wrote.

The start of May is a maelstrom of birthdays. It's as if all our parents got into bed somewhere in the month of September and did absolutely nothing except procreate. Nine months later my entire circle of friends struggled out. So almost everyone I know has a birthday in early May. My credit card is on the desk as if to prove it, and the numbers have worn off through over-use. I've bought birthday cards in batches of twelve, spent hours at the post office waiting to hear 'cashier number eight', and the Sellotape dispenser is empty again.

Then the last bit of wrapping paper is placed in the paper recycling bag to be picked up by the refuse men and shoved in with the one for all the food and the one for household waste and landfilled as one and, quite suddenly, I start to feel ill. I mean, vaguely poorly, with disparate symptoms and feelings of disquiet. Sensitive stomach, hot flushes, dry eyes, painful back, you name it, I've got it.

Then my sleep patterns are shot and I'm on the milk and biscuit meander at 4.30 a.m. Friends mention Nytol Plus and other alternative bits of old root and stalk and I smile and tell them I've taken six on one occasion and still heard every little tit in West London wake up for a major warble and a damp worm. At this juncture, people stop telling me I look well, so I interpret that as them thinking I look terrible. My hair begins to crack and dry and fly off in funny directions, so I cut it myself, disastrously, and in the mornings I look in the mirror and see looking back Ken Dodd crossed with Basil Rathbone.

I'm not happy. I'm doing all the things I usually do, and seeing all the friends I usually see. My kids are thriving, I have help in the house and my partner is adorable. There's work ahead, I'll soon have a week in Ireland and, according to my accountant, I'm fairly far from the breadline. My dog behaves reasonably well in company, and Warren the rabbit skips when I bring out his pellets . . .

All's well with the world, isn't it? All right it's almost June and the heating is on 22 degrees, the news is desperate with Israel about to be reviled by the whole world again and an able minister resigning three weeks into government because he was so scared of being outed that he bent the rules. I'm a bit spooked by Sarah Palin and her tea party and there's bugger all on the telly, but that's no reason for dis-ease.

Something is bugging me. I'm a crosspatch, unnecessarily, and people take offence at my wisecracks instead of finding them hilarious, because they sense my mood is angry. I'm not as nice as I think I am. I'm actually not nice at all. I'm judgemental and cynical and controlling and petty and I don't like me. And it is at this point that I usually, gently, bump the car into something stationary.

Then it comes in the post. The reminder from the synagogue it's fast approaching the memorial day for Jack. Whom I lived beside for thirty-five years. 29th of May 2004. *Riiight*. Of course. That'll be it. Perhaps I've been subconsciously reliving the last days of his life. That's what's been waking me up. Why do I *never* see it coming?

So I go to the synagogue and I thank the Lord for the wonders of his creation, and I go with the kids and friends to the grounds where he is buried, and put a special stone on his grave. Then I listen to the music we shared on the radio and I realize that I am not the merry widow I seem to be, my life is compartmentalized into two distinct strands. One of them is the stuff of this book with jokes and opinions and drama and comedy and love. The other is rage, remorse, powerlessness and sheer bloody frustration because that, Mrs Rosenthal, is that. There is no rewrite, no curtain call, and the body doesn't get up and walk off for a cold white wine in the star's dressing room. You are out of *control* . . . it's beyond your remit and you don't like it.

So what will I do? I'm going to reward, not berate myself. Tomorrow I'm booking trumpet lessons . . . I got one from Nats for my previous birthday. I'm going back to dance class. I'll meditate. I'll get a flat stomach. I'll paint and draw . . . volunteer for something . . . I want another chance to be better and make him proud wherever the hell he is . . .

I won't, of course. But at least, as they say in *X Factor*, it will be my dream . . .

Just for tonight, though, as I close the shutters and just relish being lonely – no, *alone* for once, I'll tell myself there's nothing amiss that a good night's sleep, a swift pulling up of boots and concluding the last page of this book won't cure. If I can't collect myself by tomorrow – I'll just have to have myself collected.

So . . . here I am, master of nothing I survey. Staff telling me what to do, rabbit eating my double-headed begonias, kids delaying me grandkids, friends telling me to stop doing stuff for strangers and do it instead for them, publisher demanding deadline decisions, director wanting lines learned, birds wanting nuts, shoes heeling, fund-raisers' space, producers' commitment, dear chap more commitment . . . Suddenly, though, I feel the sun on my skin and hope springs maternal. I am *holding my own*.

As I started a workshop of Joyce Grenfell and Ruth Draper, a little electric thrill ran through my tetchy old bones . . . not because of the work, though I'm thrilled as ever to be wearing the front-row curls and the silk, shirt-waist dress. No, the tingle of pleasure is because a dear friend in the Whittington Hospital, recovering from a broken hip, has told me that the anaesthetic has bricked her up so can she have my famous rhubarb cure? I dash to the organic shop for rhubarb and cook it slowly with ginger, lemon juice, brown sugar, a few prunes and a dash of cayenne pepper and, weyhey! Job done! Hooray and hallelujah! A few hours later, the request comes from the rest of the orthopaedic ward – 'Yeah, but wharrabout *us*, then?' – and an hour later another Tupperware container has gone off in a cab.

'If I'm never remembered for anything else in my life,' I tell my kids by text, 'I want you to remember this: your mother may never have won an Oscar, completed a marathon, dated a movie star, cooked a soufflé, or eaten a slug in the jungle with Ant and Dec; but she was one of the greatest shit-stirrers of her age.'

Picture Credits